The Empress and Mrs. Conger

The Empress and Mrs. Conger

The Uncommon Friendship of Two Women and Two Worlds

Grant Hayter-Menzies

香港大學出版社

HONG KONG UNIVERSITY PRESS

Hong Kong University Press
14/F Hing Wai Centre
7 Tin Wan Praya Road
Aberdeen
Hong Kong
www.hkupress.org

ISBN 978-988-8083-00-8

British Library Cataloguing-in-Publication Data
A catalogue copy for this book is available from the British Library

Printed and bound in China by RR Donnelley

To Sarah Buchan Jewell
1903–2009
with gratitude

and

Han Liangxi and Moyu
with love

By three methods we may learn wisdom:
first, by reflection, which is noblest;
second, by imitation, which is easiest;
and third, by experience, which is the most bitter.
— Confucius

Contents

Illustrations

(Following p. 88)

Acknowledgements

There are never enough pages available to the author to thank everyone who contributed to a book's creation. But I must tell of one person whose help in bringing her grandmother back to life was invaluable to this book and to me.

When I read that Sarah Buchan Jewell, granddaughter of Sarah Conger, had bequeathed most of her Chinese collection to several museums in Massachusetts in the early 1990s, I assumed that she had died then, or shortly thereafter. She was, after all, born in 1903. It seemed incredible to me that a woman who as a child had received gifts from the Empress Dowager Cixi could still be living a century after the dowager's death in 1908.

My partner pushed me to search for evidence that she was still alive, and I eventually found her telephone number. Then I hesitated. I was afraid that this chance to talk to the woman who was, in all likelihood, the last living person to have personally known Sarah Conger, would be thwarted; that a caretaker would tell me that Mrs. Jewell remembered nothing, or that she was not well enough to speak to me. My better half made me dial the number. "Of course you may speak to Mrs. Jewell," said a cheerful voice. And on came the 105-year-old granddaughter of Sarah Pike Conger, sounding many decades younger. I would find that in both person and personality, she was just as ageless.

When I later visited Mrs. Jewell in her home in Needham, Massachusetts, with its scroll paintings and jades and porcelains bespeaking her family's imperial Chinese past, I pulled up on my laptop the little-known photograph of her grandmother holding the hand of the empress dowager. Mrs. Jewell had never seen this picture before and she was thrilled, but even more so by the computer sitting on her lap. "These came too late for me," she told me with regret, touching the screen. "I would have so enjoyed them."

A link to the personalities of people long dead whom I had only read about, Mrs. Jewell was powerfully of the present, too—a witty and elegant lady at home in any time or place. And her memory was phenomenal. Without Mrs. Jewell's crisp recollections of Sarah Conger and her world, shared with me so generously, I could not have completed the process of painting this portrait in words—just as Katherine Carl, the first Western artist to paint the Empress Dowager Cixi, at the suggestion of Sarah Conger, painted her best portrait of her subject only after she had spent time with and grown fond of her. Had I not met Sarah Buchan Jewell and come to know her kindly heart, I could not have fully understood what was her namesake's greatest—and obviously heritable—attribute.

I offer special thanks to those whose guidance and generosity also helped make this book a reality: Laura St. Germain Adamczyk, The Wellesley College Alumnae Association; Virginia Anderson, Fogg Museum, Harvard University; Dr. Geoffrey Berridge; Roberta and Bob Blank; Dr. Timothy Brook, University of British Columbia; Winnie Chau, Hong Kong University Press; Jane Coxe; Sally Jewell Coxe, Bonobo Conservation Initiative; Dr. Pamela Kyle Crossley, Dartmouth College; Dr. Colin Day, formerly of Hong Kong University Press; Darrell Dorrington, Australian National University; Michael Duckworth, Hong Kong University Press; Jennifer Flaherty; Amanda Gustin, The Mary Baker Eddy Library; Les Hayter; James Hevia, University of Chicago; Clara Ho, Hong Kong University Press; David Hogge, Freer Gallery of Art and Arthur M. Sackler Gallery, Smithsonian Institution; Grace Ji (Ji Yayun), Leon An (An Hongyu), Robin Zhang (Zhang Zhenhua), Tony

Tong (Tong Feng), Jack Li (Li Erhui), and Jay Peng (Peng Kejie) of the Tianxiang Courtyard Hotel, Beijing; Patricia Kervick, Peabody Museum, Harvard University; Dr. Richard King, University of Victoria; Giles Li, Boston Chinatown Neighborhood Center; Lisa Lu; William Luce; Raymond Lum, Yenching Library, Harvard University; Bruce MacLaren, Peabody Essex Museum; Neal McCracken, Australian National University; Sean William Menzies; Cheryl Moneyhun, Longyear Museum; Victoria Monks, Missouri History Museum; Dr. Christopher Munn, Hong Kong University Press; Na Genzheng, *Yiheyuan* (Summer Palace, Beijing); Dr. Susan Naquin, Princeton University; Renata Osborne, Australian National University; Giles Pickford; Kathryn Press, Fogg Museum, Harvard University; Diana Preston; Leslie Prince Raimond; Rod Ross, National Archives; Harry and Patty Russell; Joseph Scheier-Dolberg, Columbia University (formerly at the Museum of Fine Arts, Boston); Jane Shea; Eddie Song; Susan and Bob Susi, Bronwen Flowers; Ellen Takata, Museum of Fine Arts, Boston; Blair Tarr, Kansas State Historical Society; Kent Tsai; Dr. David Francis Urrows, Hong Kong Baptist University; Dr. Shuo Wang, California State University Stanislaus; Simon Winchester; Jay Watkins; Eric Wolin, Peabody Essex Museum; Patrick Wright; and Wu Wei.

Special affection to Cecy, who saw me through the writing of this book—a wise and loving friend to the end—and a nod to my late maternal grandfather. Like the Congers, Earl Weston Strawser made his rural Midwest upbringing a springboard to a life of wider adventure. Like them (and like his grandson), he also loved his books.

I have made every effort to render proper names into pinyin, with the deliberate exception of spellings used in quoted material. While mindful of errors or omissions that were brought to my attention in the writing of this book, any that remain are solely my responsibility.

Introduction

Sarah Pike Conger came to China in 1898 a middle-aged woman from Iowa who knew nothing of China's people or its culture. Yet she left seven years later one of the nation's most sympathetic defenders. A survivor of the Boxer Uprising, one of history's greatest clashes between East and West, Sarah stretched out a hand to the one person who bore the most blame for the disaster, the Empress Dowager Cixi. And Cixi, who had no reason to love any foreigner, put her hand in Sarah's. This book is the story behind that gesture and the extraordinary friendship that followed.

It is also the story of how two women, born to be opposites, were able to find common ground transcending race, religion, and the fractious politics of men. That is the greatest story of the empress and Mrs. Conger, and it is told here for the first time.

* * * * *

The notion of writing about Sarah Conger and the empress dowager came to me on a visit to the latter's imperial Summer Palace outside Beijing. It was April 2008, 103 years to the month since Sarah saw China for the last time, and a few months before the Beijing Olympics, when world nations gathered in China for the first time to celebrate "One World, One Dream"—a slogan of which Sarah Conger would have approved.

Sarah has been touched on by a handful of current scholars, most at length in Elisabeth Croll's *Wise Daughters From Foreign Lands*, and within certain special contexts by James Hevia and Jonathan Spence. She flits in and out of the letters and memoirs of George E. Morrison, Princess Der Ling, Katherine Carl, and Lady Susan Townley. She appears in Pearl S. Buck's fictionalized biography of the empress dowager, *Imperial Woman*, in which Buck uncharitably attributes to Cixi the thought that Sarah looked "like a hard-faced nun." Sarah even made it to Hollywood, in her lifetime, first in the 1927 silent film *Foreign Devils*, in which she was played by stern English stage actress Emily Fitzroy, and later, in 2006, on Chinese television in the mini-series, *Princess De Ling* (Deling Gongzhu). Far from the austere, governess-like personage depicted by Pearl Buck, on television Sarah was represented as an attractive, fashionable, slightly flirty and far too young blonde—a fiction not out of place in a script that makes little use of facts. And facts are what this book is about, particularly those relative to Sarah's friendship with the empress dowager and her efforts to rehabilitate Cixi's image after the Boxer Uprising.[1]

My guide at the Summer Palace was Na Genzheng, a great-nephew of Cixi. During our tour I saw glass cases filled with gifts foreign ladies had offered Cixi over the years. The armies of Victorian bibelots appeared artless and insincere against the sophisticated elegance of the Chinese palace in which they were displayed, and seemed to symbolize the West's attitude toward China throughout modern history. Though they were given in good faith, they were selected as gifts by people who had no comprehension of the recipient or her culture—indeed, they suggested the givers were blind to the fact that China had a culture at all.

Many legends had collected around his great-aunt, Na told me, as many as there were ornaments in these display cases. Most were untrue, and none captured the Cixi that his family remembered. Their Cixi was not the evil tyrant that even now lurks in the Chinese imagination, but a kind and intelligent woman, with all the human qualities and failings of any other mortal. (She was not at all the Chinese Luddite she is often alleged to have been: she gifted Na's family with one of the more avant-garde examples of Western technology in the China of the time, an upright piano.) She was capable of amity—even her implacable enemy, the American scholar Dr. W. A. P. Martin, conceded "this good trait." It was these qualities that Cixi demonstrated to Sarah Conger and other diplomatic wives when, at her invitation, they came to the Forbidden City in February 1902, almost two years after the start of the Boxer Uprising and nearly four years after Sarah had first met the dowager face to face.[2]

When Cixi asked these women to visit her, the Boxer Uprising was still fresh in the minds of their husbands, and for good reason. After the siege, the Chinese were seen as xenophobes willing to stoop to murder, with Cixi as their figurehead. In an era in which wifely obedience was not just a meme of male-dominated society but regarded as a virtue by many of the women it controlled, the diplomats' wives, encouraged by Sarah, disobeyed their husbands by accepting Cixi's invitation. Their bravery was great, but Sarah Conger's was greater.

Unlike the other women, Sarah had survived the bullets and bombs of the fifty-five-day battle that was the Boxer Uprising, all the while filling sandbags and burying the dead. At the end of it, she still trusted in the bona fides of a potentate most Westerners saw as a throwback to the legendary female Asian tyrants—a husband-poisoner, a reactionary, a killer of Christians. Some of the foreign quarter's more cynical residents thought Sarah the dupe of the empress dowager, and it is anyone's guess as to whether this was in fact the case. But throughout her friendship with Cixi Sarah held to a simple creed. "If you look deeply enough in anyone," she told her granddaughter, "you will find the good that is there."[3]

Most people retelling or inventing stories of Cixi's murderousness had never seen her, let alone met her. Sarah had sat and talked with Cixi, holding her hand, as one woman to another. That she established such intimacy did her no favors in the eyes of most of her fellow Americans, but for Sarah, being true to her heart was worth more than kowtowing to prejudice. She worked to accomplish what she saw as her special twofold duty: the rehabilitation of the dowager's image, and the restoration of goodwill and cultural friendship between China and the West. Part of this mission involved convincing the dowager to have her portrait painted, by a female American artist, for display at the St. Louis

Exposition in April 1904—the first such image of Cixi ever created for the public eye. Sarah believed this was the best way for the world to see the dowager and, by extension China, as they really were. The portrait, given by Cixi to the United States government, was a diplomatic success at a time when few Western men, including Sarah's husband, were able to claim such for themselves.

Sarah went further. She saw Chinese women as China's untried hope for the future. From the day she entered the country, Sarah successfully befriended these women, though their homes were off limits to foreigners and the women themselves were hidden away in courtyards, crippled by bound feet and Confucian propriety. In championing Cixi, Sarah was championing them, seeking to change the world's view of not only the country's most famous and reviled woman but of all Chinese women, while opening to those women a view to a world they had never known and, in the process, opening to the west a window on China.[4]

"United," Cixi had said as she offered a conciliatory cup to the lips of Sarah and the other foreign ladies as they stood together in the Forbidden City. This was Sarah's motto, too. She had learned, as she worked in the trenches during the siege, that those gathered behind the walls of the British legation—French, British, Russian, German, Austrian, Dutch, Italian, Chinese, and Japanese—were not strangers, but one people. At the same time she found that in China, she who reverenced the Stars and Stripes, Independence Day, and Abraham Lincoln, had in her breast a poetic, patriotic Chinese heart.[5]

I

Eagle and Dragon

※

※

心有靈犀一點通

Hearts meet on the dot in a unicorn's horn

— *Poem Without Title*, Li Shangying (813–858)

1
Farmer's daughter

Born on July 24, 1843, in the Chinese year of the water rabbit, Sarah Jane Pike was reared in a place and in circumstances as far from imperial Asia as it was possible to be—the pre-Civil War American Midwest, amid the grass roots simplicity and devout Christian faith of Ohio and Illinois farming communities.

The particular brand of Christian faith in which Sarah was raised had much to do with her liberal perspective on the world. This perspective helped her appreciate the beliefs of a culture about which most Americans knew nothing, and which many Christians considered heathen. Sarah's parents, Edward William Pike and Laura Burridge, belonged to the Universalist Church. To Universalists, God was a loving creator incapable of giving life to a soul only to consign it to damnation. They encouraged recognition of the rights of women, compassion for the insane, abolition of slavery, and separation of church and state—ideals which would shape Sarah Conger's attitude toward the Chinese and, in turn, toward their ruler, the Empress Dowager Cixi.[1]

In their home in Galesburg, Illinois, in conjunction with the enlightened version of Christianity offered by Universalism, the Pikes exposed their four daughters to values that were the pillars of society in both the Midwest and their New England birthplace: constant hard work and tireless pursuit of knowledge. They also inculcated in the girls a singularly modern concept: that being a woman was no bar to any form of personal fulfillment, whether through education, a career, or an equal partnership with a husband.[2]

Laura Pike was, according to her daughter, a woman "whose whole life was filled with love and good-will." Sarah was told that as a child in wintry Vermont, her mother had raised bulb flowers indoors; when they bloomed she carried them through the snow to give to neighbors who were old or ill. Mrs. Pike's tenderness toward those in need, as well as her love of flowers—one shared with the empress dowager—was passed down to Sarah. Edward Pike, Sarah tells us, was a man whose measured judgments and tolerance she admired and tried to emulate. One of his most memorable pieces of advice was that if one wanted to be loved, one needed first to be lovable. "Later in life," Sarah wrote, "I have learned that *this* is the *secret* of *all living*" (emphasis in original).[3] But perhaps her parents' most useful message was one that Sarah returned to like a mantra all her life. "Remember," Edward and Laura often advised, "that you are just as far from other people as they are from you."[4]

Sarah entered Lombard College just before the start of the Civil War. The education she received at this Universalist coeducational institution, which had served as a venue for one of the famous Lincoln–Douglas debates in 1858, was the catalyst for everything that Sarah later believed or became. For her, education was not something one gained from a stint at a school, any more than faith was attainable by worshipping at a particular church. It was a lifelong opportunity and responsibility—the Lombard creed in a nutshell. Lombard allowed her to grow on a personal level while part of a group of young women and men as curious and ambitious as herself. She became a member of the Zetecalian Literary Society, a social club of young university women who wrote, read, and debated essays on historical topics; activities which helped her become a fluent and concise writer and researcher. Later on, she would become a strong proponent of the Chautauqua Literary and Scientific Circle, in which religious and educational devotion were simultaneously pursued to a high degree.

Characteristically, one of Sarah's strongest interests involved a branch of science long the province of males. "Astronomy was a joy to me in my school days," Sarah wrote years later. Even after she left school she continued to study the science of the stars—indeed, one of her favorite places to visit in Beijing would be Khublai Khan's Imperial Observatory. In continually educating herself, Sarah took the motto of the Zetecalian Society—*utile dulci*, "the useful with the agreeable"—as her motto for living. She might have also recognized her own development in the model articulated by Confucius to describe himself: "At fifteen, I set my heart on learning; at thirty, I was firmly established; at forty, I had no more doubts; at fifty, I knew the will of heaven; at sixty, I was ready to listen to it; and at seventy, I could follow his heart's desire without transgression of what was right." At fifteen, Sarah Pike had set her heart on learning, but also on something else. Somewhere between church and school, astronomy and apple orchards, she had met the man who was to change her life as much as she was to change his.[5]

✳ ✳ ✳ ✳ ✳

Edwin Hurd Conger was born on March 7, 1843 at Cherry Grove, Illinois. Edwin had a prominent connection to early American history: through his mother, he was descended from Mayflower pilgrims William White and Susanna Fuller. Edwin's father, Lorentus, born in New Hampshire, was both a farmer and constable in Galesburg, and if his share of worldly goods was more substantial than that of Sarah's family, there was a similar simplicity in their way of living as well as a similar depth of religious devotion: Lorentus and Mary were among the founding members of Galesburg's First Universalist Church, and had donated the land on which Lombard College was built.[6]

At six feet tall and weighing two hundred pounds, Edwin worked on his father's farm, but he also achieved high grades in school and would take top honors at Lombard. Both he and his sister, Hannah Conger, appeared so naïve and pliable they were often cast as children in college plays. But Edwin was easy to underestimate. As his correspondence demonstrates, he was a man of warmth and sentiment. He probably cracked a grin at life's ironies more often than his wife, and had in abundance the grim determination of the Midwest farmer, never certain of weather or prices but flexible enough to adjust in an emergency.[7]

Sarah and Edwin are said to have first met at Lombard College. What brought them together, besides their shared faith, is easy to guess: their similar natures, in which strong feelings ran deep beneath a calm surface, and in which was also a boundless enthusiasm coupled with a sensible practicality and love of the outdoors derived from their rural upbringing. Edwin and Sarah were a case of like attracting like; both shied away from discord, embracing peace and orderliness. There was a sense of total equality between this man and woman, which Edwin outlined years later in a letter to his daughter. "If you will have implicit and unfailing mutual confidence," he wrote, "make it a point to always consider the other more than self."[8]

Sarah still had a year to go at college when, in 1862, Edwin graduated and found himself in a flood of patriotic pressure to serve in the Civil War, which had broken out in the spring of the previous year. Nineteen-year-old Edwin enlisted as a private in Company I, 102nd Regiment of the Illinois Volunteer Infantry, one of eight men in the 1862 Lombard graduating class to do so. He fought in the Battle of Chickamauga and the siege of Atlanta, and took part in General Sherman's infamous March to the Sea. The horrors he saw and, indeed, was part of, may have helped shape his tentative first reaction thirty-eight years later to the violence overtaking Beijing in the summer of 1900.[9]

Edwin, as one of his classmates recalled, never "shunned a task because it was difficult." Soon after entering the army he was made an orderly sergeant; one of his duties, and one to which he brought his combination of fairness and discipline, was to drill the troops. Many men remembered him as the best drill master they had ever had (similar appraisals would be made by the men he commanded during the Boxer Uprising). By war's end, Edwin was promoted to company captain and was a brevetted major, "for gallant and meritorious conduct."[10]

The war and Edwin's participation in it put Sarah at risk of losing two things, the man she loved and her country. Deeply patriotic, Sarah celebrated American holidays with a religious zeal. In China she observed the Fourth of July and Thanksgiving as if they were akin to the sacred rites performed by the Chinese in their own ceremonial calendar, and

Lincoln was to her a figure as seminal to orderly society as Confucius was to the Chinese. Thus, during the Civil War, not only was she threatened with the loss of Edwin, but also with what looked like the dissolution of a nation she loved just as much—a catastrophe for a woman who revered the concept of *e pluribus unum* (out of many, one).

Nearly fifteen years after the end of the war, in late 1880, Sarah visited the National Cemetery in Richmond, Virginia. She walked the grounds with a friend who had lost family on the Confederate side of the conflict and was painfully reliving the trauma—what Abraham Lincoln called "the awful arithmetic" of war—as she passed the many grave markers lining the path. Holding the hand of her friend, Sarah felt a flood of emotion; "my heart sank within me," she remembered. "Human sympathy gave its best to soothe and allay the anguish in my dear friend's heart, for I loved her."[11] Two decades later, Sarah would feel this same sympathy for another on the losing side of a conflict, this time in faraway China. "It matters not what misconceived ideas caused this great calamity," she would write later of the Boxer Uprising and the toll it took on the Chinese. "The result is the same."[12]

✳ ✳ ✳ ✳ ✳

An engagement in the mid-nineteenth century could be expected to last for several years or until the husband-to-be had established himself as able to support a family, and Edwin and Sarah probably already had what was then called "an understanding" even before he left for battle. Edwin was mustered out of the army in June 1865, then enrolled in Albany Law School in New York state (where he first met the man who was to determine his and Sarah's Chinese destiny, future US president William F. McKinley). On June 21, 1866, following Edwin's graduation, the couple married, and they settled in Galesburg, Illinois, where Edwin was admitted to the bar.[13]

In 1868, the Congers moved to Dexter, Iowa, where Edwin's parents had bought land and where his father had set up a bank. Edwin bought a farm and busied himself with stock, farming, and banking. It was in Dexter that the Congers' first child, a boy named Lorentus, for his paternal grandfather, was born in 1870.[14] The world of the nineteenth century, even in up-to-date America, was a dangerous place for babies. The lack of antibiotics or common knowledge of how germs were spread, and a lack of proper medical care when needed militated against a child's reaching adulthood. Sarah is not known to have referred to her only son in any published writings, and information about him from elsewhere is sparse. But his death in 1877 was a terrible loss. It was also one that Sarah, when she came to know the Empress Dowager Cixi, would discover she shared with that powerful woman.[15]

But the year 1877 was also significant for the Congers in a more positive way: that year, Edwin took up his first elected position as treasurer of Dallas county, and the Congers celebrated the birth of their daughter Laura, a brilliant girl who was to accompany her parents on many a future adventure in foreign lands. What actually brought about Edwin's move from the private life of a farming lawyer to the public stage of local politics is another mystery in the Congers' story; perhaps his talent for organization, which he used to such positive effect in his stock raising as well as in his banking activities, needed bigger challenges.[16]

Edwin was elected Iowa state treasurer in 1880 and again in 1882. Three years later, he was sent to Washington, D.C. as Republican congressman from Iowa and served through the Forty-Ninth, Fiftieth, and Fifty-First Congresses; in the last, he was an able chairman of the Committee of Coinage, Weights, and Measures. "He was not an orator," recalled one old friend, but "he had a straightforward, convincing style of speaking, which commanded attention in the House."[17]

Moving to Washington, D.C. was a thrill for Sarah. Not only was she delighted to be in the capital of the United States, with its patriotic associations, but with Washington already becoming a powerhouse of policies spreading forth to change the world, for better or worse, the city had the buzz of energy that Sarah, for all her quiet ways, yearned for. She spent her first weeks visiting all the departments of state, wanting to see just how the governmental machinery worked.[18]

For all that the Congers were not a glittering young power-couple, with sterling family connections or a fortune behind them (qualities as necessary in Gilded Age Washington, D.C. as pink champagne), they proved popular, and were friends of presidents and members of the public alike. There was a solid soberness about them, a radiant goodwill and authenticity. You knew that if Edwin, with his silver Lincolnian chin beard and his guileless blue eyes, told you he would help you, you need not worry that he would forget or renege; and if Sarah, with her graying hair dyed unapologetically dark and her keen gaze softened by a ready smile, sought or accepted your friendship, you had a friend you could trust, confide in, and lean on. These were characteristics they developed not in Washington drawing rooms but in the farming communities and Universalist congregations of their youth. And while there were those in Washington, D.C. and elsewhere who found the Congers old-fashioned or unsophisticated, theirs were strengths on which others would come to lean in the difficult days ahead.

✳ ✳ ✳ ✳ ✳

When Edwin was appointed by President Benjamin Harrison to the position of Envoy Extraordinary and Minister Plenipotentiary to Brazil on September 27, 1890, he and Sarah were not yet fifty years old and were still in the prime of their lives. "When I went to Brazil," Sarah wrote later, "I was always comparing and contrasting that country and her people with my country and my people; and to me, mine were always superior." Though Sarah did not know it, Brazil was the beginning of a career for her, too, one in addition to those she had already fulfilled as a mother and diplomat's wife. For the first time, she would see how the rest of the world lived.[19]

Sarah had left Washington, D.C., with all its marble, for a lush and fragile green paradise. For close to ninety years, Brazil had been a monarchy, thanks to Napoleon Bonaparte, whose advent on the European political horizon sent the Portuguese court running to the safety of their far-flung Brazilian colony. They set up housekeeping in Rio de Janeiro and never returned to Portugal; the last of the line, Pedro II, had been removed from the throne in a coup d'état in November 1889, and General Deodoro da Fonseca became the first president of a nation which, until 1967, was called the Republic of the United States of Brazil. Because the air in Rio was held to be thick with yellow fever, Edwin and Sarah would live three thousand feet above the port city in Petropolis, the former summer resort of Emperor Pedro II. As one traveler wrote:

> Suppose you could put a range of hills 3,000 feet high just back
> of New York or Philadelphia and away up on their tops build a
> beautiful city of say 20,000 inhabitants. Suppose you could reach
> this by a short ride across the most beautiful bay in the world,
> and climb the hills by a cog-road like that which goes up Mount
> Washington. If you can imagine this, you have Petropolis.[20]

Petropolis was a town of 25,000 people, filled with lovely houses belonging to well-to-do Brazilians or expatriates. Across from the pink-walled palace of the ex-emperors stood the American legation, a simple single-storey stone and stucco villa, its deep front portico supported by Doric pillars. The gardens beside the villa were rich with camellias as tall as trees, rhododendrons the size of hayricks, splashes of multicolored azaleas, leaning towers of palm trees, and orange and banana trees, from which the legation cook plucked fruit for the day's meals.[21]

The fragility of this paradise became apparent soon after the Congers' arrival. In what has been called "one of the most bizarre episodes of the Age of Empire," the new republic was threatened first by a revolt, in 1891, of pro-monarchists and merchants unsettled by the quadruple abolition of slavery, the monarchy, the aristocracy, and the supremacy of the Catholic church, and then by the 1893 blockade of Rio's harbor by a similarly disaffected and pro-aristocratic navy. This was an early test for Edwin as diplomat, but for Sarah, another kind of test was already in the making.[22] She recalled later,

> I traveled south of the equator, and my book knowledge was
> put to the test . . . Everything was new to me, people, climate,
> vegetation; and not only these, but above me were new heavens.
> The mid-heaven constellations were there, but upside down . . . I
> realized more fully than ever before how much depends upon our
> outlook. The heavens had not changed, but my position in regard
> to them had changed, and I had much more to learn about them.[23]

As she wrote to Mary Baker Eddy, whose faith, Christian Science, Sarah had adopted a few years earlier, there was much to enjoy in Brazil:

> I love this land with its ever glowing, ever changing beauty . . . The
> sunsets are often brilliant beyond anything that I ever saw. The

birds and insects come to partake of this spirit of beauty and *they* are brilliant too.[24]

Daughter Laura, who had come to live with her parents in Petropolis, took to the country like a native. To better serve as her father's secretary she learned Portuguese during the first three years of Edwin's appointment. She also "made a serious and practical study of the intricacies of diplomatic procedure," thus relieving "her father of many of the more burdensome details of his duty."[25]

But for Sarah, something was not right. Her familiar universe, inside and out, had been turned upside down. "There seems to be," she wrote, using the euphemistic language derived from Mrs. Eddy's writings, "an unfamiliar phase of mortal mind I am here to meet . . . I am battling self." It was a crisis of conscience. A devout Christian Scientist believed that only the most vigilant oversight of thought and motive could keep one's perfect mind—Mrs. Eddy's fragment of God—from running astray. Sarah's letters and diary entries from this period until after she left China a decade later demonstrate the discipline with which she performed these searches for motivations within herself that were not absolutely honest or fair. It was this uncompromising lens, through which she would examine her soul in China, that she first turned on herself in Brazil. Looking within her heart to see what "thought treasures that I was bearing with me," Sarah found "to my surprise [that] my treasury was empty."[26]

"I soon learned," she wrote, "that the attitude of superiority I had taken made it impossible to accumulate anything." Sarah believed herself blinded to the rich variations of another culture by pride in her American lifestyle. She was not part of this new world, and it was not that world's fault, she felt, but her own. "What I see in the people [of Brazil]," Sarah wrote, "I cannot say. *I do not know . . . What is it?* This I am trying quietly & patiently to learn & to meet, & to overcome" (emphasis in original).[27]

With Edwin's reappointment to Brazil in 1897, Sarah made up her mind to "[descend] from my imaginary height with the determination to seek with open eyes and a willing heart" what was waiting to be found among the exotic flowers and birds, exotic people and customs of Brazil. "There is one brotherhood," Sarah was to write to Mrs. Eddy, underlining every word. "Under the same canopy, housed by the same loving Father & Mother God, we are brothers and sisters of one home."[28]

But the Congers would not to be in Brazil long enough for Sarah to test her new creed. She would have to travel farther to find the brotherhood and the home she longed to join. When she did, she would find her creed, and her faith, challenged almost beyond endurance.

2
Mother of China

China had not had many friends among the presidents of the United States, and the current executive, William McKinley, was not one to deviate too radically from tradition. In the past the American government had operated on the premise of never giving something for nothing. Since the American trading ship *Empress of China* first dropped anchor in Canton in 1784, Americans had had much to offer the Chinese, from ginseng to otter furs—not to mention the opium from which they, like the British, made their largest fortunes—and had profited greatly. (Chinese merchants had been following the same business plan, making fortunes off Americans fascinated with exotica from the Orient.)

Having achieved this toehold in Asia, American merchants pursued "jackal diplomacy" in the wake of British aggression, though to set themselves apart from the English they came bearing a variety of "improvements" meant to aid the Chinese. Religious Americans prayed for the day when the Chinese could take the redemptive Jesus into their heathen hearts. That many Chinese, then as now, regarded this as interference of a particularly pointed kind made little difference to the missionaries who began to pour into the countryside, bolstered by diplomatic demands made and achieved by the American government to protect their interests. American presidents tended to take the same paternalistic attitude toward the Chinese as the missionaries, though this did not extend to the Chinese on their own shores, whose influx was strictly controlled and curbed at every point.[1]

Just why President McKinley asked Edwin to take the post of United States minister to China is not known. Mark Twain later lumped McKinley together with Tsar Nicholas II and Kaiser Wilhelm II as self-appointed exporters of what he called "The Blessings-of-Civilization Trust," profiting from "the People that Sit in Darkness" in China, India, and the Philippines. Aside from Brazil, Edwin had no other international experience, and no obvious dealings with the American imperialism that was at the heart of much of McKinley's foreign policy. But they were chums from law school, and McKinley's administration was characterized by the use of double standards in assessing qualifications of those nominated for diplomatic posts. Instead of choosing someone with at least some passing knowledge of the Far East, and more than a passing knowledge of at least the French language, McKinley selected Edwin, who would have to learn on the job under the most complex and difficult circumstances.[2] The post Edwin would fill had been ably but benignly held by the affable southern-born Midwesterner, Lieutenant Colonel Charles Denby. That Denby was a warm admirer of the Empress Dowager Cixi could well have been a factor in his removal from the position. A new man, uncompromised by contact with the dowager's blandishments, may have seemed more appropriate. In this decision, at least, Edwin did not hesitate: nineteen days into the new year of 1898, he accepted McKinley's offer.[3]

✳ ✳ ✳ ✳ ✳

When the Congers arrived in Shanghai that spring, China was officially under the rule of the twenty-seven-year-old Guangxu emperor, the slender, quiet, and headstrong nephew of the Empress Dowager Cixi and tenth in the line of Qing Sons of Heaven. Cixi had officially retired as empress in 1889, when she was almost sixty-three years of age and had reigned as imperial regent from behind the curtain for over half that time. She handed the reins of government over to Guangxu, spending what were supposed to be her golden years in the remote splendors of Yiheyuan (the Garden of Nurtured Harmony, also known as the New Summer Palace), located several miles outside Beijing.

Yiheyuan would have been the perfect place to nurture harmony, had there been any between aunt and nephew. Thus far, Cixi's control over the throne, and Guangxu's age and education in Confucian reverence toward elders, had prevented outright rebellion. But for a front row seat to the dramatic undoing of all the traditional intergenerational safeguards, the Congers could not have timed their arrival in Beijing more perfectly. An explosion between the two ruling entities—the result of friction not just between an elderly woman and a willful young man, but also between the conservative past and the liberal future—was about to spill out of the Forbidden City and into the streets of Beijing. One of the more striking ironies was that aunt and nephew had a great deal in common—a rise to power through unorthodox means and a similarly hard-headed will to wield it.

The received birth date for Cixi is November 29, 1835 (year of the wood sheep), but where her birth took place is a mystery. Even her former lady-in-waiting, Princess Der Ling, who had many intimate conversations with the elderly Cixi between 1903 and 1905, and wrote a biography of the dowager in 1929, sidesteps all specifics about Cixi's birthplace or where she was living when summoned to the Forbidden City.[4]

The diplomat Daniele Varé, Cixi's biographer in the 1930s, visited Beijing's Pewter Lane (Xila hutong) in search of the house where his subject was said to have spent her childhood, but found only the single-storey pavilions that characterize surviving *hutong* houses in Beijing today. "In any Western country they would have marked her habitation with a tablet," he wrote. "Here no one remembers, and no one seems to care." This is possibly because no one believed that the empress dowager had really been born there.[5] All indications, though, are that she was brought up in just such a modest establishment. Isaac Headland was told that Cixi's father was "a small military official," and that the neediness of the family was such that Cixi had to serve as nursemaid for her younger siblings. Headland was also told that as a child Cixi played in the streets, where she was especially fond of "puppet plays [shadow theatre], trained mice shows, bear shows and 'Punch and Judy,'" suggesting that her well known obsession with theatre started early.[6] We now know that whatever their poverty, Cixi's family was noble: her father, Kueixiang, was a descendant of Nurhaci, the first ruler of the Manchu imperial house. This made him an imperial alternate, of lineage so designated to mark it off from the ruling imperial lineage. Cixi was the first known imperial alternate to find a place among the imperial concubines.[7]

Cixi was sixteen years old when she entered the palace in September 1851. She had the approved "melon-seed" face, a smooth oval tapering at the chin, a winsome smile that even as she aged retained the smile of a child and, for contrast, eyes that were at once keen and mournful— the eyes of a woman whose life was to embody the sardonic Chinese curse, "May you live in interesting times." Most sources agree she was not a model of scholarship at this time of her life. In the China of the mid-nineteenth century, few girls received the sort of education which had been afforded Sarah Pike in Civil War America. Sons ruled the household; daughters were "guests" awaiting marriage into another family. Yet the fact that Cixi's imperial finishing school included not only lessons in reading but also painting and fine calligraphy, and that she proved such an adept student, says as much about her inborn intelligence as it does her ambition. (Though, in fact, it is not entirely clear that ambition, the "vice" so often attributed to Cixi, was ever one of her governing characteristics.)[8]

She ascended to the imperial bedchamber not a moment too soon. A fractured empire was the inheritance of the Xianfeng emperor in 1850: that year, the Taiping Rebellion, an anti-Manchu movement led by an eccentric who believed himself the brother of Jesus Christ, was establishing hegemony over Guangxi province. By 1853, just when Cixi was getting accustomed to life in the Forbidden City harem, Hong Xiuquan and his "long hair" followers had made the old Ming capital of Nanjing their base of power. Their next target for takeover was Qing Beijing.

Exploiting these circumstances, Queen Victoria's foreign secretary, Lord Palmerston, used what one writer describes as a policy of deliberate collision: "Rude surprises were grasped as great opportunities, and armed force was used to guarantee the outcome, while the public at home was led to believe it was all part of a grand design." It was a design of power over the Chinese which was not just given political weight but was attributed to the superior will of the Christian God.[9]

Thirteen years after the First Opium War, the second was again a result of such a "rude surprise." The British had a longer wish list after this second victory: a legation in Beijing; access to Tianjin, Beijing's port on the Yellow Sea; permission for foreigners to buy property inland; and, of course, that opium be made legal in China. Xianfeng's deputy in Guangzhou, Commissioner Ye Mingzhen, was a xenophobe to the core. Though there is evidence that he made efforts to co-operate with them, Ye could be as hard-nosed as the foreigners he hated. His inflexibility allowed Hong Kong Governor Sir John Bowring and Harry Parkes, an interpreter acting as consul in Guangzhou, to pursue a collision course, a strategy that had gained Britain so much in the past. Thus began the British bombardment of Guangzhou, followed by Palmerston's next collisionist tactic, sending Lord Elgin to China to occupy more ports. An allied army was formed, which secured Guangzhou and headed for Beijing.[10]

The June 1858 Treaty of Tianjin legalized opium, and demanded yet more indemnity money—six million silver taels—from a nation already bankrupt. But before ratification, Xianfeng's request that the foreign envoys come to Beijing not up the Beihe River but overland from Dagu was taken amiss by the British. Lord Elgin attacked the Dagu forts but was repelled, and Elgin led another expedition in the summer of 1860. Talks involving Harry Parkes and imperial negotiators broke down, and Parkes and his companions were taken captive. When the prisoners were not given up, the French converged on Beijing and the Summer Palace. "Fearful lest the terrible barbarians should capture him in Peking," wrote Philip Sergeant, "the Emperor resolved on flight." Xianfeng and his court (including Cixi, her son, the emperor's primary consort Cian, concubines, officials, and eunuchs) had been hiding at the Old Summer Palace (also known as Yuanmingyuan or the Garden of Perfect Brightness). Here there were acres of pleasure pavilions stuffed with silks and treasures; the compound had been enlarged and beautified by the Qianlong emperor in the eighteenth century with foreign-style marble palaces designed by Jesuit architects. At the news that the foreign devils were at the gates of the capital, Xianfeng insisted that the court set forth for Jehol (Chengde), the imperial hunting lodge north of the Great Wall. The supremely realistic Cixi must have understood that this was no hunting trip but the final curtain on her husband's reign.[11]

The court left for Jehol before dawn on September 22, 1860. Prince Gong, Xianfeng's adroit half-brother, was left behind in Beijing to negotiate with the foreigners, "the only wise political act of [Xianfeng's] life." In the first week in October, after the French and some Sikh cavalry marched into the abandoned Yuanmingyuan, the retribution began: "not only looting, but wholesale and wanton smashing and trampling underfoot for the pleasure of destruction." Lord Elgin professed to be disgusted by the vandalism, yet came to the conclusion that because all the items of value had already been stripped from the palaces, the army had the right to "mark by a solemn act of retribution the horror and indignation with which we were inspired by the perpetration of a great crime," namely the imprisonment and deaths of the captured men. As Philip Sergeant has pointed out, by this same logic King Leopold's palace in Ostend would have had to be burned to expiate for Belgian atrocities in the Congo.[12] As a result, one of the world's architectural wonders was put to the torch. Contrary to Lord Elgin's remarks, not only was the palace beautiful from without, it was also filled with beauty. As one of the French officers present for the destruction explained later, what he and the others saw in abandoned pavilions could only be described using ink made of "all known precious stones [dissolved] in liquid gold."[13]

Treasures stolen from Yuanmingyuan appeared on the auction block shortly after—a dog from the imperial Pekingese kennels was brought to England and given to Queen Victoria, who dubbed it "Looty." Of the fabled pavilions at Yuanmingyuan, only fragments of elegantly carved marble remained, scattered across acres of torn landscape, to be picked apart and used by farmers and scavengers for less aesthetic purposes. "[The end of Yuanmingyuan] was the beginning of two important phases of the Empress Dowager's life," wrote Professor Headland and his wife—"her affliction and her power." This event was also to shape Cixi's reaction to and handling of the Boxer Uprising almost forty years later.[14]

In Jehol, news of the destruction and of the concessions wrung from Prince Gong seemed to drive the final nail into the Xianfeng emperor's coffin. In August 1861, he was on his deathbed. Although the birth of a male heir had made it more likely that the Xianfeng emperor would nominate his son to be the next ruler of the Manchu empire, primogeniture was not practiced by the imperial house, and the delirious Xianfeng could just as easily have named a nephew. Xianfeng had chosen eight regents, two of whom, Prince Yi and Sushun, were Cixi's sworn enemies. Just before Xianfeng died, Cixi rushed into his room, carrying the three-year-old boy, and stood at the bed, saying to the emperor, "Here is your son." The question implied by that flat statement hung heavily in the air. "Of course he will succeed to the throne," was the emperor's response, as Cixi recalled it when relating the incident many years later.[15]

It was not even clear that the Xianfeng emperor's dying wish would be honored. No Qing emperor had died with only one male heir—after an emperor had "ascended the dragon to become a guest on high," there had always been bloody fraternal squabbles, with cadres of potential emperors clawing their way to the dragon throne.[16] Cixi's concerns were more personal. Should the regents put her son out of the running, she could look forward to imprisonment, forced suicide, or outright execution. And before Xianfeng's body had cooled, Cixi and Cian had become virtual captives of Prince Yi and Sushun, the regents for the young emperor. But if they thought Cixi was to be bamboozled, they were seriously mistaken. She had spent her youth not in indolence but in learning. Whatever his other failings, the Xianfeng emperor had acknowledged her intelligence: he had allowed her to work with him, giving her a window into the workings of the empire and the mechanics of court politics. The self-preservation that drove her to barge into the emperor's death chamber with her son would not let her give up this fight. Cixi told Sushun that she was no mere concubine but the mother of the emperor, and would never accept such an unfair arrangement. She then convinced Cian to join her against the "Gang of Eight."

Cixi and Cian held the trump card in this game, because they had somehow retained one of the two seals—the "Seal of Lawfully Transmitted Authority"—without which no edicts or decrees could be ratified. Even when Sushun placed the women under house arrest, depriving them of food and water till they agreed to seal his decree, plans for his downfall were already spinning in Cixi's brain. The court prepared to return to Beijing, where tradition demanded that the boy be the first to meet his ancestor's coffined remains.[17] Cixi had communicated with

Prince Gong in Beijing, so once the regents set foot in the capital, they were quickly rounded up. Counter-edicts suspending the Gang of Eight's authority and appointing the dowager empresses in their place were issued in the young emperor's name, and sealed with the Great Seal. All eight regents were executed, Sushun by beheading in the humiliating venue of the common execution ground in the vegetable market. The child emperor's new reign name, Tongzhi or "Joint Government," described the new arrangement, with Cixi and Cian as co-empresses dowager and Prince Gong as joint regent, and it says something about Cixi that this is often overlooked. She did not, as is frequently charged, instantly take over sole power. "Historical judgments vilifying Cixi as a usurping empress in the Han Chinese mode should be reexamined," writes Evelyn Rawski. Cixi's tradition of joint rule with her brothers-in-law, Prince Gong and Prince Chun, "may be seen as a historical repetition of the Manchu tradition of cooperation between imperial widows and their brothers-in-law."[18]

✳ ✳ ✳ ✳ ✳

Now Cixi's time of real power began, but with it fresh afflictions took root, in a pattern that was to be repeated.

"It may be said with emphasis," wrote Colonel Charles Denby, the American minister to China just prior to Edwin Conger, "that the Empress Dowager has been the first of her race to apprehend the problem of the relation of China to the outer world, and to make use of this relation to strengthen her dynasty and promote material progress." Arriving at this awareness of just how to interact with an unfriendly outside world, especially one that wanted to eviscerate China, required a great deal of trial and error from the Empress Dowager Cixi. In the thirty-seven years before Sarah Conger's arrival in China in July 1898, Cixi had become the most powerful woman in the world next to Queen Victoria, one of the few foreign leaders she admired. Cixi and Cian, until the latter's death in 1881, ruled "behind the curtain" as the Tongzhi emperor grew up through a wayward, unstable, and impetuous youth. He was fond of the idea of reform but had no clear idea how to make use of it. He died of smallpox at age eighteen (a death later laid at Cixi's doorstep), leaving no heir. No doubt terrified of revisiting the succession crisis that had surrounded the death of Xianfeng, and feeling the need to consolidate her own family's power around the throne, Cixi nominated another heir, Zaitian, son of her sister and Prince Chun. She did so with such urgency she ignored the tradition according to which an emperor's heir had to be from a generation after his own, so he could worship in proper hierarchical order at the ancestral altar. This break with tradition was to dog her later on.[19]

Zaitian became the Guangxu emperor in 1875. While finding him more stable than her late son had been, Cixi may have overdone the job of making him fit to rule: she encouraged the young man's energetic but imperious nature more than may have been safe. Guangxu did not limit himself to the purview of his own nation, but sought knowledge of the forbidden world outside it—this was helpful to him, fearsome for Cixi. She had also underestimated the Guangxu emperor's self-will. Plagued by ill health but intelligent and impatient (a trait for which his aunt was notorious), the Guangxu emperor had been married off to Yehenara, a niece of Cixi's, who was, like him, interested in the world outside the Forbidden City. But the young emperor preferred the company of one of two sister concubines, a young woman known as the Pearl (Zhenfei, or "Precious Concubine"). An aristocrat of the Tatala clan, the Pearl, with her sister, had been well educated. Unlike her less ambitious sister, however, the Pearl was just as prone as the Guangxu emperor was to rubbing Cixi the wrong way.

In 1889, Cixi turned over the reins of empire to Guangxu and withdrew into part-time retirement at Yiheyuan, enjoying her holiday from the throne but watching and waiting to see how her pupil carried out his imperial duties. Nine years later, at the same time as Sarah and Edwin Conger were arriving in steaming Beijing, Cixi's eagle eye had seen quite enough to worry her. The simmering pot that was the struggle between her and Guangxu, between the conservatives and the reformers, and between past and future, was ready to boil over.

3
High walls

On June 23, 1898, the Congers' steamer put in at Shanghai, where they were whisked off to the Foreign Settlement. This area west of the famous waterfront Bund was crowded with what were the tallest buildings in China and vessels from a dozen nations were moored along its bank. The settlement stretched along the Huangpu River and inland to the west, centering around the Shanghai Race Club and fashionable Bubbling Well Road. The French had a concession all their own to the south of the Foreign Settlement. The Chinese City lay in a small area south of these settlements' bisecting line, Avenue Édouard VII.

The Treaty of Nanjing, following the First Opium War, made Shanghai possible, in terms of its foreign population. By granting Great Britain "most favored nation" status, China raised the expectations of other nations involved in trade who now desired the same favors. These nations were granted their concessions, and with the real estate came extraterritoriality. This meant that if a Frenchman, Englishman, or American committed a crime in Shanghai they could only be tried by their own national courts which were set up within the concessions to deal with such matters. In other words, foreigners in Shanghai, a city synonymous with crime, could indulge in it all they wanted, knowing the Chinese father of a raped girl or Chinese merchant they had cheated could never pursue them.[1]

It was from a window of her hotel that Sarah received her first harsh glimpse of the Chinese laboring classes. The sight of men pulling heavy carts or running foreigners around in rickshaws shocked her: "They do the work of beasts and are treated as beasts," she wrote to her sister. "The wheelbarrow men and others, who do work elsewhere apportioned to beasts and mechanical contrivances, eat little else than two bowls of rice a day, and wear little clothing." Never one to shy from asking questions, Sarah talked to people who lived in Shanghai—most of them probably her husband's colleagues—to discover the true state of the laborers' situation. She was told that though these men seemed to her to be working like animals, they were gainfully and willingly employed. They did jobs which, however difficult they seemed to her, fulfilled a real need in the urban economy. And they were eating food that had served their ancestors well for thousands of years, whether hoeing fields or building the Great Wall. Assuredly a Chinese man who pulled a rickshaw or pushed a wheelbarrow (another form of human transport in China) lived a life not to be envied, though this was a fact over which it would not have occurred to most expatriates in China to linger. "Yet these toilers are strong," Sarah observed, "do their work well, and are of good cheer."[2] China was not America, Sarah realized, but a land and a people unto themselves. "It proves itself an axiom—'There are no idle people in China,'" she wrote. The Chinese had to be seen and judged by their own standards, Sarah realized, not through the lenses or laws of other nations. But she was to see something else, too: how some Chinese who went abroad brought back many of their own prejudices intact, untouched by contact with Western freedoms.[3]

The Congers were visited, as per custom, by Shanghai's highest Chinese official, the *daodai* or intendant of circuit, who later invited them to dinner, for a meal that was half Chinese and half Western, in alternating courses. Sarah is silent on the topic of how well she or Edwin handled the Chinese portion of the menu, not to mention the chopsticks. (Sarah was never to master them, though she was to become fond of Chinese cuisine.)[4] But she was charmed by the *daodai*'s fluent

English, especially when she learned he had been educated in the United States. When Sarah noticed that his wife was not present she asked him why. The *daodai* answered frankly: "My people do not approve." That there should be disapproval of an official's wife attending a reception for honored guests simply because she was a woman came as a shock to Sarah—it was as if on one of Edwin's visits to the White House he should be compelled to leave Sarah at home because it was improper for her to show her face before American government officials. This was a stark first glimpse into the restricted existence of Chinese women, for whom the walls of the family compound, the bound feet in fashion among Han ladies, and a host of societal restrictions made ventures into the street outside, let alone the greater world, very rare events. It was also Sarah's first experience of the sad irony of the lives of many foreign-educated Chinese who returned to China. This man who spoke English like an American because he had gone to college there (to his benefit), was not able to bring American ideas of gender equality to China, for the benefit of his Chinese wife.[5]

✳ ✳ ✳ ✳ ✳

The Congers spent over a week in Shanghai. They then boarded their train for Tianjin, Beijing's port on the Yellow Sea, which they reached on July 4. The American consul gave a party in celebration, a touch all the more appreciated in this the most foreign place the Congers had ever visited. At the Beijing station, which lay five miles from the capital, a trio of staff from the American legation met the couple with sedan chairs, Beijing carts, *mafu* (grooms for the horses), coolies to carry bags and boxes, and carts to carry the bigger items. In one long procession, the Americans began their trek to fabled Beijing over what many foreigners (and Chinese) considered one of the worst roads on earth.

A decade earlier, English author Alicia Little found travel over the thirteen miles from Tongzhou to Beijing harrowing in all aspects. Riding in a springless cart pulled by a trudging donkey, she was subject to "holes and ruts, into which we dropped with a veritable concussion, not a jolt." Holding on to the sides, she lost her glasses several times, then decided to get out and walk in the dust, only to find herself surrounded by touts, peddlers, and beggars, all doing their best to sell her something. With them came a number of other travelers—camels bearing bricks of tea to Beijing or heading south to pick up more. Mrs. Little's first impression of Beijing was of dirt and chaos. "I . . . began to wonder how long Peking could go on," she wrote, "accumulating filth within its walls without breeding a Black Death or other pestilence."[6]

On the other hand, American author Eliza Ruhama Scidmore, not so respectful of the Chinese as Mrs. Little, nonetheless found her first sight of the city an unparalleled thrill. "Peking is the most incredible, impossible, anomalous and surprising place in the world," Scidmore wrote of her visit, which occurred around the time of the Congers' arrival. The city was at one and the same time an international capital of a once great empire and "a permanent Tatar encampment, a fortified garrison of nomad bannermen." The walls and gates she rightly described as the city's greatest features, only looming above the traveler's head after she had already crossed the broad plain on which the city, so like that nomad encampment, squarely sat. Beijing, to Scidmore, seemed as ephemeral as a camp of Mongolian yurts.[7]

Already three thousand years old when Edwin and Sarah arrived, Beijing (literally the "Northern Capital") had survived several major name and dynastic changes over the millennia of its existence. Lying at nearly the same latitude as Rome, and just 120 feet above sea level, the city benefited from the dry climate of northern Zhili province. But it also suffered, as it does to this day, from its proximity to the Gobi Desert, just north of the Great Wall which is some forty miles from the city's walls. In the spring, sandstorms turned the skies a deep yellow; the narrow alleys or *hutong* and the broad boulevards alike were filled with an ochre "fog" which the burning of coal for cooking, heating, and workshops only made worse.[8]

Even foreigners who hated Beijing's smells and its climate marveled over the shimmering yellow roof tiles of the imperial palaces in the Forbidden City complex, which sat like square-cut golden jewels boxed within walls the shade of faded crimson velvet, a sacred city within a profane one. Imperial custom decreed that no house rise higher than the emperor's own, meaning that few of Beijing's buildings were higher than the many trees lining streets and standing in courtyards. Through the branches, the green tiles of princely dwellings and the pale gray of common ones occasionally thrust an upturned eave or rooftop dragon, while the roof ridges of temples and grand houses crawled with a procession of animals prosaic and fantastic all chasing evil Prince Min astride his chicken off the curving edge. Foreigners were struck by the vivid contrast between the gilded and rainbow-painted shop signs sticking out at right angles above crude holes in the wall, and what could be found within: men and women sold everything from candied fruits on sticks to animals spun from hot sugar; butcher shops and markets offered all manner of animals for the dinner table, from the homely to the exotic; and a variety of services, from the brushing of titles on book spines, to the trimming of queues and shaving of foreheads, to the making of shoes, clothing, rugs, pillows, knives, calligraphic and scenic scrolls, cosmetics, and health and longevity medicines, all sat alongside the ever-present tea shops and bakeries. Buddhists, Daoists, Confucianists, Muslims, Christians, and Jews had lived together for centuries in a harmony that would have been the envy of Western capitals.

Over all this, above the curling rooftops of the Forbidden City, one saw the purple smudge of the distant Western Hills, studded with temples and the pleasure haunts of foreigners, glimmering in the summer heat or shimmering with snow in winter. And one could hear the clanging of camel bells and the low booming of temple bells, the hurry, chaos, variety, and energy of the city's teeming populace.

In her brief account of first entering Beijing, Sarah says little about the city itself. But there were two aspects that spurred her curiosity: the many walls (behind which lived the secluded Chinese ladies she longed to meet and know) and the many graveyards. China seemed to her, indeed, to be made up of little more than the latter, "anywhere and everywhere, [they] lay along our route to the city." She was not alone: to many foreigners coming to China for the first time, "the authority of the dead was everywhere."[9]

While in Sarah's America the concept of park-like cemeteries helped soften the harsh edge of death by comforting the living who visited their dead, Chinese graveyards were designed for the dead alone. Ancient Daoist sages had decreed that the direction in which an ancestor was laid to rest, the condition of the soil above and below, and the presence or absence of beneficial water or stones, all played a crucial role in the luck or lack of it of the deceased's survivors. This meant that wherever *feng shui*, as the geomantic method was called, established a site as auspicious, there the dead would be buried. With a population of 400 million, China did not have endless plots of land to devote to cemeteries, so they were often sited in full view of roadways or buildings. Knowing this, foreign powers would, in time, use their destruction as another method of punishing the Chinese people, acts that would move Sarah to outrage.[10]

The walls obsessed her most—she might have agreed with China scholar John Hay, who wrote: "The plan of Beijing is a construction of boundaries," a "fractured series of layers." "China has fortified herself against the outside world as well as against her own people," Sarah observed. "How I long to go behind these high walls and see something of the Chinese home life! Can it be that good fortune will ever open these locked gates and invite me to enter?" This was a lot to expect before she had even settled in Beijing. But the image of Shanghai wives kept in hiding while their husbands had free run of the world had stayed with her. She now looked at walls as something peculiarly male and confining, and at the lives of the women within those walls as the key to freeing the mysteries China posed to her at every turn—and, perhaps, the key to freeing China of the unseen walls impeding its progress. Sarah determined that, with time and luck, she would get behind these walls, bringing the world with her and introducing China's women to the world.[11]

✳   ✳   ✳   ✳   ✳

The area known to foreigners as the Legation Quarter was called by the Chinese something much more evocative—the "Eastern Lane of the Mingling of Peoples" (*Dongjiaomin xiang*). Located east of the Qianmen Gate on the Tartar City's southern wall, the area dated back to the time of the Mongol Yuan dynasty, when it was used as a stopping place for foreign traders. It was also the city's gateway for goods brought in from southern China, including tea. The lopsided rectangle of its footprint was bisected from north to south by the euphemistically named Jade Canal, a waterway fed by the pleasure lakes situated west of the Forbidden City but believed by foreigners to be an imperial sewer drain. Some found the entire district distasteful. "For the nearly forty years that the fine flowers of European diplomacy have been transplanted to Peking," sniffed Eliza Scidmore, "they have been content to wallow along this filthy Legation street . . . the highway before their doors a general sewer and dumping-ground for offensive refuse of every kind."[12]

Perhaps Sarah expected to find in her new home something of what the British had, a Chinese palace once the home of an imperial duke, fitted with Western "improvements," but retaining many of its original, crimson-pillared, gilded charms. But compared to the British, French, or Russian legations, the American was unremarkable. A friend of Sarah's, the young American artist Cecile Payen, who lived in the legation compound during the Boxer Uprising, was less charitable:

> The houses, originally Chinese, are small one-story structures, and the rooms are very dark . . . The compound is very crowded, which is a great disadvantage, for in Peking there are no pleasure-promenades, and you never think of going out in the streets for a stroll. The place is guarded at night by a watchman who makes his rounds beating two hollow pieces of wood, whether to let the inmates know he is doing his duty, or to warn malefactors of his approach, I cannot learn.[13]

The Congers' quarters lay along one side of a tree-filled courtyard. Inside the gray-tiled buildings, which were set with incongruous Western-style mullioned glass windows, were high-ceilinged Chinese rooms clumsily divided into more or less recognizably Western living and dining spaces using screens, potted palms, and an army of mismatched Victorian settees, marble-topped tables, pier-glasses, and chairs divorced from long-gone dining suites, squeezed in among crimson pillars rising to ornate blue and green painted ceilings. Hidden away in the southeast corner of the compound, directly adjacent to the Tartar Wall on the south and the Jade Canal and Water Gate on the east, was a famous temple, the Sanguanmiao or the Temple of the Three Officials. This was the last place of worship of the last emperor of the Ming dynasty, Chongzhen, who after praying for guidance at this temple hanged himself on Prospect Hill behind the Forbidden City. The temple was no refuge for an emperor, but it would become an unlikely but beloved home for the Congers in another few years' time.[14]

The crowdedness of the American legation noted by Cecile was partly due to the superabundance of servants (a total of fifty) and staff. For a first secretary, Edwin had the wealthy, cosmopolitan, and multilingual New Yorker, Herbert Squiers. New to the diplomatic service, Squiers lived with his elegant wife, Harriet, in the white brick, European-style building in the compound which also housed the legation's business office. The second secretary, W. E. Bainbridge and his wife, also lived in the compound, along with the interpreter, F. D. Cheshire, who had taken to wearing a queue and Chinese clothing "so as to be better able to mix with [the Chinese] and study the language," remembered Miss Payen. Each of these men and their families, plus Edwin and Sarah, had the large number of servants believed necessary at that time and in that place.[15]

For all they were older than most of the diplomats in Beijing, the Congers were rank upstarts on the diplomatic pecking order—their country did not even own its own legation compound. According to Eliza Scidmore, while the "picked diplomats of all Europe" were sent to Beijing to do service, "sustained by the certainty of promotions and rewards after a useful term," the American minister earned little and could expect less. He is "crowded in small rented premises, is paid about a fourth as much as the other envoys, and, coming untrained to his career, has the cheerful certainty of being put out of office as soon as he has learned his business and another President is elected."[16]

Diplomatic Americans in Beijing clearly felt they were not held in very high regard. "Foreign society here is divided into three distinct sets," recalled Cecile Payen: "the diplomatic, which is very cold and formal, the customs, with Sir Robert Hart at its head, which is the most sociable, and the missionaries, who form a society of their own."[17]

Sir Claude MacDonald was not the doyen or most senior member of the group of foreigners—that honor belonged to the elderly, optimistic Marquis Don Bernardo de Cologan of Spain, squinting his cloudy eyes against the Chinese sun. But Sir Claude bore himself like one, with his tall, pencil-thin figure, quizzical expression, and stiff waxed moustache. He would show great courage when his life depended on it, but he had a faulty memory and an apparent overall lack of interest in details that would cause problems for everyone in time. Lady McDonald (Ethel), was a handsome, somewhat stern, and no-nonsense Englishwoman who would prove her mettle under enemy fire as well as in the diplomatic fray: it was she who would first seek an audience for the foreign diplomats' wives with the Empress Dowager Cixi. Like de Cologan, the Austrian minister Baron Moritz Czikann von Wahlborn would also stand out in difficult circumstances, though for different reasons and very much in spite of his obvious view of Beijing as a nauseating stepping stone to better things. Czikann's first secretary, Arthur von Rosthorn, who with his wife would echo Sarah's sympathy for the Chinese, would show far more character.[18]

The French minister, Stéphen Pichon, was a charming and alert man who, however, could not refrain from sharing his innermost fears with all and sundry, putting firmly set British teeth on edge during the Boxer troubles. He also had a boyish streak, displayed in photographs taken of him in August 1900 lolling on an abandoned imperial throne. It has been pointed out that Pichon and Edwin were the only republicans present among the baronets, counts, and marquises. But where Edwin swam in these coroneted waters as easily as he might in a swimming hole back in Iowa—from naivety as much as American nonchalance—Pichon was full of middle-class complexes. Unhelpfully, his friendly wife, the daughter of a restaurateur, was often made the butt of jokes among the supposedly better class of diplomatic society in Beijing, entrenching more harmful factions within the tiny community.

As important for his diplomatic prowess as for his nation's proximity to (and designs on) China, Mikhail de Giers proved himself a redoubtable Russian minister, never venturing an opinion or sharing an observation, and comfortable in his cloak of mystery like a painted Chinese mountain wreathed in mists. His wife wore a permanent knowing smile that complemented her husband's inscrutability. Presenting the opposite extreme was the voluble, officious, and violent Baron Clemens von Ketteler, German minister and a middle-aged career diplomat, who considered himself a lofty specialist in *les choses chinoises* cast among lessers of education and caste. Yet he was habitually cruel to Chinese people in ways that led him, step by step, to the muzzle of a Chinese gun. His young American wife, heiress to the Ledyard railway fortune, hated

Beijing as much as Lady MacDonald did, and in her own way made as much fun of the Chinese as her fellow aristocrats did of Madame Pichon.

This little international community, in which Edwin and Sarah arrived as newcomers knowing nothing of the challenges or opportunities, was a motley crew at best to pilot the unsteady ship of foreign diplomacy on a Chinese sea growing choppier by the day. "Never before," one historian points out, "had the diplomatic corps [in Beijing] been so collectively ignorant of and insensitive toward the Chinese body politic."[19]

✳ ✳ ✳ ✳ ✳

For Sarah, the uniform grayness of the American compound and perhaps what seemed an unrelenting aura of untidiness throughout the city moved even this perennially hopeful woman to write that what she saw was not pre-possessing. But, being Sarah, she determined to make the best of the situation, which is why she first went to visit her kitchen.

Few foreign diplomats' wives (save, perhaps, for Madame Pichon) ever saw the interior of their kitchens or even knew where the kitchens were, but Sarah was no typical diplomatic lady. She had spent her early married life dealing with that room, which in a Midwest home was the source of a housewife's pride. Her impression of the American legation was not improved by the sight of where the legation's food was cooked. She was, in fact, "heart-sick":

> Across one end was a piece of masonry about six feet long, three feet wide, and two and one-half feet high. This masonry had three small holes in the top, with loose bricks placed about them. At the front were corresponding holes for the fire. There was no chimney! High in the room was an opening for the smoke to escape. There was an old-fashioned, foreign brick oven in a corner near this Chinese range.[20]

Sarah could not believe that a simple meal, let alone the many courses required for formal dinners, could ever be produced in this "kitchen." Edwin suggested she have the sort of frank discussion she might have had with a servant in her Des Moines home, and his advice was, as Sarah often acknowledged, excellent, but it also led to a surprise. First Cook was an artist, and a proud one. Far from cringing before this nervous American memsahib, First Cook told Sarah that she was worrying herself over nothing.[21]

Sarah was not so sure. "At first," she reflected later, "I tried to have [the Chinese servants] learn my way of doing." Soon after the Congers arrived, Sarah took it upon herself to reorganize the legation's accounts, so that instead of each household department purchasing its own coal or food stores, Sarah would buy in quantity for everyone to use as needed. The servants did their best to function within this strange system of strict accountability. But the changes Sarah had ordered soon caused more chaos than they were worth. Nothing was right, the servants told her—one of the countless problems was that the coal she had ordered in would not burn. Actually, nothing was that different from before, except for one important detail. What the servants really missed, Sarah discovered, was something Chinese people seldom spoke of publicly. It was a staple of Chinese trade: the "squeeze," a practice by which the purchaser of items for a third party skimmed off a profit. The servants could not do this if Sarah made the purchases for them. Shocked at first, Sarah realized that imposing her—the foreign world's—way on her Chinese servants not only deprived them of a source of income that was as much a part of doing business as the handshake (written contracts being uncommon in China), but ultimately cost the legation more in the long run. In this case it was more expensive to disrupt a routine and tradition that was centuries old than it was to retain it.[22]

Sarah had a similar moment of insight around this same time. She had noticed that wallpaper in one of the reception rooms needed replacing. The servants told her there was no way to match it. "No got," she records their reply, "no have Peking." But all was not lost. "Chinaman can make," they insisted. Thinking in terms of the lifespan of wallpaper patterns, which in America was as short as that of the season's fashions, Sarah could not understand how this could be done. But shortly afterward, First Boy Lu brought in an old man, who stood in the room studying the wall for a while, then went away. He returned in a few days with sheets of wallpaper painted to look exactly like the sections that needed replacing, apparently even matching the original paper's faded pigmentation. Of everything she would come to admire in the Chinese, it was this god-in-the-details approach that Sarah enjoyed most. She had already noticed that foreign banks employed Chinese "for their most important detail work." Her bank manager told her he hired Chinese for three reasons: "they are honest, self-possessed, and accurate," traits in which foreign workers were evidently deficient. Their ability to concentrate, though surrounded by distraction, echoed Sarah's own credo: steadiness in any storm. They were steady even in the storm of Sarah's initial misgivings. Where there were points about which she was adamant, and where she put her case both firmly and logically, the servants lent a ready ear and were more than willing to compromise. This was because when learning to let her staff use their own methods, Sarah had also mastered the subtle Chinese art of adapting, like bamboo to the wind.[23]

"The Chinese system of living is so intricate and so well learned," Sarah concluded, "and adhered to by all classes, that it 'passeth understanding.'" Sarah was aware that she was asking the Chinese to live by a rule foreign to them. "My ideas of right," she wrote to a friend, "should not be so arbitrary as to deprive them of a day's wages." The heavens she had seen upside down in Brazil were still puzzling to her, but she was beginning to recognize and appreciate their new pattern.[24]

4

Chinese Christians

Almost four years before the Congers' arrival in Beijing, in November 1894, the Empress Dowager Cixi, then in her third year of retirement, was presented with a gift which, as one of her biographers puts it with pointed understatement, "is supposed to have led indirectly to very important developments."[1]

Following the lead of the missionaries who had converted them, Chinese Protestant women throughout the empire had raised a subscription to help pay for an elegantly printed edition of the New Testament, translated into Chinese and bound in silver repoussé with a scene of Christ rising to heaven, to be given to Cixi for her birthday. Unlike the Jesuits, who in the China of the late Ming and early Qing dynasties had seen the wisdom and the expediency of incorporating Chinese and Christian systems of faith and worship in their efforts to convert the Chinese, the Protestants who had swarmed into China from Britain and America in the nineteenth century proved to be largely tone-deaf to the culture that hosted them. What Cixi already knew of Christianity was hardly likely to dispose her toward it. She had lived, after all, through the Taiping Rebellion, in which a failed scholar of the

Confucian classics turned to a sketchy knowledge of Christianity in recasting himself as a Jesus-like freedom-fighter against Manchu rule (and was assisted by foreign Christians interested in booty, saving souls, or both).

Nor did Cixi like the notion of foreigners coming to China to sway the Chinese away from their ancient religious allegiances. Cixi was a devout Buddhist, scrupulously adhering to the rites, to which she added the more mystical rituals of Daoism. As she told her lady-in-waiting, Der Ling, there were many foreigners who were "very nice and polite," but she saw in Christianity a threat not just to Buddhist belief but to the basic structure of Chinese culture. Christianity was a "new idea," a fad, which influenced the young and the ignorant to "chop up their Ancestral Tablets and burn them. I know many families here who have broken up because of the missionaries, who are always influencing the young people to believe their religion."[2]

The specter of foreigners as drug pushers extended to macabre tales that missionaries used Chinese children's eyes as ingredients in their potions. Even when Der Ling told Cixi that her own father, diplomat Yu Keng, had met some of these children and discovered they had been taken to the missions by their families *because* of their condition, in the hope they would be helped there, and that the children had been coached by the local prefect, the old lady was still not entirely convinced. There were few such liberal voices at court to help broaden her view. Yet it was really not the missionaries Cixi disliked most—it was Chinese converts. "These Chinese Christians are the worst people in China!" she told her lady-in-waiting. It was they, she believed, who stirred up civil unrest by refusing to obey the laws that had been part of Chinese society for millennia, disrupting the Confucian structure of containment and order, and of respect for the authority of emperor and parents. What made Christianity especially repugnant to devout Chinese was the absence of the rite of recognition and duty toward one's ancestors. Unhappy ancestral ghosts were condemned to roam the land and were the disrupters of the harmony toward which all ritual in China strove. And of course, the worst thing about the Christians, especially to Cixi, was that their allegiance to the emperor as living god was compromised by their conversion to the worship of the single god of the Christian Bible. It was this compromised allegiance that would lead the throne, in a few years, closer to disaster than it had ever been before.[3]

So in presenting a copy of the New Testament to Cixi, Chinese Christians and their missionary advisors, as well as the foreign ministers of Britain and the United States who personally offered the gift to the Zongli Yamen (Chinese Foreign Office), did not understand with what apprehension their Christian Pandora's box might be received. Cixi issued a polite acknowledgement, sent gifts to the missionary women responsible for organizing the project, and that might have been that. Guangxu, however, had heard about the New Testament sitting unread in the Zongli Yamen, and he "ordered copies of both New and Old Testaments in Chinese from the American Bible Society at Peking, and set to work with the Palace eunuchs to read them." This was not the beginning of Guangxu's interest in all things foreign, but it was the point at which his voracious curiosity about the West began to swallow whole every translated European book he could find, increasing his understanding of how the world outside China functioned, with its collection of monarchs and presidents, empires and republics. A flame was kindled in Guangxu for all things foreign, but most of all for all the things that China did not possess, summed up by the single word "reform."[4]

✳   ✳   ✳   ✳   ✳

"There is a Japanese expression, 'fire-thieves,'" wrote Cixi's earliest biographer, Philip Sergeant, "denoting those who take advantage of a conflagration to steal property from the burning houses." Such was the reaction on the part of several foreign nations with their sights set on China, as a result of the concessions wrung by Germany from the Chinese government.[5]

On November 1, 1897, a pair of German, Roman Catholic missionaries were set upon by a crowd and murdered in the coastal province of Shandong. Attacks on missionaries had been rising since the middle of the nineteenth century, often in response to an increase in missionary activity. This had been a factor in the attack in the summer of 1891 on a Methodist mission in Wuxi on the Yangzi River, in which missionaries were murdered by anti-foreign, anti-Christian rioters. Jiangsu, the province in which the attack occurred, had only four Christian missions, but it was sandwiched between Hubei which ranked second among the mission-populated provinces with fifteen, and Guangdong, which boasted over twenty as a result of its longer history of foreign and Christian contact. Shandong, where the German missionaries were murdered in 1897, was a smaller province than Hubei or Guangdong but had fully a dozen Christian missions. Coupled with the province's heritage as the birthplace of Confucius and home to a number of sites sacred to Daoists, it is reasonable to assume that by 1897 the tectonic plates of Chinese and foreign culture, and more specifically of Chinese and foreign religion, had finally begun to grate against one another.[6]

Though no one ever discovered just who the murderers were, whether they were rogue elements acting on the general unrest in the province, or members of a particular secret society bent on removing foreign influences, Germany sent a fleet speeding toward Jiaozhou Bay, Shandong's harbor and another of the province's revered sites (from here, the Buddhist monk Faxien had set out for India in AD 414 to bring Buddhist scriptures and relics back to China). Occupying Qingdao, the German government proceeded to make demands of the Chinese authorities. They wanted the missionary killers executed, the local officials punished, and the provincial governor sacked. This only fanned the flames. The Germans then demanded and received a ninety-nine-year lease of Jiaozhou Bay and coal mining rights, among other privileges. No sooner were these awarded than other nations stepped up to complain and make their own demands. First Russia, then Britain and France argued their cases for concessions, and received them. China lost four of the greatest harbors on its coast.[7]

Even as his aunt took China more seriously than most people believed, the Guangxu emperor proved the reality of inherited tendencies in his theatrical reaction to this fresh carving up of Chinese soil for the European tea table. "To repair a broken self-image and to rehabilitate a mutilated spirit," writes Luke S. K. Kwong, "Kuang-hsu's [Guangxu's] only chance was the attainment of dynastic revitalization through his imperial role." Thus it was through his frustration at the slow pace of reform, his highly emotional temperament, and what seemed to be the right timing to strike out on his own as ruler, that Guangxu fell in with Kang Youwei, one of the most controversial figures in late Qing China.[8]

Born in 1858 in Guangdong province, Kang was an example of both the positive and negative effects of foreign influence on a scholar steeped in the Confucian traditions he desired to reform. Later hailed by many Chinese as a reformer who helped lay the foundations of the modern Chinese state, Kang was indeed that. He advocated reforms across a broad spectrum of social and political needs, including calling for modernization of the army, postal system, the judiciary, and education (including the abolition of the examination system on which the hopes of so many would-be bureaucrats and their families had rested for several centuries, and on which so many were dashed). He was especially outraged by the low status of Chinese women, believing that improving their status would strengthen China as well as lift the nation's standing in the eyes of foreigners—a concept he ironically shared with the Empress Dowager Cixi, his implacable enemy, and which was fulfilled, to a point, later in the twentieth century by Mao Zedong's communist government.[9]

The fatal flaw in this genius of the new and improved is one shared by many trailblazers: that of identifying too closely with one's own reforms. Kang was that other cliché, a great thinker with a great ego to match. When taken into the Guangxu emperor's confidence, he clearly did not offer his assistance clothed in objectivity; his own past resentments against the Qing regime played an overarching (and overreaching) role in the events that were to send him in flight from Qing justice and result in the executions of colleagues too brave or too blinded by his rhetoric to flee China with him.

The Guangxu emperor gazed at the array of reforms urged on him by Kang and his followers like a child given free reign over a candy store. At first, it must have seemed to Cixi the natural excitement of a boy king finally allowed to rule, and as he made his dutiful visits to the Summer Palace and reported on his progress, she offered her advice, as per her role and prerogative. But she began to suspect that something else was afoot—that hands other than her nephew's were grabbing at the sweets and, most alarmingly, were intent on depriving her of her freedom to do the same.

✳ ✳ ✳ ✳ ✳

For decades, American diplomats had always made use of a particular temple, the Sanshan'an or Three Hills Nunnery, a Ming-era compound fifteen miles away from town, as a retreat from the dust and heat of Beijing in summer. The Sanshan'an was one of eight temples staggered up the Western Hills, nicknamed by the Chinese *cuiwei shan* (the blue-green tinted mountains). Given the sprawl and smog of modern-day Beijing, the Western Hills are sometimes hard to see, let alone imagine from the perspective of a century or more ago. In the Congers' time, though, they would still have appeared as one early twentieth-century admirer described them: standing out "against the pure and tender blue" of morning, their forested slopes turning purple and then black at evening "against a background of fiery sky."[10]

Surrounded by the Cui, Pinpo, and Lushi Hills, the Sanshan'an was built on a "natural shelf of the mountain-side," recalled an American guest of the Congers. The temple had a terrace running along its length, "from which we look right out on the world beneath us, down the valley towards Peking." Positioned on the veranda with a good field glass, Sarah could see all traffic crossing the plain around Beijing. If she knew when Edwin was coming home from the city, she could follow the dust raised by his retinue as they crossed the flatlands. If you turned and looked up behind the terrace, you saw Mount Bruce towering above the rooftops of the temple; from the lower slopes you could see the golden copings of the Empress Dowager's pleasure spot, the new Summer Palace, glimmering in the distance.[11]

At the doorway to the temple was a carved tablet, a "cloud and water stone" which, when splashed with water, seemed to reveal endless vistas of mountains and mists populated by figures animal and human. Perhaps thinking of this tablet, with its obdurate yet permeable surface, Sarah wrote to a nephew, "There is a wonderful book opened before me." It was a book she would open further when she and Edwin set off on September 12 for a whirlwind trip of three days through several thousand years of Chinese history.[12]

The Congers' group for their short trip was comprised of Sarah and Edwin, their daughter Laura and her cousin Mary Pierce, four "donkey-men," and five legation servants: the first *mafu* or stableman, Number One Boy Lu, Number Two Boy Liu, the senior cook, and a coolie to do the various odd jobs. There were three ponies, ridden by Edwin, Laura, and Mary, the two girls sitting on cushion-like Chinese saddles of dark blue velvet trimmed in red. Sarah sat in a mule litter, a light sedan chair mounted between two animals and driven by minders on either side. Other than the clatter of hooves, the monosyllabic orders of the minders, and the occasional remarks and laughter between the girls, the trip was one of peaceful quiet threaded by the chiming strings of bells worn around the ponies' necks.[13]

What Sarah described as the "little army" descended from the gentle incline of the Western Hills to the flatlands around the capital. They skirted the northwestern city wall, probably drove across the well-paved road leading to Cixi's Summer Palace, and perhaps even followed it for a time. The flatness of the landscape reminded Sarah of her native Midwest. She marveled at all the corn, beans, millet, and buckwheat grown in allotments dwarfed by those she knew from Iowa farms, and yet rich with yield (she may not have known yet that the Chinese, unlike American farmers, used extremely potent human waste as fertilizer). She took note of how every inch of ground was utilized to the fullest, none wasted on a homestead for farmers or barns for their animals. If these farmers were given the massive acreage devoted to American farms, she wondered, what further glories could they achieve?

The party stopped for the night at an inn, which Sarah picturesquely described as "dooryard and barnyard all in one." If Sarah thought the old Chinese buildings of the American legation a trifle primitive, at least there she had such familiar comforts as Western furniture, glass windows, heating, light, and a modicum of privacy. At the inn, she found herself in a little room, sparsely furnished, its papered windows blind to the sunset-lit world outside. Their bed was a *kang*, the ubiquitous northern Chinese brick and stucco stove that could heat a room and the people lying on it, as well as serve as seating and storage space. Sarah had never lived in such primitive conditions on the farms of her girlhood, but in another way she realized that even on this rough journey she and Edwin were still spoiled in the extreme: Lu remembered to bring not just utensils, cups, plates, and tea for impromptu tiffin, but also blankets and pillows, carpets and chairs for their room. The coolie washed the plates that Number Two Boy Liu fetched away, and laid out and made up the Congers' beds. Used to American household help, with their independent characters, Sarah appreciated her solicitous and selfless Chinese servants. "They are so quiet, attentive, careful, tasteful, and exact about their work," she recorded, "that they seem more like well-bred girls than men." Against the poise, unflustered calm, and thoughtfulness of these male servants, Sarah clearly felt even she cut an obtuse figure, as she realized that sensitivity and an eye for beauty were not exclusively the province of well-bred girls.[14]

Throughout that first night, Sarah recalled waking periodically to the distant soft tolling of the bells of the camels plodding endlessly down from Mongolia, their scruffy backs loaded with coal for the stoves of Beijing. It was "a dream melody all unreal to us."[15]

Next morning, after First Cook served breakfast, they were off for the final fourteen miles to the Great Wall. Sarah gave up the litter to the girls so she could ride alongside Edwin. "It was up, up, up all the way, climbing a mountainous road," on one side the cliffs rising sheer overhead, on the other a river of rocks and clear splashing water. They shared the road with the camels whose bells they had heard the night before, along with flocks of sheep and lines of pack mules bundled with goods for the Beijing markets: wool, animal hides, brick tea, fruit, wheat, fodder, cotton, and a hundred other commodities. Among these crowds of animals were silent Mongols and Chinese, their serious faces seemingly impervious to the glorious scenery around them.[16]

The Congers would have had glimpses of the Wall—the occasional crenellated curve bending along a distant escarpment—before they actually reached it. But even as they went through the Badaling Gate and up the Wall proper, the full impact of the structure was withheld until they had climbed the steep gray brick steps to the top, climbed higher still (on certain inclines a challenge even for the hardy Congers), turned around and looked back. It was then that Sarah really saw a "coiling, climbing, leaping thing" unfolding before her. This wall, she wrote, "is wonderful indeed!"[17]

In the West, the Wall was more a construct of myth than of bricks and mortar, a symbol of the Chinese emperor's supernatural ability to call forth men and resources to make a whim a reality, without counting costs in money or in human life. Sarah had read enough about the Wall (probably in her friend Dr. W. A. P. Martin's 1894 book, *A Cycle of Cathay*) to know that it was first built over two centuries before the birth of Christ, that it began at the coastal town of Shanhaiguan, a stone reptile curving up from the ocean and over plains and mountains 1,500 miles into the Gobi Desert north of Tibet. She knew that it had been built by the first emperor, a great ruler and a dreadful man, who sent conscripts, many of them scholars who had never performed manual labor, to their deaths in order to finish the Wall in ten years' time; those who died in their workplace were immured within it, giving the Wall another distinction as the longest graveyard in the world. Sarah knew that this first emperor gave China his name and united its little kingdoms into an empire, yet was one of the most infamous book burners of world history—contradictions in Chinese history and within the Chinese themselves which Sarah would learn more about over the coming years.[18]

High atop the Great Wall, in one of the guard towers spaced out across the serrated brick ridge, the Congers sat down for tiffin, all their legation china, silver, and linen spread out over the crumbling gray bricks that wriggled their way into the Gobi. The only sign of life other than themselves came when, having finished their meal, they climbed down one of the ramps to the Mongolian side, where even the stunted trees and rough scrub seemed different from the flora on the Chinese side a few yards to the south. "Here came quietly along an orderly drove of about two hundred swine from the mountains of Mongolia," Sarah recalled. As she watched them stumbling and grunting along, kept together by the sticks of their Mongolian herders, she noticed that the pigs all wore four leather "socks" to protect their feet from the flinty stones in the path. "Foolish, do you say?" Sarah asked her reader in a letter describing the experience. Maybe so in Iowa, where pigs were usually crowded into sties, those dirty antechambers to the slaughterhouse. "Not one of them seemed foot sore," she went on, "and they traveled at their master's bidding without rebellion." It certainly took patience to sew and put on what amounted to eight hundred little swine socks, but it was also a smart economist who knew that healthy pigs were happier pigs, and apt to fetch the better price in the swine markets of Beijing. "I call this a wonderful phase of patience and economy," Sarah opined.[19]

Seeing the pigs in their leather socks made Sarah more reluctant to accept the stories her fellow foreigners told her of Chinese cruelty to animals. She liked to tell about a day in the garden of the Three Hills Nunnery when she had happened on a snake. She called for the gardener to kill it. "Instead of inflicting a blow, he carefully, with his broom, directed it to a hole in the wall," Sarah recalled. "I did not understand this consideration given to reptiles and asked my boy Wang why they were not killed. He replied: 'Chinaman no kill snake, Chinaman good to snake, snake good to Chinaman. Chinaman kills snake, snake kill Chinaman." Cruelty, Sarah observed, "is a dark thread woven into the fabric of every nation"—by no means only that of China. Indeed, she noted, cruelty could be found even within herself. "One of the richest lessons I have learned in the Far East," she wrote later, "is to root out of my own character what I condemn in the character of others."[20]

✳   ✳   ✳   ✳   ✳

The Congers passed another night at the inn, rising before dawn for a seven-o'clock departure. The carts and most of the servants peeled off for Changpingchou (now Changping), a walled town to the south of the tomb of the Yongle emperor, builder of the Forbidden City. Sarah, Edwin, and the girls struck east for the tomb itself.

In 1898, none of the tombs had been opened, certainly not for the viewing public. The grandeur of the underground chambers and their contents were only faintly hinted at in the structures above—Yongle's being the grandest of them all, it was a natural draw. Called the Changling or Long Hall, Yongle's tomb lay on a site the emperor had chosen with care. The grounds were filled with ceremonial buildings—the white marble Hall of Eminent Gratitude, the Ming Pavilion, and the Treasure City or mausoleum—all linked by courtyards and surrounded by evergreen trees. Sarah approached the place with awe. "For five hundred years this structure has stood the angry storms and the burning sun," she wrote of the Hall of Eminent Gratitude, with its forest of sixty-two towering columns of aromatic *nanmu* (cedar) trees, "and looks as though it might brave them for two thousand more."[21]

Sarah looked out from Yongle's enormous spirit tablet in a pavilion high on a hill above the tomb. Past the tops of cedars at least as old as the tablet, rustling in the otherwise soundless air, she looked upon a true city of the dead. Yet she had evidence of a living energy as palpable as the warmth and movement of a living thing. On their way to the spirit tablet, the Congers had passed through a courtyard where a heavily carved fountain in which water still flowed had been set. Stopping briefly, the servants had dabbed their handkerchiefs into the water, which was believed to have healing properties, and pressed the damp cloth to their eyes—an example of what many foreigners derided as native superstition. But Sarah looked on with fascination. In such a potent atmosphere, she could not blame her servants for thinking the water from the emperor's fountain would heal them. Here was proof of a belief, a faith, so powerful it had lived on in the memories of these people, their parents, grandparents, and more distant ancestors. "Those glazed yellow walls and roofs," wrote Sarah, "are still reflecting light with a glow."[22]

Sarah pondered what had always fascinated her about human history: the power of great thoughts to manifest great works. The "thought" of Qin Shihuangdi may have led to the execution of scholars and the burning of books, but it had also manifested the Great Wall, a thought made visible not just as an enormous landmark across the face of China but also as an iconic image across the minds and memories of countless human beings, those who had seen it and walked on it, and those who had only imagined and dreamed about it. "The quality of that thought-force which placed those giant monoliths centuries ago has held them there," she wrote. And no matter what happened, "with this inherent power through and through them," these manifestations of thought could not collapse. "Recorded history is only the memory of expression of thought," she insisted. "Some of these thoughts bear so much of stable truth and eternal life in them that they stand the test of time."[23]

More and more, Sarah was coming to believe that a nation that could raise such superhuman monuments, capable of surviving the storms of nature and of mankind itself, was not a nation to be despised but admired, emulated rather than preached to. And it was definitely not a nation to be taken for granted.

5
Daws in peacock's feathers

When the Congers returned from the Great Wall, the Beijing air was already pungent with an incendiary collision of emotions, all roused by the decrees issued by the Guangxu emperor. Anxiety and excitement, hope and fear, increased with the number of reforms implemented, and spurred on both factions for and against those reforms. The secrecy and mystery which had always been a source of power for the imperial throne now worked against it; nobody had answers, just opinions, which gave rise to rumors, and these became more fantastical with the passing of time, destabilizing imperial authority.

As these groups began to form into two larger factions, those for reform and those against it, lines were drawn between the camps of the empress dowager and her nephew. And they were drawn early, as Sir Robert Hart observed. "People are ranging themselves," he wrote in December 1895, "some behind the Emperor—others behind the Empress Dowager, and it looks as if one of these illustrious personages would have to push the other to the wall presently."[1]

It was not solely a matter of contention between different groups of Chinese. The conservative faction that blamed liberal reformers surrounding the emperor also blamed the foreigners (including the Japanese) whose Western notions gave rise to the reforms in the first place. This in turn focused long-held resentments on missionaries now stationed in villages and towns up and down eastern China, and it was the ominous news of troubles for the missionaries in one of these enclaves that, together with the clashes closer to Beijing, convinced Sarah on September 20 to join Edwin at the American legation, where he had gone to attend to business.

Three days later, after the quashing of the coup, the outraged empress dowager imprisoned as many of Guangxu's reformer associates as her police could find, called her nephew on the carpet for his unfilial plotting, placed him under a loose form of house arrest, and resumed governance in his name. The reforms Guangxu had shepherded in were dismantled, to rise another day at a pace Cixi felt more appropriate to imperial speed limits. Cixi did not do this without some applause from high places in the foreign community. "She is a wonderful woman," wrote Sir Robert Hart after hearing the news, "and she has bowled over the Emperor by as astonishing a coup d'état as the one with which she placed him on the throne."[2]

The executions began. In the early hours of September 26, all of Guangxu's captured associates, except for Kang Youwei and Liang Qichao (both of whom had lucky escapes, thanks to Guangxu's warning), were beheaded in the vegetable market in Beijing. Three days later, Sarah heard that the Guangxu emperor had tried to escape the Forbidden City. "He reached the wall," she records, "but was brought back and imprisoned on an island in the imperial grounds." The place of the emperor's "imprisonment" was Yingtai, an artificial island which sat off the shore of the South Sea, in the so-called Sea Palaces complex (Zhongnanhai) west of the Forbidden City. Yingtai was covered with pleasure pavilions, to one of which, a building both Guangxu and Cixi had used as an office, Guangxu made his retreat. Far from being imprisoned, however (and as Sterling Seagrave points out, when was Guangxu not a prisoner of the throne?), Guangxu merely went into seclusion, much as he had done after China had been beaten by Japan in 1895, three years earlier. "It is a matter of record," Seagrave writes, "that there was an interruption in his routine of only three days, evidently caused by dismay and disillusion, not by torture and imprisonment." Guangxu's unseating and the rumors of his fate that swept through Beijing in the aftermath set nerves on edge, and explosions were inevitable. But that these would take direct aim at the American legation came as a shock.[3]

On September 30, British and American legation staff were leaving the railway station outside the walls of the city, on their way back to their compounds, when they were "attacked by a mob," as Sarah heard it. They hurried to a Chinese policeman, but either misunderstood his directions or were shooed away as they claimed. According to Sarah, missionaries among them tried to reason with the crowd in Chinese, to no avail. They were harried as they went down the streets. When the "mob" saw them leaving in closed chairs and carts, they "ran for them with yells, stones, clubs and clods of dirt." The chair-bearers understandably dropped their passengers and ran, and it was this, not direct combat with the attackers, that left one chair occupant with broken ribs and others with torn clothing. Sarah heard later that the assailants yelled "foreign devils!", a common enough epithet that most foreigners could count on having thrown at them at least a few times while they were in China. But they also screamed a word which, a little over a year later, would become all too terrifying to those besieged in the foreign legations: *"Sha!"*, meaning "kill."[4]

Edwin sent word immediately to the Chinese Foreign Office, in tandem with ministers of other nations, requesting protection for all foreigners. At least part of the international community's fear had to do with economics. As Sir Robert Hart wrote in early October, the "restlessness" and accompanying instability would put a crimp in trade, "revenue will fall off," China would have to default on loan payments, and "all the world will step in and joint-control ensue." No nation, not even the British or French, really wanted to seize that tiger by the tail.[5]

The rumors and the threats of violence continued. On October 1, Sarah heard that the Guangxu emperor had been poisoned, a piece of news which, when it reached the populace, resulted in even more belligerence toward all things foreign. It would not have improved the general Chinese mood to find out on October 5 that English marines stationed at Tianjin were preparing to head for Beijing, even as they could only have cheered the follow-up report that Chinese officials had ordered them and their guns off the train. This same day, Sarah shuddered at the news, again unofficial but subsequently borne out by the facts, that Cixi had had fourteen eunuchs strangled—they had either been too friendly toward the emperor, had played roles in his reforms, or had been part of an escape plot that came to light, nobody knew what to believe.

The next day, English marines succeeded in getting through to Beijing, as did Russian and German troops, marching up Legation Street with an escort of Chinese officials. For all that this military presence eased the worries of most in the foreign legations, Sarah could not help but feel a cold foreboding at the sight of troops displaying themselves and their arms in so brazen a fashion. She had an intuitive fear that rather than discouraging troublemakers, the foreign troops' appearance in Beijing would only fan the flames higher—after all, not since the invasion of Beijing by the Anglo-French army in 1860 had foreign soldiers marched into the city. "It is a new sight, and a sad one," she recorded, "to see these foreign troops march into this capital city. Can we realize what such a condition means to them?"—"them" being the Chinese, who cautiously stood back to watch the soldiers flaunt their brass.[6]

Sarah had more opportunity to doubt the efficacy of Western crisis response when a cable arrived from Washington in the middle of October, calmly stating that the troubles in Beijing were over and that Cixi and her nephew were now "working in harmony" toward a resolution of their conflicted interests. Sarah could only wonder at what was either embarrassing ignorance or cynical politicking on the part of the diplomatic corps in the American capital. Not only was there no harmony between the dowager and the emperor, but Cixi was already considering how to completely remove Guangxu in favor of the son of a conservative "Iron Hat" prince of the blood. The unrest continued to such a degree that Edwin finally called in a corps of American marines to protect the legation compound. Diplomatic deafness was not unique to the United States. In November, British Admiral Lord Charles Beresford was in China at the invitation of the Associated Chambers of Commerce to look into the ramifications for American and European business should China break up. Beresford suggested to Lord Salisbury, the conservative British prime minister, that he would like to make a pact with Yuan Shikai to take Beijing and put Cixi under arrest, placing the

Chinese government under Sir Claude MacDonald's control. Salisbury's response was chillingly aristocratic: "The idea would have been attractive at the beginning of the century," he wrote to Beresford. Sir Claude was not much more enthused, rather more bluntly recommending to Beresford that he "stick to trade and commerce."[7]

By the time the American troops arrived in early November (only nine at first as, according to Eliza Scidmore, "the want of actual roof-area to shelter more guards" obliged Edwin to keep the remainder ninety miles away in Tianjin), more rumors had drifted over the Forbidden City's walls. Sarah heard that Cixi was now frightened by what was happening; at the same time she heard that Cixi had had a eunuch executed for showing pity toward the miserable young emperor. Conflicting accounts pointed to the only fact of which anyone could be sure: nobody really knew what was happening in the imperial palace (a trial run for the information breakdown that fueled the Boxer Uprising). Even canny Sir Robert Hart believed it when he was told that Cixi had six candidates for the position of crown prince lined up in the Forbidden City, one of them to be chosen as the emperor's replacement. According to his source, this would happen sooner rather than later: "it is said that one of them will be Emperor before the end of the month."[8]

Cixi certainly was scared. What Sir Claude MacDonald called "Shanghai rumours" (Kang Youwei's writings) had become ominous enough for him to recommend to Cixi that a foreign doctor be brought to the palace to examine Guangxu. To distance herself from the increasingly sticky calumny that she was having the Guangxu emperor poisoned, Cixi took Sir Claude's advice and permitted the medical visit. The gesture was not, in the end, much more than pro forma: the only available physician was Dr. Dethève, from the French legation, and taking the frightened young man's pulse and listening to his heart, while Cixi hovered in the background asking questions, was the extent of the examination. Dethève did find out from court doctors and even, apparently, from Cixi herself that the emperor suffered from dysfunction in his renal and reproductive organs, the latter of which was judged to make him unable to father children. But for Cixi's purposes, at least, this visit showed that the emperor was still alive.[9]

More violence flared, this time around the railroads, which the

Chinese believed upset the balance of *qi* and disturbed the spirits of the earth. A crowd set upon some foreign railroad inspectors; three foreigners were injured in the attack. Sarah believed that this incident was the work of "undisciplined Chinese soldiers from the interior," rather than ordinary Chinese, and she was probably right—twelve thousand troops under the command of Muslim General Dong Fuxiang were camped three miles outside the walls of Beijing with Cixi's permission, for reasons never fully explained to the worried foreign diplomats. Sarah then witnessed, again with mixed feelings, another display of foreign military bravado as the eighteen American marines under the orders of Edwin marched into the city dragging a Gatling gun behind them. The men and their gun were put up in the crowded compound, and then appear to have waited for an attack that, as it happened, never came. What was Edwin preparing for? We do not know what credible information he had, and Sarah does not venture into this territory in her diaries.

As the atmosphere began to cool, someone had the idea of posing all the various legations' guards together for a photograph in the grounds of the British legation—whether for purposes of camaraderie or for a show of force to the Chinese government is not known. Of the eight groups, only the Americans, eager to make a show of their patriotism, brought their flag. When lots were drawn to decide who would have the honor of standing in the middle, the Americans won. The photograph, published in Sarah's *Letters from China,* shows eight different companies of marines in the uniforms of their respective nations, posed against the architectural miscellany of the British legation buildings, Stars and Stripes thrusting up prominently from the ranks of the Americans. But as much as she loved her country's flag, it was not the high note of emotion that stayed with Sarah as much as the sight of the co-operative brotherhood of nations arrayed on the parade ground that morning. "Was there ever such a picture?" she exclaimed. "The marines of eight nations peacefully standing side by side in a foreign land."[10]

The sense of safety brought by this international military conglomerate was brief and illusory, not so much because they were technically outnumbered should the Chinese army, as evidently feared, decide to sweep into the Legation Quarter, but because of the age-old curse of Asia, disease. Sarah had invited guests to the legation for a

Thanksgiving dinner of fifty-six settings—American missionaries and marines who, like the missionaries, were far from home and were no doubt pleased by the novelty of emulating the half-mythical 1621 pilgrim meal. Partway through dinner, Edwin was approached by an orderly with some unnerving news—one of the marines was ill, and not from what he had eaten: he had smallpox.[11]

It is not known whether Edwin, Sarah, or Laura had ever been immunized against what was then still an almost always fatal disease; immunization was certainly a common enough procedure in their day and a desirable one for diplomats and their families. As a Christian Scientist, Sarah technically avoided the trappings of *materia medica*, but if given the chance to be immunized it is likely her good sense, and Edwin's, would have prevailed. The real threat, however, was not so much to them as to the safety of the American legation: if one marine was ill, others might be infected, too.[12] There had been some form of inoculation in China since the eleventh century, and the close quarters in which most Beijingers lived ensured a sizable population of smallpox survivors and, thus, pockets of immunity. But smallpox could sweep through the ranks of boys from the American hinterlands like fire through a prairie.[13]

Never one to hide anything, Edwin chose to tell his guests the matter-of-fact truth; perhaps because of this, no panic ensued. The missionaries coolly took the news in, while the marines, far from fleeing the afflicted man, gathered around him. "His comrades fearlessly stood by him," Sarah recalled, "tenderly prepared his reclining chair, and tucked the covers about him," doing so at their own peril.[14] A few weeks later, at the Nantang Cathedral Hospital, the marine died, and was buried in the English cemetery outside the western city wall, "with all the honors that kind, true friends could give him," Sarah wrote. "We all mourn his loss." How many of the other infected men died Sarah does not say. But the little force guarding the legation, and those living within it, had a lucky escape.[15]

So, indeed, when the threat diminished, had the diplomats of the Legation Quarter. In writing of the upheaval after the Hundred Days of Reform, just prior to the Boxer Uprising, ever-skeptical Eliza Scidmore painted an ominous picture: that "the little community of foreign diplomats, shut like rats in a trap in a double-walled city of an estimated million three hundred thousand fanatic, foreign-hating Chinese, with a more hostile and lawless army of sixty thousand vicious Chinese soldiers without the walls and scattered over the country toward Tientsin," was a sitting duck should the Chinese decide they were really finished with the foreigners for good.[16]

Scidmore was putting the situation lightly. Despite the legations' repeated demands to disband, Dong Fuxiang's men remained. Sir Robert Hart naïvely dismissed the significance, likening Dong's men to thievish crows masquerading in peacock plumes. But it was clear that this army gave increased confidence to the imperial court and, by extension, to the people. An unwonted assertiveness began to weave a new pattern in which, like a crowded Chinese tapestry, there was no longer a place for foreign devils.[17]

6

Imperial audience

"The wives and the ladies of the diplomatic corps had never been recognized," wrote Eliza Scidmore, "during the thirty-eight years that Legations had been established at Peking." That was about to change. On the frigid morning of December 13, 1898, Sarah and the wives of six other foreign ministers were up and primping before the sun had risen. They had been invited by the Empress Dowager for an audience in Zhongnanhai, the Sea Palaces complex.[1]

The idea had been broached over six months earlier. In May 1898, Prince Henry of Prussia, the light-hearted younger brother of Kaiser Wilhelm II, was granted an audience, Cixi's first known meeting with a foreign male. We know that Lady MacDonald, the British minister's wife, asked the prince if he would put in a good word with the court on behalf of the foreign ladies, who wished to be presented to Her Majesty. Since her resumption of power in the Guangxu emperor's name, Cixi's availability for audiences was greatly reduced, so a delay followed while court astrologers and *feng shui* specialists sought the most auspicious date for such a meeting. Cixi's watch-and-wait nature probably also played a part. She needed time to think Lady MacDonald's request over, and had to find that time in between the minor cataclysm of quashing of the Hundred Days of Reform and tightening control of the radical conservatives at court, who may have put pressure on her not to meet with foreigners at all. According to Sir Robert Hart, the ladies themselves caused much of the trouble by not being ready on the day Cixi asked for them, disagreeing on a translator, and being held up because the first secretaries' wives and daughters wanted to be included. It was "another instance," pointed out Sir Robert, "of the way international jealousies and individual crankiness shunt China on to a wrong line the moment she wants to get on a right one!"[2]

Finally, the day arrived, and at 10 a.m., a Chinese escort rode up to each legation to fetch the wives of the ministers. Two sartorial standouts were Lady MacDonald in bold stripes and Russian Madame de Giers in a hat with plumes spouting like a public fountain. The other ladies (Baroness von Heyking, Mme Pichon, and Mme Knobel) were draped in enough bright yardage for a velvet circus tent. Only the Japanese minister's wife, Mme Yano, in a sedate kimono, and Sarah, in dark silks, treated the occasion as one for understatement. Each lady folded her skirts and plumes into her sedan chair and, hoisted by five bearers, and each with two grooms on horseback, started from the British legation at 11 a.m. for the jouncing trip to the Sea Palaces.

On reaching the first gate (Xinhuamen), the ladies were seated in open court chairs lined in red satin, the Chinese color of happiness, which many of them must have been feeling. They did not progress far. Just inside the next gate, they stepped from their chairs into a train coach, a gift from France to China that was, unsuccessfully, meant to be a promotional gesture. Ironically this carriage, which Lady MacDonald remembered as "worn and shabby," had no "fire-wheel cart" to pull it, but instead was pushed by eunuchs dressed all in black, like the stage attendants at a kabuki play. The coach was rolled a short distance before stopping for a reception with officials. The ladies then made their way to the audience hall.[3]

Complaints about what venue was appropriate for the reception of "foreign devils" at the imperial court dated back to Lord Macartney's audience with the Qianlong emperor in the late eighteenth century. The Ziguangge or Pavilion of Purple Light had been used by Cixi's son the

Tongzhi emperor for foreign audiences; being among the Sea Palaces, it was located away from the sacred inner precincts of the Forbidden City proper. But Cixi had another reason for choosing this venue: she did not like the Forbidden City. She was put off by the darkness and gloom of the Ming-period buildings. The Forbidden City was also discomforting to her because it was literally a museum, not just of Chinese history but of Cixi's own humble beginnings.[4]

The audience hall was somewhat small, so the ladies had to work to maintain the strict formation demanded by diplomatic etiquette. "We stood according to rank," Sarah recalled, referring to each woman's seniority of time served in Beijing. The *London Illustrated News* offered to its readers an artist's rendering of this first encounter: Cixi on her throne, to which the foreign ladies had to gain access via a railing and steps up to a dais, with Guangxu sitting meekly to one side. While Lady MacDonald paid her respects, the heads of the six other women (the Japanese minister's wife conspicuous for her lack of towering European headwear), seen from behind, were lined up looking on. The interpreter presented each of them to Prince Qing, who then introduced them to the emperor and empress dowager. Though not mentioned by Sarah, Cixi's chief eunuch, the infamous squeeze-master Li Lianying, would also have been present.[5]

Lady MacDonald delivered a short speech, translated for the listening imperials. Each lady was then brought to the Guangxu emperor's throne, where she curtseyed and took his narrow outstretched hand. Guangxu inspired in foreign women a sympathy that most men who met him did not share—where males tended to judge him weak, women saw a helpless boy, trapped by illness and the trappings of rank.[6] This was certainly his first time meeting a foreign woman, as it was Cixi's. "It is stated, and said to be true," Sarah wrote she had heard, "that Her Majesty, the Empress Dowager, had never seen a foreign lady, and that a foreign lady had never seen her." But all reports indicate that Cixi showed little reserve when the meeting finally occurred. Her welcome was more voluble than the emperor's: she took the ladies' hands warmly, greeting them in Chinese.

Neither Sarah nor Ethel MacDonald tells us what Cixi was wearing when they first met, but thanks to more detailed accounts of similar occasions by other eye-witnesses, we may hazard a few guesses. She would have worn an imposing *tianzi*, the Manchu headdress shaped like a large, flat bow a foot across and made of black satin or horsehair, which sat atop the head. *Tianzi* were typically adorned with flowers, real and silk, jewels of pale jade, dazzling blue kingfisher feather ornaments, and dangling pieces of gold or silver with pearls. We know from Princess Der Ling and the photographs of Cixi taken by Der Ling's brother that Cixi's *tianzi* were elaborate and their adornments often changed throughout the day. We may be quite certain Cixi was sporting one of her more exquisite embroidered robes, which she tended to change depending on her visitors or her mood. She would have worn claw-like fingernail protectors, made of gold or silver and embellished with jade and other precious stones and cloisonné, on her fourth and fifth fingers. Lady MacDonald later remembered Cixi's "harsh voice, disagreeable to listen to," but this may be explained by the Dowager's unfamiliarity in addressing a roomful of women who were not servants or officials. None of the other women, including Sarah, left record of such a voice; Sir Robert Hart found it sweet and girlish, which perhaps Cixi took pains to affect when speaking to him.[7]

After greeting the ladies, Cixi took gold rings set with pearls and placed them on the women's fingers—Sarah was to relish showing off hers on her return to America the following year. Backing away, and bowing, as instructed, the ladies were guided out of the imperial presences to a dining room, where they were offered a table filled with Chinese delicacies. When the ladies were returned to the audience hall, they found the dowager once again, this time seated in a throne chair covered in yellow silk. As this provided a better vantage point from which to study Cixi from closer quarters, Sarah bent an appraising eye. She had been told the Chinese were cruel; she had also been given to understand that Cixi herself was cruel—an impression the executions and rumored incarceration of the emperor following the end of the Hundred Days of Reform in no way dispelled. But now, looking at Cixi face to face, Sarah was what can only be described as astonished and disarmed. "She was bright and happy," she recorded, "and her face glowed with good will. There was no trace of cruelty to be seen . . . She extended both hands towards each lady, then touching herself, said with much enthusiastic earnestness, 'One family; all one family.'" Sarah was so charmed, that when Cixi presented the Guangxu emperor's plain wife, the young Empress Longyu, Sarah could only remember her as being "beautiful."[8]

Cixi then walked to a little theatre, where the ladies were beckoned to join her. Here they were permitted to watch a performance of the Beijing opera for which Cixi had a passion. Sarah does not state whether or not she and the other ladies were constrained by etiquette to stand during the performance (Cixi herself would have reclined behind silk scrims), but it is probable that the ladies did so, as no one, not even those who were "all one family," was permitted to sit in the empress dowager's presence. If this was already uncomfortable, their many-layered Victorian clothing would have been put to the test where the December chill was concerned. The Sea Palaces were icy in winter, the rooms heated only by indoor charcoal braziers that filled the air with carbon monoxide but little warmth. Throughout the hour or so in the theatre, interpreters did their best to explain to the foreign ladies the quick action and colorful plots over the clanging gongs of the orchestra and the falsetto arias of the male performers.[9]

When the performance was over, the ladies were brought back to the dining-hall, where Cixi was again waiting for them. As tea was served, the dowager walked with a cup to each lady, sipped from it, then tipped the rim toward her seven guests, murmuring with a smile, "One family; all one family." More presents followed, including bolts of vivid silks which would be put to a rougher use than intended in a little over a year's time. Then the ladies made their way back through the courtyards to their red satin chairs, and home to their respective legations.[10]

Lady MacDonald wrote with some perception of the imperial woman who had granted her the audience she desired:

> I should say the Dowager-Empress was a woman of some strength
> of character, certainly genial and kindly . . . [Her interpreter,
> Henry Cockburn's] opinion of the Dowager-Empress was what
> I may call the generally accepted one. My husband had requested
> him to take a careful note of all that passed, especially with a view
> of endeavouring to arrive at some estimate of her character. On
> his return he reported that all his previously conceived notions
> had been upset by what he had seen and heard, and he summed
> up her character in four words: "amiability verging on weakness!"[11]

Amiable Cixi was, but it was not weakness that moved her to grant this audience—it had taken a fair amount of courage, and perhaps an equal amount of realpolitik. As when she freely invited the French doctor to come to the Forbidden City to examine the emperor, it was the politically savvy thing to do to beckon the wives of the foreign ministers for a glimpse of her private world. This was the same world their nations had despoiled in 1860, but this time the clatter of barbarian languages in the Forbidden City's courtyards would be by invitation instead of invasion. Who better to invite for that first glimpse than the barbarians' women? "The Chinese say," wrote a male missionary in the 1830s, "that foreign sailors, foreign firearms, and foreign females are the great exciters of all disturbances, and therefore are forbidden to enter their confines." Cixi may well have enjoyed challenging and exploiting that shared Asian and Western misogyny, which had failed to hold her back, and might be an interesting foil to what she may have seen as the more circumscribed lives of supposedly liberated "modern" Western women.[12]

Cixi would have understood that these women from Paris and St. Petersburg, Des Moines and Berlin, were no more where they were because of their own special talents or abilities than she was as empress dowager. Yet she knew that the woman who shares a bed with a powerful man is herself a powerful woman—in the intimate darkness of the marital bedroom, even a Chinese wife could communicate on equal terms with her husband. The dowager's well-developed survival instincts told her that the way to charm these foreign women's husbands was through their wives. If Cixi's performance—for such it was—before the foreign wives was successful in charming and relaxing them, they would carry this goodwill back to the connubial bedroom, tiny pebbles dropped into a deep pond, sending out ever greater concentric circles of influence in her favor. Whatever doubts the male contingent of foreign diplomacy may have held about the event, and there were some, the overall response was positive.

Unfortunately, Cixi would not be able to have the articles in the foreign press about herself or her court translated daily until the advent of the multilingual Princess Der Ling, her lady-in-waiting from 1903–05, which meant she probably knew nothing about the column space the *New York Times* offered to the audience in its edition of December 15, 1898, describing Cixi for the most part in agreeable tones. The article reported an incident that Sarah did not mention and that would have surely amused Cixi had she known of it: how the dowager, "in a burst of womanly emotion embraced her visitors."[13]

Some, of course, could not see anything positive in any meeting of East and West. George Morrison's editor, Valentine Chirol, inveighed in a letter on the impropriety of "exposing the representatives of refined European womanhood to the ribald jests of Palace eunuchs and the offensive curiosity of Chinese Mandarins."[14]

On her return home, Sarah was met by Number One Boy Lu, "who tried to impress on me what a great thing had come into my life. He said, 'Madame, much great thing come to you. Emperor come down from Heaven. No foreign lady see him, few Chinese men . . . You are very blessed." Sarah agreed. But seeing the extremely restricted life of the Guangxu emperor at first hand, she wondered something else: "How can this great Empire grow in strength and glory when her rulers are in such bondage?"[15] Yet Sarah was dazzled by the glowing face and warm hands of the empress dowager. She especially exulted in the singularly feminist tenor of the visit. "Only think!" Sarah wrote ecstatically to her sister. "China, after centuries and centuries of locked doors, has now set them ajar! . . . English was the first language spoken at Court to Their Majesties by foreign women . . . [English which] in its purity has been carried to the very throne of China by a woman." She realized that now that the door was ajar, if only a crack, she might find her way through it again. At Cixi's court, as perhaps nowhere else in China, it was a privilege to be a woman.[16]

7
Christmas in Beijing

If American Thanksgiving, with its enshrinement of family togetherness at the time of harvest, was one celebration in which the Chinese could theoretically enjoy a shared interest, Christmas was another matter altogether. It honored, after all, the birth of Jesus, the god of the foreigners most missionaries were so eager the Chinese should accept over Confucius, Laozi, or the Buddha.

Christians and their faith had existed in some part of China since the Tang dynasty, when a "mission" of Nestorian Christians made its way over the Silk Road to Shanxi and the Tang capital, Chang'an. It was the Western wing of the faith, Catholicism, which ultimately gained the upper hand among Christian sects in China. Part of this was due to the assimilationist credo of Jesuits like Matteo Ricci, who like many of his successors adopted Chinese dress and language and searched for links between his faith and the belief system of the Chinese, the better to help the latter understand Christianity. Some members of the imperial family converted—even the Kangxi emperor, before his turnabout rejection of Christianity, wrote a poem about the crucifixion. Jesuits were useful for more practical matters, too—they designed the quasi-European palaces of Yuanmingyuan, brought astronomical instruments to Beijing, and regulated the Chinese calendar.[1]

The Jesuits' Protestant successors, however, often offered little to the Chinese beyond the concept of hellfire and damnation. Confucian education instilled a "strong sense of moral responsibility, inseparable from guilt consciousness," writes Julia Ching, so that many Chinese simply shifted from one guilt concept to another when they converted. As Sarah saw the irony of Westerners sharing the good tidings of Christ, the peacemaker, via less than peaceful means, she wrote to a nephew in the winter of 1899, "Would that more of the Christ-spirit could be shown [to the Chinese] by these people coming from Christian lands!"[2]

Sarah was at the other end of the spectrum from American missionaries like the Reverend Francis E. Clark, who trivialized Chinese beliefs by likening the burning of incense in temples to the folksy American rural superstition of nailing a horseshoe over the farmyard door. "Everything in these temples is dirty and disorderly," Clark wrote in his book *Our Journey Around the World* in a chapter titled "The Sordid Spirit of Buddhism." He went on to say, "[the worshippers] bustle around in the most business-like way, buy their incense, light it, place it in the proper receptacle, and then go off perfectly satisfied that they have done their duty." Sarah, who admired practicality with a touch of the sublime, would have disagreed. As she often asked in her letters, was faith as much a part of the average Christian's daily life as it was for the average Chinese? As Sarah pointed out,

> Spirits are in everything with them, while we so often think the power is in matter . . . in their gods or Buddhas [*sic*] are found in each part of the body some material thing representing a thought—to illustrate—in the eyes are looking glasses—in the heart pearls—in the stomach or bowels money etc. You see, their thoughts are *Reflection—Value—Plenty*. (emphasis in original)

This use of symbols was, she increasingly believed, proof that the Chinese were as spiritual as Christians, and possibly more so.[3] She especially approved of Chinese ancestor worship. "This worship has its virtuous and elevating effect upon these people," Sarah recorded. "They show their parents the greatest respect and consideration while with them, and visit their tombs with a living thought." Unlike many foreign women in China, who obsessed about the smells and dirt and could only imagine that a full dose of Christian teaching and Western soap and water would save the souls and the bodies of the Chinese, Sarah was content to let the people in whose country she was a guest live as they needed and wanted to live—if they asked for help, she would give it, but would not force it upon anyone. And perhaps uniquely among religious foreigners in China, she applied the standards of the Chinese to biblical personages, not only the other way around. Many missionaries would ask themselves, "Were the Syrians [in the Bible] as untaught, as primitive, as animal-like as the Chinese?" But for Sarah the strength and faith of the modern Chinese served as proof that the incredible acts lauded in the Bible, in which the transformative power of belief played a role, could actually have occurred as described.[4]

Sarah did sometimes feel a sense of spiritual solitariness in China, but she did not recruit anyone to her cause. She kept to her principle of living by example, as a few missionaries she admired did and, coincidentally, as Laozi adjured—that the true sage "spreads his teaching without talking." As Sarah explained, "It was my watchful prayer to *live* my blessed Faith in all my intercourse with [the missionaries] and with the Chinese. I met them on their ground and strove to learn of them . . ." She held that it was in this way that "I learned some of my most valuable lessons in China."[5]

"I wish that I could know what these Chinese think," Sarah wrote to a niece in America. "I look at them and wonder what is under the calm surface. Sometimes I see them unobserved and they are merry, full of fun, and have innate grace. In everything our standpoints and modes of action differ. We seem to be travelling in different directions—growing further apart. Will the time ever come when we shall be of one mind?"[6]

✳ ✳ ✳ ✳ ✳

Christian foreigners in Beijing were by no means bereft of Christmas trappings, yet it was still a holiday they had to make for themselves. Some dwelled on what to them seemed differences made the more stark by how they and non-Christian Chinese chose to spend December 25. In a letter home about her holiday, Sarah wrote to her sister not so much about how different Christmas was in China as about how strangely familiar it seemed. On opening the legation's front door on Christmas morning, Sarah described how she and Edwin found that gifts had arrived in the night. At each side of the low steps that led up from the courtyard was "a little tree in a pretty painted porcelain pot. These trees were decorated with many styles of most intricately cut paper people, animals, birds, bats and flowers in colors," she wrote. "On the soil of the pots were clay birds beautifully covered in feathers, and by the side of one pot was a good-sized toy Peking pug dog, chained."[7]

Not many foreign observers would have understood how the bat, that creature associated in the West with abandoned houses and graveyards, would find itself on a Christmas tree. But Sarah, perhaps because she was never able to grasp the written language itself, was an eager student of what she called the "language" of Chinese symbols. Summoning Number One Boy Lu, she went with him out to the courtyard and asked him about the ornaments on the trees, and listened as he explained the symbology. "Everything, trees and all that was upon them, brought their message," Sarah wrote. She recorded that the Chinese character for "bat," *fu*, was a homophone for the character for "happiness"; the birds (probably sparrows, that endemic nester in the eaves of Beijing) symbolized love and loyalty; and each flower had its own code for good luck, wealth, or long life. Even the dog had a meaning. In Chinese folklore, a dog coming to one's house was an auspicious sign, an indication that good fortune was on its way. That the dog tied to the tree was a Pekingese added a Buddhist symbological dimension, for legend held that the Buddha had created it from a lion that begged to be made small enough to court a favorite marmoset, yet still retain its great heart and courage. The little dog symbolized the brave constancy of true love. "We appreciated the kind thoughts that prompted the gifts," Sarah recorded; but as she learned the trees' deeper implications, she realized that "everything has an underlying meaning." She marveled that "the simplest things are not 'common' when you hear what they say to you."[8]

With Sarah's understanding of this "language" came a sense that she needed to protect it. She does not state why, but she clearly felt that her Chinese Christmas trees, if left displayed for guests to the legation to see, would not meet with the same appreciation she and Edwin felt for them.

So they each took a painted porcelain pot and set the trees down in their library, placing them alongside "our other dear gifts." There Sarah sat, for a long time, studying them. "I can never tell you what a field of thought opened up in me," she wrote her sister, "as I sat meditating upon that scene before me . . . Into that Christmas room a new thing entered; it brought a soft light in its simplicity that lighted anew all that was there." She added, "Do you think it strange that I am becoming interested in these people?"[9]

To her sister, also a Christian Scientist with a metaphysical bent, Sarah's interest in the Chinese would not have seemed strange, nor would it to anyone who had read Darwin's conclusion on the equality of races. Advancing as a civilized being, Darwin wrote, individuals group themselves into communities, and "the simplest reason would tell each individual that he ought to extend his social instincts and sympathies to all members of the same nation, though personally unknown to him. This point being once reached, there is only an artificial barrier to prevent his sympathies extending to the men of all nations and races."[10]

But that "artificial barrier" was an obdurate one. To many who did not know Sarah Conger, in and out of China, her increasing fascination with China would indeed have appeared peculiar, even threatening— the wags of the diplomatic quarter might have described her as "going native." Sarah was far from going native—she never seems to have even tried on any of the Chinese robes and gowns she collected, let alone used chopsticks. According to her granddaughter, she subscribed to the theory that learning the Chinese language was somehow indelicate for a foreign lady (or thought to be so by a foreign lady's husband), though she learned to transcribe the names and titles of her Chinese friends with an admirable command of the principles of Wade-Giles romanization. Even when, in coming years, Sarah went so far toward recognizing at least the beauty of the instruments of Chinese worship as to set up "an immense golden God in the library," Edwin noted how just before their foreign guests arrived for Christmas dinner she "deftly covered it up for the evening"—just as she had done when concealing the Chinese Christmas trees from the same guests' gaze. She was obviously never quite sure of her fellow foreigners' reaction to her sympathy toward China and the Chinese. Yet Sarah was coming to a realization that was rare even for well-traveled and sophisticated Westerners. She saw how much she shared with a people with whom she had assumed foreigners had nothing in common. That included what only appeared to be differences in religion. She already knew that to judge a people based on one's own religion was not only unjust, it was ignorant. "The rituals or sayings of a religion do not make up the real character of persons or nations," Sarah wrote. "All religions have some of the true and good in their teachings and the value of these teachings depends upon the depth to which they enter the hearts and minds of their advocates."[11]

As she sat in the library studying her Chinese Christmas trees, Sarah knew that she and the Chinese did understand one very important shared language, that did not require study of the hundreds of characters necessary to read a newspaper or the thousands needed to decode the poetry of Li Bai—they shared the language of appreciating beauty, the syntax of which leaned on the heart, not the words, of the speaker. Only by carefully following "the intricate thought-methods of the Chinese," Sarah concluded, could one ever hope to "reach accurate conclusions about China," or about its people. Like a Daoist adept, Sarah was becoming comfortable with mystery, sensing, like the mystics of Christian, Hindu, Buddhist, Jewish, and Muslim faiths that "the Mystery of mysteries is the Door of all essence." And she knew, more and more—to paraphrase an old Biblical homily well known to her— that only by the fruits of the Chinese people's culture would foreigners ever come to know them.[12]

✳   ✳   ✳   ✳   ✳

Sarah had been to court, but she still did not know how Chinese people really lived. "I wish that I could see these ladies in their home life," she wrote home wistfully. Her primary contact came through her servants, who were by no means ordinary Chinese, trained as they were to show only a pleasing face to their employers. Her other tiny view, like a hole poked in a paper window, came through the Chinese she encountered through her charity work, notably with the Woman's Winter Refuge.[13]

The women at the refuge were those who had no family to look after them, women who were elderly, destitute, and—worst of all—childless.

A woman's situation in China could be summed up in the words of the poet Fu Xuan, who lived in the third century BCE: "How sad it is to be a woman! Nothing on earth is held so cheap." Little had changed. "The honor of a woman is her child-bearing," Sarah wrote of what she had learned, "and the more boys the greater the honor." When she was not answering to her father and elder brother, a Chinese woman was answering to her husband and then her eldest son. After marriage, at which ceremony the bride and groom usually first set eyes on each other, a woman's legal status was low, far lower than that of her mother-in-law and far, far below that of her husband. If he abused his wife, he was given less punishment than if he had slapped a perfect stranger; he could commit adultery under his wife's nose and take as many concubines as he could afford.[14]

On a practical level none but the lowest class of woman worked— no lady exposed herself to the unseemly gaze of the male-dominated marketplace, or disobeyed her male relatives by doing so—and such work as a childless widow could get was rarely well-paying. "Women almost never earned money," wrote one Western scholar of China, "and even when they derived some income from weaving, spinning, or embroidery, it went to the family and only the father, husband or father-in-law could dispose of it," the only exception being the eldest son if the mother was a widow.[15]

Ida Pruitt's friend Mrs. Ning described the fate of one abandoned elderly woman in the China of the nineteenth century. "One day when I was begging and feeling sad in my heart," Mrs. Ning recalled, "I saw an old woman begging on the street. She was crawling on her hands and knees like a four-footed animal." The woman Mrs. Ning saw had once been a person of substance, with her own home. Her husband had died young, and she had hired herself out as seamstress to wealthy official families. The son she worked to put through school also died young, and her grandson was a wastrel who sold everything but the spectacles his grandmother needed to wear when sewing. Then these too were taken from her, and she ended up in the street. She tried to commit suicide by leaping from a bridge. Mrs. Ning saw her, laughed at by people above. No one made an effort to help her. The Chinese assumed that the unfortunate's family would take the situation in hand—if not, a stranger's fate was not one's business. In Chinese society, a family was supposed to look after its own, and if it did not, it was unlucky to get involved. Only when a foreign missionary saw the miserable old lady was she taken in and given medical treatment and food, but died a few days later and was buried, simply but with dignity, at the mission.[16]

To the abandoned lady of Mrs. Ning's recollections, who had spent the end of her life shivering in doorways, anything with a roof would have seemed the height of luxury. As Sarah would discover on another errand of mercy in which sympathy and reality collided, in a world where a *kang* with no pillows was heaven next to dying under a bridge, there was still much for a sympathetic but naïve American to learn. Sarah was particularly interested in the role of children in Chinese families, admiring their obedience to their elders, and their manners which were more graceful and considerate than those of many an adult foreigner. "Love for children," Sarah recorded, "is one of greatest passions [of the Chinese] and it seems to be a redeeming one." She knew that while sons were most desirable, to have no children at all was a calamity, because there would be no descendants to sweep their graves or offer sacrifices to their spirit tablets. But Sarah found out that even if a couple was childless, they could still save the situation by adopting a child— or buying one. This sale of children—which, remarkably, she does not judge—gave Sarah an idea she came to regret.[17]

One day, her second amah approached her and said, "First amah have little baby boy." Sarah had not been aware that her first amah was even pregnant, and asked if she might see the baby. Her first amah showed Sarah "a small, bright-looking child," which was held inside the coat of a strange man. She asked the woman where the baby had come from and how it came to be hers. "I have no baby," the amah told her, "this man have many, can't feed 'em. I buy baby." Her sister, already nursing an infant of her own, had agreed to take the baby until it was old enough for first amah to take into her own care.[18]

The legation was also hosting a visiting guest from Shanghai at this time, a woman who had brought along her own amah. This servant, probably hearing how easy it was to obtain a child in Beijing, asked if she could go out into the city to buy a baby girl. As she told Sarah, she was in an unhappy marriage made worse by the lack of children, and had heard from a servant (Sarah's first amah?) that there was a family willing to let their little girl go cheaply. But when the woman returned to the legation, Sarah found out that the transaction had not been a success; the child was not to be had so cheaply after all. "She seemed to be a good woman," Sarah recalled, "so I said, 'I will go to a mission and see what I can do for you there.'"[19]

During a recent visit to a mission school, Sarah had seen "hundreds of street children" in the Sunday school class, orphans without much hope of being adopted by ordinary Chinese as they were now, by virtue of their being housed by the mission, Christian by association if not yet by baptism. This interest in her welfare from an important foreign woman made the amah very happy. "Oh, thankee, missie, I very glad," she said. "I take girl, pay school, and she grow nice girl. I get nice husband her, and they go my house, and they give me chow when I old."[20]

The two missionaries that Sarah met with later, who had been in China for thirty years and spoke the language fluently, sat and "patiently" listened to her story of the childless servant. These were not women accustomed to giving anyone a soft landing. Confronting Sarah with their combined street-smarts, they told her what they thought of her good Samaritanism. "People here have to be very careful in giving what they call assistance," the ladies advised. Assuming the amah was telling the truth about her situation (which Sarah had naïvely not doubted for an instant), and that she was allowed to adopt a girl from the mission, something could still go wrong, and in China when such a thing happened it tainted everyone concerned, including the mission, the missionaries, and Sarah. And what if she was not telling the truth? "She may be filling up the dance houses," they said, "or she may wish the child for a worse fate"—surely the first time that Sarah Conger had been cautioned about contributing to child prostitution. And there was a possible fate even worse than these: if the father were so unprincipled as to take a fancy to his own step-child, there was nothing the mother could do to stop him. Everything in the house belonged to him, they warned, including the adopted girl, whom he might put to unspeakable uses.[21]

As a world opened to her that she had never conceived of, Sarah must have shuddered. "It is better to let them do their own work in their own way," Sarah was told, advice she had already taken to heart where her servants were concerned, "unless you know just what you are doing, and for whom."[22]

"I returned home wiser," Sarah recorded, "and these words stared me in the face with a piercing, living glow: 'Mind your own business and let others mind theirs'"—the credo, actually, of any Chinese stepping over a dying beggar in a Beijing street. As Sarah would write in her old age, having learned the Chinese way, "Help those who would help themselves."[23]

8
Unlocking the gates

Sarah began to wander deeper into Beijing in the winter and spring of 1899, where she discovered a site which fascinated her more than any of the palaces or temples: the Imperial Observatory.[1]

The movement of stars and planets and the bright patterns of the constellations had been of interest to Sarah since childhood—from the flat Midwest plains, she had only to look up at night to see the skies transfigured by the hour. She loved, too, the fact that many of the greatest minds of past centuries had watched the stars for answers. As Sarah wrote to a nephew,

> Every age seems to have reverently recognized the heavens as a watchful, changeable, never-failing friend, always true to man physically and spiritually. The Life, Truth, Love that never fails is so indelibly stamped in the brilliant heavens that all mankind has recognized it, looked up to it, and humbly clasped its proffered, helping hand.

Once she discovered the Imperial Observatory,[2] built on the southeast corner of the old city wall in 1296 during the reign of Khublai Khan, she could not stop coming back. Under the Mongols, the observatory (largely the work of Muslim astronomers) had consisted of a tower with a quadrant for determining the altitude of celestial bodies. A century and a quarter later, the city walls were pulled down and re-erected further south and east, leaving the observatory on its remaining corner of city wall. In 1674, bronze astronomical instruments were designed by Jesuit priest Ferdinand Verbiest at the command of the Kangxi emperor, who was not yet an enemy of Christians and their innovations. Verbiest designed six instruments in total—a quadrant, celestial globe, an altazimuth (similar to a quadrant), an ecliptic armilla to measure longitude and latitude, a sextant, and a zodiacal armilla that showed the geocentric astronomy of the time, a herd of celestial bodies trailing around the earth with the twelve signs of the zodiac encircling them. Fifteen years later, a theodolite was added, with another armilla thirty years after that. Louis XIV, France's Sun King, was appropriately said to have contributed a second altazimuth.[3]

When Sarah came to see them, all these instruments were still in place, as was the Ming-era water clock in a chamber at the base of the observatory. Climbing to the platform fifty feet above the street, Sarah was enthralled by two things: the antiquity of the spot, and the fact that most of the extant instruments on the platform were not Chinese at all. As Sarah moved among the graceful silhouettes, starkly outlined against the jumbled backdrop of the city below, she who knew how they were meant to be used could not get over the fact that they still functioned, easily shifting on their pivots. "They are always exposed to the changes of the seasons," she recorded, "always in the open, yet they are without corrosion." She attributed this imperviousness to the material the instruments were made from, gold mixed into the bronze, which made them a form of astronomical jewelry, alfresco art with their superbly molded dragons and Chinese designs. "Each line," she marveled, "seems to stand out as boldly and accurately as if in the first year of its long existence."[4] Though she only visited the observatory by day, Sarah easily imagined court astronomers standing atop the wall, moving the instruments that were "so nicely poised upon their axes," following the "myriads of bright lights" through the aspects of which "simple and complex problems could be solved."[5]

"My thought," she told a nephew, when describing one of these observatory visits, "reaches out to know more. All that this vast universe has said, is saying, and will continue to say to mankind, will never be known. The vibrations of the sunbeams tone and intensify the rich and varied colorings of nature in all their grandeur." Just as the great scientists and explorers whom Sarah admired had loved the mysteries of the universe as much as they loved uncovering the truth behind them, so it was that she was most fascinated by the mysteries of China that she could least fathom, and it was these that would most elicit both her sympathy and her admiration. But what also moved her was the fact that here, for a moment in time, was prime evidence that there had been a brotherhood of thought in China—that what had allowed the worlds of East and West to briefly co-operate to create these instruments of beauty and usefulness might occur again, if East and West worked hard enough to achieve it.[6]

But even as she tried to dwell on this positive image, it was around this same time that Sarah came to a painful conclusion, which she dared to share only with her sister in America. "I do not wonder," she confided, "that the Chinese hate the foreigner."[7]

✳ ✳ ✳ ✳ ✳

In March, when northern China was still in the grip of the receding winter, but flowers that in Des Moines were still asleep were already beginning to bud, Sarah took guests from the American legation on her first trip outside the city since the troubles of the previous fall. She chose two religious sites, possibly thinking they would be more accessible, if not more elevating, to her guests. But she was to discover in so doing that the distance between herself and her fellow foreigners was widening even as that between herself and the Chinese was abating.

Built on the Anting Plain north of the city wall, on the site of a shrine constructed during the Liao dynasty, the Yellow Temple was first consecrated in 1652 by the Shunzhi emperor, as a residence for a visiting dalai lama. A "western" section for lamas from Tibet and Mongolia was built by the Kangxi emperor nearly seventy years later, in expiation for the death of a Mongolian living buddha, who had been struck down during an audience with the emperor by one of the imperial retainers for failing to stand on Kangxi's entrance. A marble stupa or reliquary had been added to the pleasantly tree-filled grounds in 1780, after a visiting panchen lama, second in authority to the dalai lama, died of smallpox in Beijing. The deceased prelate was sent back to Lhasa in a gold coffin, but the clothes he had died in were buried in the stupa.[8]

When allied forces stormed Beijing in 1860, Sir Hope Grant had camped out in the so-called "travelers' palace" meant for the dalai lama. Perhaps because of this, the temple grounds were used by foreigners in Beijing as a place for picnics. Indeed, by 1899 it was common to see foreigners clambering over the various statues, posing for souvenir photographs in attitudes of giddiness that jarred with the temple's sacred setting. Photos taken by young Lancelot Giles, a student interpreter at the British legation, show groups of foreign ladies in summery chintz and their dapper bowler-topped male companions lolling over the Yellow Temple's stupa; another, taken at the so-called Tomb of the Princess (actually the burial place of two of the Jiaqing emperor's daughters) is conspicuous for featuring worthies of the Legation Quarter astride the ceremonial stone animals and balustrades, like children who have discovered a new amusement park.[9]

Though in poor repair when Sarah took her guests through it, the Yellow Temple was still a locus of Buddhist festivals, with brightly colored prayer flags fluttering above activities religious and commercial convened by the monks who lived there. (Years later, one inveterate traveler would pay the going price of two viewings for a dollar charged by the monks to see "dead priests ... kept in wooden boxes like gramophone cabinets.")[10]

Sarah's party consisted of twelve people, of five different nationalities, traveling on ponies or in chairs over the rough roads. Some of the group were young and frisky: "the riders had their frolics in speeding their horses," Sarah recorded, "then in the shade of some trees they waited for the coming of the chairs." She watched with sympathetic concern as the bearers tried to keep up.[11]

Marveling at the marble stupa, with its thirteen panels representing the Buddhist heavens, its gleaming gilded cupola, and carved scenes from the life of the panchen lama, Sarah seems to have had the embarrassing experience known to every tour guide when she looked into the faces of her guests and found little trace of interest or understanding. Indeed some of them were not even with her but were spurring their ponies across the temple grounds or wandering off in chattering knots among the trees. While she and a few others of the party stayed "to listen for answers to [our] questions," she noted, "others would look, pass on and out and feel no inspiration."[12]

The eighteenth-century Bell Temple lay amid the quiet farms that Sarah had admired on her trip to the Great Wall in September. From ancient times it had a shrine, but did not become famous until a bell considered the greatest feat of bronze casting in China was hung in it. This bell, transferred from the Temple of Longevity (Wanshousi) in Beijing, was cast in the reign of the Yongle emperor, who desired a bell of such size and volume as could be heard for one hundred *li* (thirty miles).[13]

There must have been more pony racing on the way to the Bell Temple, because in her letter describing the day Sarah pointedly notes how, after reaching the site, the *mafu* assigned to each rider "walked the horses quietly for about thirty minutes" before taking off their saddles and bridles, watering, feeding, and stabling them. The Chinese were again proving to her eyes, at least, that they were more sensible of the animals' welfare than the supposedly more humane foreigners who rode them.[14]

At the temple the group was amazed to find tables filled with flowers and sweets, and laid with legation china, silver, and linen. It was the work of Wang, the legation's new number one boy, who was proving to be a real artist in these and other matters of domestic entertainment. "My servants had done it themselves," Sarah recorded, like a proud mother. "I let them do it in their own way. The guests exclaimed 'Marvelous! Marvelous!'" After tiffin, everyone moved on to see the Great Bell. She was told, as she passed under it, that the bell, at fifty-three and a half tons, was second in size to only one other on earth (the great Tsar Bell in Moscow, considerably younger), but as a hanging bell it was the largest of its kind. "We looked at it, we felt of it," she marveled. "It was really there, hanging from that immense frame of mighty timbers." For Sarah, it was "that historic, talking thing," a keen old sage speaking wisdom of the ages. Among Chinese, only the emperor himself had the power to command the bell be rung. Yet for their foreign guests, the keepers of the bell graciously made an exception, striking it with its immense timber clapper.

As Sarah wrote, "This monster bell sang to us a song of days gone by. It struck eternity's chord." For the first time during the morning's outing, it appeared the "five nationalities" in Sarah's party were also awestruck enough to stand still and listen to the "historic, talking thing."[15]

With Wang beside her, Sarah climbed a haphazard staircase until she was looking straight at the crown of the bell. In order to prevent the bell from breaking when struck with too much force, and to regulate its tones, a hole had been left in its top. Handing Sarah a string of cash that he had brought from home, Wang told her, "Make wish, throw cash at hole top bell; hole receive cash, good luck." This proved easier said than done: Sarah tossed several strings, each with a wish, and though most of them ran down the sides of the bell, she got some through the hole. In any event, she was happy to see that the most immediate recipient of good luck was the young temple-boy, who busily collected the coins off the floor below.[16]

To Sarah, the bell "sounds a sweet welcome and a cheering goodbye." But she also noted that not everyone could hear its message, even those standing next to it. "These tones vary," she pointed out diplomatically, "in proportion to the quality of the sounding board receiving them." There were clearly, in her view, too few foreign sounding boards in Beijing of the required sensitivity.[17]

✳ ✳ ✳ ✳ ✳

The attitudes many foreigners showed toward the Chinese continued to trouble Sarah. Living among the nationals of several countries, she enjoyed the different characteristics of Austrians, Belgians, Dutch, English, French, Germans, Italians, Japanese, Russians, and Spanish, but against the backdrop of a people who, like the Chinese, seemed so purely what they were, the many differences stood out starkly, as did each nations' particular response to the Chinese. "Many times," Sarah confided to her sister her first winter, "I feel ashamed that we do not appear more like civilized people. Our ignorance and extreme prejudices make us appear in a bad and untrue light; we are really better than we seem." But it seemed to her that in too few instances foreigners made an effort to show their better side.[18]

The Chinese, too, had their prejudices, as Sarah discovered first hand. It was what to a woman like herself was among the greatest sins of omission—the almost total absence of middle-class Chinese women from the life of the capital, from its markets, theaters, and temples. She had already experienced this ostracism in Shanghai. Of the "better classes" of Chinese women, Sarah was told, "they do not labor; a life-work is done if they bear even one or two children." It pained her that even another woman, albeit a foreign one, could not visit them, given the strictures on their freedom created by their men. "I wish that I could see these ladies in their home life," she wrote her sister, who was of the same mind where women's rights were concerned. "If I ever do, I will let you rejoice with me."[19] Sarah had her chance during a visit to the legation by Viceroy Li Hongzhang.

Li was in his mid-seventies when Sarah first met him in April 1899, when he was far from the energetic and dashing mandarin who had played the interchangeable games of war and politics for the better part of his long life. All Sarah saw in 1899 was a stooped old man with attentive manners toward her and showing a respect for Edwin which he often showed toward Americans. Li was that creature Sarah Conger greatly admired, even if she did not know all the unsavory facts of how he managed to accomplish it: he was a survivor. Son of an official of provincial rank in Anwei, Li had been a strapping young man, six feet tall and with an excellent brain. He attained the *jinshi* degree in the metropolitan examinations in Beijing at age twenty-four and fought soon after against the Taiping rebels, whose effort to establish a "Heavenly Kingdom of Great Peace" had cost China millions of lives and made it easier for foreign interlopers to fill the vacuum. With General Zeng Guofan as his mentor and example, Li learned and used street-fighting techniques, making use of ruffian armies who were at their best under such conditions. When the rebellion was ended, Li was forty-nine years old and in his prime.

Becoming viceroy of Zhili, a mere step away from Beijing and the power held by the co-empresses dowager Cian and Cixi, Li became a favorite of the latter's, though often enough he displeased her to the extent of being demoted and sent forever from the imperial presence—until she needed him again. And Li needed Cixi's protection because he had enemies everywhere in China, some of whom rightly suspected he was not entirely looking out for China's best interests, whether in provincial deals or in his parleys with Russian and Japanese envoys, and some of whom wanted a slice of the same pie. Li had friends among both the Americans like Charles Denby, Edwin's predecessor at the American legation, and the British like Sir Robert Hart of the Maritime Customs, and he leaned on them for advice he either used or sought for the purpose of deepening their friendship. After a stroke in 1888 and the death of his beloved principal wife, followed by the Sino-Japanese War in 1894–95, Li should have been a broken man, but that he could travel around the globe in 1896 on a goodwill mission, taking in the courts of Queen Victoria, Kaiser Wilhelm II, Tsar Nicholas II, and the White House of President Grover Cleveland, showed there was still fire in the belly of the old diplomat. Li knew where a smiling face and gentle demeanor did him the most good—at the homespun American legation, amid the Congers' no-nonsense Midwestern manners.[20]

Li met with Edwin probably as much to determine the Americans' response to the political situation in the aftermath of the Hundred Days of Reform as to pay a courtesy call. During the visit, Wang told Sarah that Li wanted to meet her, Laura, and the female guests of the legation. They presented themselves and greeted the famous old statesman, who seemed so "unusually happy" that Sarah made a bold move. "I ventured to say, 'Your Excellency, Li Hung Chang, if in accordance with your thought, and that of your family, I should be much pleased to pay my respects to Lady Li.'" This request was translated, and digested slowly by Li. The Lady Li Sarah referred to was probably Ding Xiang, a favorite concubine of Li's. He gave a laconic reply: "I will see." It was not much to give Sarah hope, but the next day a message arrived from William Pethick, Li's American secretary, saying that Lady Li and family "would be pleased to receive the ladies of the American Legation."[21]

Besides Sarah, the visitors comprised four other women, including Laura, requiring five chairs, twenty-four bearers, four outriders, and Wang, a veritable parade that took forty-five minutes to traverse the crowded streets to the red-doored gate of the Li mansion. William Pethick met them there and escorted them into the courtyard, where they were greeted by Viceroy Li's youngest son. This would have been only one of many courtyards in the Li compound.

Beijing's courtyard houses or *siheyuan* were multigenerational microcosms of a family, with several courtyards sheltering as many generations as the family coffers could afford. The number of courtyards was an indicator of a man's wealth and status. Beyond the front gates, with their flanking carved marble lions (denoting civil rank) or drums (military rank), past the spirit screen that kept out ghosts (which, being unable to turn corners, could float no further), one entered an intimate space full of potted plants and plantings in beds—wisteria, forsythia, lilacs, dragon-claw willow, flowering fruit trees, and trailing vines. Through a round moongate the visitor might step into a second courtyard framed in pavilions with crimson pillars and elaborate carved eaves painted in orange and green, the ceiling beams and joists decorated with cartouches of floating goldfish, idealized landscapes, or Buddhist symbols. Beyond this would be another doorway, perhaps shaped like a vase, an open fan, or a leaf, where another courtyard offered more flowers and trees, a pool for fish, or the abstract handsomeness of standing scholar's stones carved with snippets of poetry. These doors were the only openings in the inner walls, aside from fancifully shaped "leak windows" giving a view from one quadrant of the garden into another. In the furthest courtyards the women lived, far from where male visitors might accidentally see them, in a quiet broken only by servants' chatter or the laughter of children. Each family unit lived in its own sheltered space, as private from one another in their own apartments as the compound itself was from the streets on the other side of the walls. Yet even in the first courtyard, once the red gates closed to the *hutong* outside, the noisy world of men, what poets called "the red dust," could not intrude on one's privacy, flowers, and orderliness. This was Sarah's first experience of such a home until she entered an abandoned one after the end of the Boxer Uprising.

Li's son guided the Conger party over the threshold of a pavilion not far from the main entrance of the compound, where Lady Li, his wife, and a cousin, stood to welcome their guests. "These ladies were dressed in the richest of Chinese attire," Sarah recorded, "choice satin embroideries and brocades and the finest of foreign jewels." It was a scene of particularly potent irony not unlike the reception in Shanghai. The formal manners and traditional dress of the Li women stood in contrast to the foreign jewelry they wore to please their foreign guests, as did the foreign furniture on which they were asked to be seated. Perhaps most ironic of all, one ancient tradition seemed especially out of place: all the women, despite their efforts to be modern, had bound feet.[22]

Sarah expressed her admiration of the ladies' garments, prompting Li's son to tease her by saying that men could wear "pretty colors" as well as women. The era when European men could garb themselves like peacocks had gone out with the French Revolution, but Sarah could not have agreed more. "Bright colors complement gentlemen as well as ladies," she told the young man. In a letter describing the visit, once she had gathered more thoughts on the subject, she would go further—that it was wrong to make Chinese, male or female, feel they should wear anything but what they preferred by custom or choice, an attitude decidedly the opposite of that held by both pro-Western foreigners and ultra-Westernizing Chinese.[23]

With Li's son translating, the women exchanged pleasantries, sipped tea, and studied one another for all of thirty minutes. Sarah had dreamed of this moment, of being invited into an authentic Chinese home and seeing how its ladies lived, and we may assume the Li women were just as intrigued by the visit, considering they had met very few foreign women. But the pervasiveness of her own culture, even here behind Chinese walls, troubled Sarah. She had hoped to see "purely Chinese rooms," where the women lived out their lives in their traditional way, looking after their children, making music, or embroidering. Such a home was a woman's world but ironically one over which she had no control—another factor that fascinated Sarah, brought up to consider herself the equal of any man, a determiner of her own destiny, with the freedom to do as she pleased.

It was easy to project both ideals and condemnation on the Chinese. Eliza Scidmore once visited a Manchu household of high rank, full of preconceptions about women who she was sure would be "uneducated, secluded," sitting in darkness smoking opium, only to discover the sober and intelligent ladies discussing the newly discovered cathode ray. Sarah had arrived at the Li residence expecting to find herself enveloped in the traditional Chinese world she craved, only to find it all too foreign-inflected. Like an ethnographer on a field trip, she had hoped the ladies would carry on with their everyday life at home as if Sarah were not there. Pride, "face," and decorum all militated against such an experience. So when she left the Li mansion, though happy to have been received, Sarah did so feeling that her mission—to get to the heart of the Chinese woman's life—was not yet accomplished, and that it was somehow a failure on her part to get as close to the Li women as she desired.[24]

Yet she had done more good than she realized. A week after her visit to Lady Li, Sarah received a return call from Li's son. He brought with him his wife and sister, along with the cousin who had been present at the earlier visit. In accordance with custom, Lady Li was not able to leave her own home to accompany them, but sent along her greetings. This disappointed Sarah, but when Li's son told her that neither his wife nor his sister had ever entered a foreign home (not that the Congers' legation drawing room was all that different from Lady Li's own), she was thrilled to show them her hospitality. Dressed in all their Chinese finery, and with the omnipresent foreign jewels, the Li women stayed nearly an hour, for the same polite conversation and tea drinking that had characterized Sarah's visit to the Li mansion. When they departed, Sarah noted that Li junior's sister took precedence in the line of chairs, even over his own wife—a pecking order that would never have been countenanced in America, where if a man's unmarried sister lived with him and his wife she usually took a subordinate, even servile role. As with so many Chinese customs, which seemed to run counter to Western ones, this fascinated Sarah but did not repel her—after all, would she be happy if the Li women criticized her own customs and habits without trying to understand them first? It was, Sarah believed, no one's business to try to change another culture, unless that culture wanted the changes itself.

Beyond the fact that it had happened, and had lasted twice as long as her own visit to the Li mansion, the women's visit gave Sarah the satisfaction of having had a call returned to her by highly placed Chinese ladies. She had hope that more was possible. Just how lucky she was to have received a visit at all was made clear to her later, when William Pethick, who was becoming more and more a kind of unofficial advisor to her on Chinese customs, smilingly told Sarah that in receiving the Li ladies she had achieved a kind of social coup. What had happened at the American legation had never happened before. In allowing his daughter to visit the American legation, said Pethick, Viceroy Li had bestowed on

Sarah and Edwin a rare honor. "Viceroy Li Hung Chang is very strict about his daughter," Pethick remarked. "He forbids her going out, but has let her come here. This is a compliment to the American minister and his country."[25]

Sarah may have made more progress than she knew; but she did know there was still further to go: a world in which a mature, intelligent woman was not allowed to explore was a world in need of big changes, whether the men who manned the gates wanted them or not. "I prophesy," she recorded, "that [China] will in time unlock her barred gates and mingle and intermingle with other peoples," in so doing to "cooperate in the great struggle for a better and higher civilization"—words that would return to haunt her in the great struggle that was coming in another year's time.[26]

1. Sarah Pike Conger as she appeared during her husband's tenure as Iowa congressman in the 1880s. Author's collection.

2. An 1885 campaign button for Edwin Hurd Conger, Iowa congressman and future minister to China. Author's collection.

3. Lombard College's "Old Main." It is the only extant building from the Lincoln–Douglas debates of 1858, and would have looked much like this when Edwin Conger and Sarah Pike were students at Lombard. Rex Cherrington Collection.

4. Laura Conger Buchan, Sarah's daughter, a young woman whose fragility belied a powerful intelligence and a will of steel that faltered only briefly during the fifty-five-day siege of the British legation. Author's collection.

5. View from the Tartar wall looking north, showing buildings belonging to the American legation on the left, the arched porches of the residence of the British minister further along, the Jade Canal running to the east of both, and the rooftops of the Forbidden City palace complex in the distance. Where the Chinese are standing on the wall (below) was very near the most embattled portion of the fortifications during the Boxer siege in July–August 1900. The temple that served as the Congers' home for their last years in Beijing lay just to the left of the figure in dark clothing. Author's collection.

6. The drawing room of the American legation in Beijing, post-1900. Formerly known as the Sanguanmiao, where the last Ming emperor prayed before committing suicide in 1644, the building was used as a home by the Congers while the new American legation was constructed. Temporary as it was, it was the closest Sarah ever came to living in a real Chinese house, and as such was the home closest to her heart. Author's collection.

7. American doctor, and friend of Edwin and Sarah Conger, N. S. Hopkins on the Great Wall of China with two lady companions, pre-1900, showing the ruinous condition of parts of the fortification. This photograph was fixed atop paperweight-sized slices of Great Wall brick and sold in silk-bound boxes for the benefit of medical services in China. Author's collection.

8. From left, Sarah Conger, Laura Conger Buchan, and Edwin Conger at the Three Hills Nunnery in the Western Hills, the ancient temple that was the American legation's summer retreat (pre-1900). Russell Collection.

9. A view of the Beijing Observatory before 1900. The thirteenth-century structure, with its foreign-designed instruments of the seventeenth and eighteenth centuries, was one of Sarah's favorite places and a symbol to her of what the two great peoples of West and East could achieve when they worked together. Author's collection.

10. A Manchu funeral in Beijing, circa 1925. Leave out the telegraph wires and this could be a procession from a century earlier—a mix of East and West, modern and ancient, that was part of Sarah Conger's daily experience in Beijing. Author's collection.

11. Members of the diplomatic corps sitting on the sacred animal sculptures at the Tomb of the Princesses outside Beijing, circa 1900. The Giles Pickford Collection. ©Australian National University.

12. The diplomatic wives who attended the first audience with the empress dowager in December 1898. Sarah Conger is fourth from right, with Lady MacDonald in stripes standing to the fore. Author's collection.

13. The northeast corner of the Forbidden City's moated wall. Behind this mysterious structure lay the empress dowager's most private pavilions and courtyards, the so-called Retirement Palaces. Photograph: Les Hayter.

14. The Congers' Number One Boy, Wang (far right) and his family. "The very best of *the best*," Sarah wrote of him. Author's collection.

15. Sketch from a photograph showing, from left, Edwin Conger, painter Cecile Payen, and servant having tiffin atop the Great Wall, May 1900. This was their last calm before the storm of the Boxer Uprising. Author's collection.

16. Cecile Payen's watercolor of Dr. Poole's bungalow at the British legation, painted in late July 1900. Payen gave the painting to Sarah Conger for her birthday, and it survived the siege. Sally Jewell Coxe Collection. Photograph: Sally Jewell Coxe.

17. The burning of the Qianmen Gate on June 18, 1900. The Giles Pickford Collection. ©Australian National University.

18. Liu Wuyuan, the teenaged messenger who made it safely the ninety miles to Tianjin with an S. O. S. from the besieged residents of the legations and back again to Beijing. The Giles Pickford Collection. ©Australian National University.

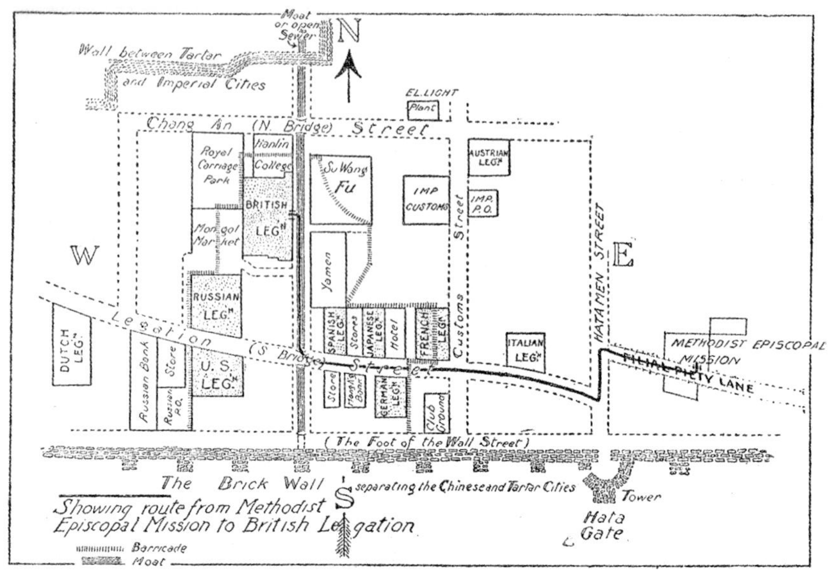

19. A map of the besieged Legation Quarter, reproduced from Ethel Hubbard's 1905 biography of missionary Mary Porter Gamewell, showing the lines of defense and the congeries of streets and alleys that surrounded the complex. Author's collection.

20. Laura Conger Buchan with the pony Wang saved from the siege dinner table. Author's collection.

21. Idealized illustration of blue-eyed Iowan Calvin Pearl Titus lifting the American flag above the Beijing city wall, bombs bursting over the Forbidden City. He received the Medal of Honor for this feat, but it was actually Sikh troops who were the first to enter the British legation. Author's collection.

22. British soldiers larking on the empress dowager's infamous Marble Boat at the Summer Palace after the flight of the imperial court in August 1900; they also went skinny dipping in the lake. Author's collection.

23. Sarah, Edwin, and Laura Conger walking toward the Forbidden City's Meridian Gate in September 1900, its palaces abandoned by the emperor, empress dowager, and their court to dust, sightseers, and kleptomaniacs. American troops stand at attention on either side. Underwood & Underwood Glass Stereograph Collection, Archives Center, National Museum of American History, Smithsonian Institution.

24. A rare shot of the empress dowager in her chair during her return to Beijing on January 7, 1902, outside the temple of the God of War. The Giles Pickford Collection. ©Australian National University.

25. Carved and gilded memorial tablet given to Edwin Conger by the grateful Chinese Christians of Beijing. The tablet is now displayed at Knox College, Lombard's successor institution. Special Collections and Archives, Knox College Library, Galesburg, Illinois.

26. The denuded platform of the Beijing Observatory—a sight that shocked and depressed Sarah Conger. The instruments were not returned by France and Germany until after World War I. The Giles Pickford Collection. ©Australian National University.

27. A view of the new American legation, its cornerstone laid by Sarah Conger on April 19, 1904. The building is now the centerpiece of Chienmen 23, a complex of restaurants, shops, and galleries in the former diplomatic quarter of Beijing. Author's collection.

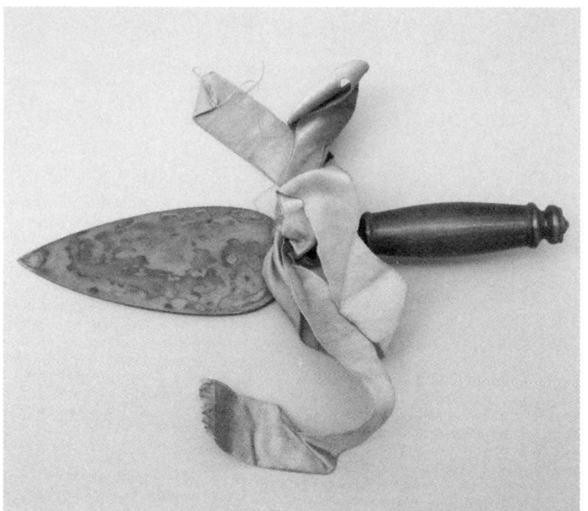

28. The silver trowel used by Sarah Conger to set the cornerstone of the new American legation. © 2011 President and Fellows of Harvard College 991-12-60/14900.

29. One of many photographs Sarah had made of guests to her famous tiffins for Chinese ladies. This shows Manchu women of high rank and includes painter Katherine Carl (third row, extreme left), with future author Princess Der Ling, her mother and sister standing just behind Sarah, who is seated (in black) beside the imperial princess, the Empress Dowager Cixi's adopted daughter. Author's collection.

30. Lao Hu, the Pekingese given to Sarah Conger by the empress dowager. The Congers brought him to their California home in 1905. Russell Collection.

31. The formidable, witty, and warm Dowager Princess K'e, one of Sarah's closest friends in Beijing and Sarah's key to private celebrations among Chinese families rarely shared with foreigners. Author's collection.

32. Sarah Conger Buchan (Mrs. Theodore E. Jewell), circa 1905, wearing the clothes made for her by Sarah Conger's friend, Mrs. Wang. Author's collection.

33. A group of Sarah's Han Chinese friends, photographed outside the American legation after tiffin, circa 1904. Sarah's friend Mrs. Wang is fourth from left; her daughter, whom Sarah loved, sits to her left on the carpet. Author's collection.

34. This gate at the Summer Palace, just off the Long Gallery beside Kunming Lake, is still remembered as the one leading to the chambers where the painter Katherine Carl lived while she worked on the empress dowager's portrait in 1904–05. Photograph: Les Hayter.

35. The first portrait of Cixi completed by Katherine Carl (1904), in a frame of carved camphorwood designed by the dowager. It was photographed at the Summer Palace by Xunling, and is still there. Freer Gallery of Art and Arthur M. Sackler Gallery Archives. Smithsonian Institution, Washington DC.

36. A view to the picture gallery at the 1904 St. Louis Exposition, showing Katherine Carl's second portrait of the empress dowager, brought to the White House after its display at the Exposition and accepted as China's gift to the United States by President Theodore Roosevelt. Courtesy of the Missouri History Museum, St. Louis, Missouri.

37. Photograph of the Empress Dowager Cixi, center, with Sarah Conger to her left, three unnamed foreign women, and Lili, daughter of the photographer, Xunling. This is the only known photograph of the empress dowager touching a foreigner. Freer Gallery of Art and Arthur M. Sackler Gallery Archives. Smithsonian Institution, Washington DC.

38. A room of the Conger house in Pasadena. To the left (beside the fireplace) is the scroll painting of chrysanthemums given to Edwin Conger by the Empress Dowager Cixi. Russell Collection.

39. A room in the Congers' Pasadena home. A portrait of their son, Lorentus, who died at age seven, can be seen on the wall. Russell Collection.

40. Sarah Pike Conger with the two most important women in her life, her granddaughter Sarah Buchan Jewell, and the latter's mother, Laura Conger Buchan. Russell Collection.

9
Gathering storm

While Sarah was celebrating the brilliant China of the past, the Empress Dowager Cixi was looking to a murkier future, via human instruments of a vintage pre-dating the bronze altazimuths at the Beijing Observatory.

Just as Cixi had not been averse, at first, to the Guangxu emperor's reforms, she had not always rejected foreign ways and things. Yuanmingyuan, the pleasure spot she had loved as the setting of her happy days as the Xianfeng emperor's favorite, would surely have also fascinated her with its European-style buildings and technology. Cixi was later to enjoy the very foreign art of photography, standing by in a darkroom as prints were developed, and working a camera herself. (She is even said to have had an interest in early moving film technology.)[1]

What she hated about foreigners in China, in the big picture, was what they seemed to be doing to undermine the authority of the dynasty. They took ever-bigger bites out of the coastline, established and entrenched Christian missions in order to recruit converts, and subverted the familial and religious traditions that had been a part of Chinese culture for millennia. In the smaller, more subjective picture, Cixi could never forgive the destruction of Yuanmingyuan by British and French troops in 1861. Even as Sarah saw beauty as the common language between cultures, Cixi could be forgiven for thinking that even the rough and ready barbarian armies should have understood and respected beauty when they saw it. That they viewed it as tinder for bonfires, or as loot, colored her view of any positive contributions foreigners might be able to make to China later on.

While she had not protested Guangxu's reforms until discovering that they came at the price of sweeping her out along with the eight-legged essay, Cixi's response was that of a woman fighting for her life on the one hand and fighting for imperial China's life on the other. And though she had quashed the Guangxu emperor's reforms when she went after those of his associates who desired her removal, she had not been able to stop the juggernaut of change. The aftermath of the Hundred Days of Reform flew not in the face of the emperor, hidden away in disillusionment and depression, but in her own. Her response to this storm unleashed by a young man unable to control it was to influence all her actions over the next eighteen months.

The storm began with words—the writings from safe exile of Kang Youwei and Liang Qichao, those two ringleaders and survivors of the plot to imprison the dowager.

To say that Kang and Liang did their best to destroy Cixi's reputation is misleading, because until late 1898 few in the West really knew enough about her, if they had ever heard of her at all, to have any cogent sense of her. Guangxu was still the emperor of China, in whose name decrees were issued and laws promulgated. Cixi ruled from behind a curtain which, though made of gauze, effectively concealed her person. Even after the Boxer Uprising thrust her into the lurid spotlight as a villain, respectable foreign newspapers and journals often joined ranks with gutter press not only in spreading tales of her depravity but getting even her name consistently wrong. When Kang and Liang began their campaign from afar, they offered the world an image of Cixi that for most people formed their first impression of her. There would not be any clear photographic images of her until one of her palace officials, Xunling, made a series of them between 1903 and 1905. While a limited number of these was soon available for sale in Shanghai (Cixi's effort to humanize herself à la Queen Victoria?), even these authentic images of Cixi were not accessible to Westerners for some years.[2]

So tales of the dowager's pecuniary and sexual depravity, coupled with Western stereotypes of Chinese women, in which rich or powerful women came to assume the chilling outlines of the suitor-killing Princess Turandot of legend, painted a fearful picture indeed. As Kang wrote from Hong Kong in letters sent to both Sir Claude MacDonald and to Edwin, Cixi was nothing but a "False Empress," "a licentious and depraved palace concubine" who cared nothing for the Chinese people, and even worse, kept the chief eunuch Li Lianying so near because he was no eunuch at all but a lover. It was not enough that Cixi was a phoney empress elevated from depraved concubinage, she also had to be a merry imperial widow. By another lover, unnamed, according to Kang, Cixi had had at least one child she intended to put on the throne (though she had never availed herself of the opportunities she had had to do so), and she had poisoned the harmless Cian and the Tongzhi emperor's wife—she had taken the evil stepmother role beyond its fairy tale circumscription. Cixi was, in short, a "usurping, murderous thief" who had, Kang told the *China Mail*, misappropriated funds allocated for the navy in order to beautify her pleasure spot, the Summer Palace, where she kept the Guangxu emperor constantly drugged. Kang's grief at his brother's and friends' executions may excuse the outbursts he delivered to the *China Mail* and the foreign legations soon after he reached the safety of Hong Kong. But this tirade became his lifelong stock in trade. And because foreigners knew so little about Cixi to begin with, the bits of mud and dung stuck, finally obliterating details of the authentic woman.[3]

While this image was shaping itself against the ignorance of the outside world, nations that had always made demands on China, and some that had yet to do so, were jockeying for position like irate customers at an understaffed Chinese takeout counter. Russia and Germany, France and Great Britain, all were pressing China's nerve points. France promised a demonstration of strong-arming if their demands in the city of Shanghai and the province of Sichuan were not acceded to; and Portugal was next in line, desiring the extension of its territory in Macao, that foreign foothold where extraterritoriality had its first flower. Belgium, unwilling to be left out of any deal that might favor France, asked for a concession at Hankou, while Spain and Japan both sidled up with their own demands. Luckily for China, virtually powerless Italy, a latecomer to the chopping block, was for the moment the biggest troublemaker, pressing for a concession at Sanmun Bay, in Zhejiang province. Where it had so often caved in, the Chinese government refused—another sign of how right Sir Robert Hart was to note an unusual, unnerving new confidence in the Chinese government and military.[4]

After the Italian threat, copies of a secret edict went out from Beijing to all high officials in the coastal provinces, ordering immediate resistance should Italy or any other foreign invader attempt to put ashore. Had Cixi's edict been shared with the foreign powers in China, and the coastal defenses been put on alert in an open fashion, Italy might well have pressed to the point of declaring war on China, a calamity Cixi (and those relying on China's loan payments) needed very much to avoid— at least for now. It could well be that she had an ally in mind should a war declaration come, for it was at this time that China was exploring an offensive/defensive alliance with Japan, her erstwhile enemy. But nothing came of this effort, because Japan itself had an eye on China. Russia, China's closest quasi-Asian neighbor, would have seemed a natural ally, and Li Hongzhang had urged Cixi to rely on the Tsar's bona fides. But the dowager distrusted the Russians (perhaps knowing that Li was taking bribes from them), intuiting that one day they would seize Manchuria and possibly more. China was, in all respects, completely alone. This isolation may explain why the dowager turned to home-grown forces to keep China for the Chinese. She had nothing else.[5]

To make the situation even worse, there was not a united body of political advice at court that Cixi could lean on, as was her prerogative in the tradition of the imperial family. Throughout that summer, instead of serving her best interests or those of the empire, two of Cixi's most prominent officials, Ronglu and Prince Qing (Yikuang), were facing off in a fatal policy disagreement that mirrored the divisions within society itself.

Prince Qing, a descendant of the Qianlong emperor who was married to a relative of Cixi's, had been handed control of the foreign office in 1884 by Li Hongzhang after another of China's crises with a foreign power—in this case France, which had grabbed Chinese territory in Indochina. Then in charge of foreign affairs, Prince Gong, Cixi's brother-in-law who had negotiated with Britain and France in 1861, was in favor of parley to avoid any military clash. Having stayed behind to face the allied forces while Xianfeng and Cixi fled to Jehol, and thus having seen the disasters wreaked on the Old Summer Palace and on Beijing, Prince Gong knew better than to engage any of the Western powers in combat. Viceroy Li agreed with him on this, and all might have been well except for the conservative faction at court, the Iron Hats, princes of the blood (like Qing), who were continually scheming for the throne or at least some enriching proximity thereto.

Several of these Manchu princes began to turn to magic. As one writer notes, they "consulted soothsayers daily, and saw themselves as legends in the making." Reality was so hard to face that it was accorded no place in daily life or, even worse, in political plotting. Prince Qing was said to be as venal a bribe-taker as Ronglu, and his vision of Chinese progress did not boast a very wide horizon. But he was a believer in the uses of constitutional monarchy and admired the personal role taken by the German kaiser and the imperial family in the affairs of their nation. Several years later he was also to be responsible for introducing the Western-educated daughters of Yu Keng to Cixi. Because these women ultimately served to open the doors of the modern world to her, and smoothed the way for Cixi's diplomatic efforts through the wives of the foreign ministers, Qing could be said to have contributed to Cixi's post-Boxer Uprising enlightenment. But that was still a long way down a very rocky road.[6]

The Iron Hats gathered strength from leaguing with the Pure Party, an uneasy mix of isolationists and pro-Westerners who shared a common cause: the foreigners were not to be parleyed with, and in an ideal world would be driven out of China forever. Because Prince Gong was seen by the conservatives as having sold out to foreign pressure in 1861, he had become *persona non grata* to these factions. When in later years the Iron Hats and their friends gained the support of the Guangxu emperor's father, Prince Chun, Gong was dislodged from power. Li, who always knew which way the winds were blowing, had promptly dropped Gong, who left politics altogether for the solace of his private garden. War erupted anyway, and France had taken Indochina without much fuss. It was the Iron Hats' ability to manipulate policy at court and within the clan that triggered events across China supportive of their anti-foreign aims.[7]

Commander of the Beijing police forces, Ronglu was one of those solidly unromantic men around whom it is easy to weave fantasies. His ancestry was the most colorful thing about him—he was a descendant of Fiongdon, the famous military commander under and favorite of Nurhaci, the founder of the Qing dynasty—though there was also a splash of color around his alleged assistance in saving Cixi and Cian from assassination on their return to Beijing from Jehol in 1862. From all accounts, Ronglu was the proverbial career policeman, a hale and hearty fellow, secretive and perhaps humorless but never asleep at the wheel, a man who looked out for his friends, and probably understood the criminal mind so well because he could, if necessary, think like a criminal too. Like many of his breed, he would have had allegiances that crossed boundaries political and personal—he was, after all, a friend to the Christian, Westernized Yu Keng, whom he had urged Cixi to post to the safety of Paris when it was clear that the conservatives, and the Boxers, were gaining traction at court.[8]

A clash between Prince Qing and Ronglu was inevitable. While the latter was as traditional a Manchu aristocrat as the Iron Hats were, he had a more pragmatic attitude toward the West and Westerners, especially where things military were concerned, and unlike Qing, who was always basically a puppet of others, Ronglu was his own man. Ronglu owed his rise not so much to his background or to any particular talents as to the fact that he was favored by Cixi, a status that conferred as many drawbacks as benefits—whomever had Cixi's favor was very powerful, and was envied, factors guaranteed to raise the ire of the princes of the blood. It was not that Ronglu had any treasonous love for foreigners, beyond admiration of their superior military organization. But he, like his friend Prince Gong, knew that whenever China had engaged their military forces, it had lost—not just palaces looted of treasures and put to the torch, but huge slices of territory, so that much of the Chinese coastline was in the hands of foreign nationals and corporations. If it is true, as some writers have claimed, that Ronglu and Cixi were parties to a romantic affair, requited or not, it is even more in keeping with the man's loyal nature to have protected her against her own failures of judgment. If he tried to thwart Cixi's unfortunate procession toward disaster, he clearly did not succeed, and may, in the end, have decided to march along with her, if only to protect her from herself until the bitter end.

✳   ✳   ✳   ✳   ✳

Irony in imperial China took a form as lavish as the meals on the imperial dining table, in few instances more so than in the advent of Tsaiyi, also known as Prince Duan.

As Edwin reported to Washington as early as June 1899:

> [Duan] is known to be malignantly antiforeign, a patron of the Boxers, and has many of them in his division of the army. His policy toward them cannot, therefore, be expected to be a repressive one, but must mean continual persecution and attacks upon missionaries and their followers, destruction of their property, hindrance of trade, and constant menace and danger to all foreigners and foreign interests.[9]

Though a nephew of Prince Gong, that man of cool reason, Prince Duan was one of hot-headed reaction. Where Gong tried to preserve what was left of the Qing patrimony, Duan desired complete restoration of its forever-lost glories, beginning with the annihilation of all foreigners in the empire. Duan brought the Boxers to Cixi's court, where they put on colorful performances of kung fu moves and apparent imperviousness to bullets and sword-blades. They shored up the conservatives' irrational faith in their ability to do even more—drive the hated foreigners into the sea.

Though a prince of high rank, Duan preferred the dirty streets of Beijing and the dirty company of thugs whom he tried to emulate in every way. Princess Der Ling had met him in Beijing in the late 1890s, when he and several of his bravos came to the house of her father, Yu Keng, and had seen him for what he was: "a degenerate." He was possessed of wealth and lands, and as an Iron Hat prince had reached as far up the slippery summit of imperial Manchu dignity as he could do without actually slipping onto the throne itself. What made him especially repugnant to Der Ling were two things—his habit of slumming with thuggish young men through whom he built a coterie devoted to the Boxer "cause," and his physical dangerousness. Duan poked about Yu Keng's home on what was clearly a reconnaissance mission to discover whether the family was Christian (they were). Duan's motives became evident to Yu Keng when, in Paris in the first days of the Boxer unrest, he heard that Duan had personally looted and burned the house down.[10]

After the demotion of Guangxu, Cixi had been restrained by advisors and by foreign diplomatic pressure from dethroning him entirely. That did not keep her from looking for a crown prince to take his place. The Guangxu emperor's coronation as heir to Tongzhi had not been technically legal, since they were of the same generation: only an heir from the next generation down could properly worship at his ancestor's shrine. In choosing Pujun, Duan's teenaged son, Cixi was not improving on this record of breaking the rules, but it "was not the first time nor yet the last," wrote Der Ling, "that she saw fit to override custom and tradition." Dr. Marian Headland, American physician to the Manchu aristocracy, believed Cixi was actually forced into choosing Pujun, "the son and grandson of ultra conservative princes," a faction developing more and more power at court. There was certainly madness behind the method of choice, because Pujun, from all accounts, was no better a boy than his father was a man. Der Ling knew him to be "a troublemaker of the first water from the moment he appeared at court." He broke the age-old rule by which after dark the only genitally-functional male permitted within the palace precincts was the emperor. Flings with serving-maids were the natural consequence of his presence. One maid, as she was being readied for whipping for some infraction of Cixi's rules, was found to be wearing Pujun's underwear. Worse still, Pujun was known to actually push around the Guangxu emperor, an act of unparalleled *lèse-majesté*.[11]

According to the Shanghai correspondent of the *Daily Mail*, Ronglu had caused an uproar at a council of ministers by declaring the need for "suppression of the Boxers promptly." When Cixi gave her support to this view, says the report, Prince Duan and Kangyi created "a scene of disorder," both of them walking out of the council (without imperial permission) to a chorus of "Down with foreigners!" "The effect was electrical," says the report. "The palace officials of all sorts and most of the populace [*sic*] took up the cause of Tuan and his agents and immediately put the Emperor and the Dowager Empress under restraints." This image of Cixi and Guangxu held in shackles by a band of terrorists is not so much of note for what it described in July 1900, when the report appeared in the *New York Times*, as it is for how accurately it depicted the overall truth of Cixi's situation from the beginning to the end of the Boxer disaster.[12]

That Cixi would fall in with a group of unreasonable, reactionary, ultra-nationalist Luddites whose plans spelled certain suicide for the empire she sought to preserve has still to be explained. She was by nature a watcher, a waiter, a cautious observer. This was how she had survived her rise at the imperial court, and this was how she still stayed on top. Alicia Little caught a glimpse of this Cixi as the dowager alighted from the imperial train in April 1903. "The most striking thing about her," she wrote, "is her stillness," adding that for all Cixi's utter quietude, "one felt the magnetic power of the woman." Standing in the eye of a storm she had helped to stir, though possibly never predicted would escalate into the cyclone it became, did Cixi stand too still?[13]

✳ ✳ ✳ ✳ ✳

As passions and plots were stirring in the dusty *gaoliang* fields of countryside and the crowded hot streets of town, the Congers and their American staff and guests were comfortably ensconced at Three Hills Nunnery. It was the Fourth of July, the anniversary of their second summer and their first full year in China.

The Americans watched from the terrace as servants returned from Beijing bearing strings of firecrackers, armfuls of rockets, and double-cannon crackers, which in China went by the colorful names of *yanhua* ("smoke flowers") and *baozhu* ("cannon bamboo"). The servants later helped hoist "our large American flag," which "waved the good tidings of our Independence Day to the great city below."[14]

Early on the morning of the fourth, Secretary Bainbridge carried cannon crackers up the side of Mount Bruce and began to let them off, one after another, while from the terrace below the Congers and company fired their own armaments. It was, Sarah remembered, "as though a battle were raging." Sitting at breakfast later, the Americans sang "My country, 'tis of thee," letting the sounds of Yankee freedom ring from a Chinese mountainside. Though they had left their framed Declaration of Independence hanging on a wall of Edwin's office at the legation, someone had remembered to bring the Constitution, and each read from it words that to the people of imperial China were as foreign as the Confucian classics were to the average American: "We the people . . ." who will not suffer tyrants gladly, who will pay with their blood to make a more perfect union—all for one and one for all.[15]

The servants brought out string firecrackers, festooned from the tops of long poles, and lit them. The calm mountain air was filled with hundreds of cracking pops. Peering over the terrace through the smoke, Sarah discovered that several little country boys had gathered beneath, drawn by the sound. To the Chinese, firecrackers were not so much sparkly detonations of celebration as charms to ward off the malign spirits which were believed to populate the air and bring bad luck to the living, especially on celebratory holidays. It would be interesting to know if the boys standing below the terrace were wondering not whether they could get their hands on the fireworks but if the foreign devils were trying to ward off demons even worse than they were themselves.

As the long golden day drew on to cool evening, Sarah wrote,

> We sat under the bright folds of our national colors and talked over the many events that have brought their untold sorrows, joys and responsibilities to our country as a whole, and to her people individually. Many rapid steps have been taken in the past year. May time prove that these steps were taken upward and onward and that they brought blessings to humanity. May the acknowledgement and praises extended to us by sister nations encourage and urge us on to better deeds.[16]

They all had reason to feel that life was good, the contented Americans celebrating on the nunnery terrace. Rapid steps had indeed been taken, after a few initial stumbles. Sarah and Edwin had arrived in China just in time for an imperial coup and the upheaval that followed. The coming of foreign troops had seemed to calm the troubled waters, and it must have been reassuring, as much as Sarah disliked warfare, to know that if upheaval came again, these soldiers could be relied on to calm things down.

On a personal level, Sarah could count her small but significant diplomatic triumphs as blessings—the audience with the charming

Empress Dowager Cixi, in whose face was "no trace of cruelty," and being welcomed into a Chinese home by the ladies she had so wished to know. She had learned from her servants and her work with missionaries about both high Chinese culture and the seamier side of Chinese life—all part of the education she had set herself to achieve. And she had discovered that far from being a people with whom she had nothing in common, never a day went by that did not offer more evidence that she and the Chinese touched on many common points, particularly through mutual appreciation for beauty.

Reading Sarah's letters and diary entries from this golden summer, you can almost hear her giving a sigh over the pleasant Chinese design not just of the porcelains and embroideries she was now collecting, but the deepening Chinese design of her life. Neither she nor any of the others seated on the terrace that fourth of July, nor even those Chinese in the fields and in the streets whispering a sedition they must have doubted would ever flower into rebellion, would have believed the events they all would live through, and many die during, only a year later. Come the summer of 1900, the Declaration of Independence hanging proudly on Edwin's office wall would be shot through by a Chinese bullet. The enlightened concept in both the Declaration and Constitution of "we the people" overcoming the tyranny of a single ruler would metamorphose into the people recast as tyranny itself, an echo of the age-old Chinese belief that if the emperor had lost the mandate of heaven, it was his subjects' responsibility to drive him from the throne. And the "better deeds" Sarah hoped the world would aspire to would be replaced by a desperate and agonizing struggle for individual survival—the ultimate test of those "love thoughts" by which she had hoped to enter the hearts and minds of the Chinese.[17]

II
Battle in Beijing

*

*

*Only in war do we have no regard for expense, difficulty or danger;
we are ready to try anything.*

— Imperial Manchu prince's comment to Jesuit missionary
(July 1788; quoted in Waley-Cohen, *The Sextants of Beijing*, 181)

10
Shadow Boxers

Aside from being thoroughly American (born in Washington, D.C., no less), Dr. Robert Coltman was the antithesis of Sarah Conger. If she saw the poetry of China, Coltman only had eyes for prose.

A long-time resident in China, who had learned the language fluently, and far better acquainted than Sarah with Chinese customs common and arcane, Coltman nonetheless cast a gimlet eye on the Chinese people and their Manchu overlords. Combining a nineteenth-century doctor's fussy fastidiousness with the competitive edginess of a journalist, in which capacity he had served since 1895 as correspondent for the *Chicago Record*, he subscribed to many of the same value judgments held dear by other foreigners in China. In this view, the nation was a hive of unsanitary superstition and habits, and the government a comedy performed by idiots for a populace of fools. Coltman reserved for Cixi a guarded respect that easily morphed into contempt for what he considered her feminine weaknesses and appetite for self-aggrandizement.

Coltman and Sarah did share one strong opinion concerning relations between foreigners and the Chinese: that the Boxer Uprising had not been without provocation. But always a man for running down first causes, Coltman believed he could pinpoint the uprising's opening shot in the turbulent fall of 1898, when the empress dowager's resumption of power and the placement in Beijing of General Dong Fuxiang and his Muslim troops raised fears among foreigners in the capital. "I refer to the riot at Lukouch'iao," Coltman wrote, "known to the English-speaking world as Marco Polo bridge, from its having been accurately described by that early traveler."[1]

Situated at the northern terminus of the Hankou–Beijing railway some ten miles south of Beijing, and linked to the railway from Tianjin at Fengtai, the area around the bridge was a locus of political struggle among diplomats of Russia, France, and Britain, all of whom hoped to gain control of it. On October 24, 1898, Coltman was called down to Fengtai by an urgent telegram, to come and help the resident engineers, A. G. Cox and Captain Norregaard, who had been injured in a riot at the iron bridge they had built near the old Marco Polo bridge. Coltman found the men "roughly used." Cox told him how he, Norregaard, and some guests had followed up their tiffin with a walk to the iron bridge, only to find at the other end a group of Dong Fuxiang's Gansu soldiers who shouted insults at the foreign men. One of Cox's guests, a man named Campbell who was fluent in Chinese, asked the soldiers to let them cross. An officer intervened to let the foreigners pass, but when the men returned to the bridge the soldiers began to stone them. The foreigners shoved their way through, blinded by blood. Norregaard shot his revolver into the air. When this sent the soldiers fleeing, the men stumbled across the bridge and back to Fengtai.

But this was not what sent chills up Robert Coltman's spine. That sensation began in Beijing, in Imbeck's Hotel in the Legation Quarter. Coltman was invited to meet there with Hu Zhifen, governor of Beijing. He had been appointed by Cixi as special commissioner to go to the Marco Polo bridge and launch an enquiry into what she understood to be the wanton shooting of Chinese soldiers by Captain Norregaard. Hu asked Coltman to come with him to the Gansu soldiers' camp to examine the alleged bullet wounds. While Coltman did not much relish strolling into an encampment of known haters of foreigners, he went— "there was a spice of adventure about the undertaking," he recalled. He took a revolver, coldly reasoning that if any trouble arose he would take Governor Hu hostage, "believing as I did that the Empress' special commissioner's person would be sacred in the eyes of her generals" (if not in those of Dr. Robert Coltman). He would also be able to give a foreigner's testimony (considered by other foreigners to be superior to that of any Chinese) that the Chinese soldiers had been the aggressors.[2]

With his Smith & Wesson six-shooter in his pocket, Coltman took the train to Lugouqiao, where he and Governor Hu were met at the iron bridge by Gansu soldiers. Hu interrogated the bridge watchmen and asked about the incident involving Cox, Norregaard, and their guests. (One watchman, who blatantly blamed the Gansu soldiers, was later murdered by them.) At a nearby inn, in his vested authority as representative of the empress dowager, Hu called for the general and colonels of the Gansu regiments quartered in the area to come to him immediately. But there was no respect for Cixi among the Gansu officers or their men. One of the colonels seized his chance and "commenced a most venomous speech against the introduction of railways in China." He declared that the railways had ruined the livelihood of carters, boatmen, and coolies who lived by the wheelbarrow or rickshaw. He "wound up his rather long discourse by declaring that the abolishing of railways and driving into the sea of every foreigner was the duty of every loyal subject of the empire." Hu, all respect for his office forgotten, could hardly get a word in edgewise. He was, thought Coltman, also uncomfortable that he had brought along with him not just a foreign devil but one who understood everything they said. But Coltman had other thoughts to ponder:

> To me it was a revelation. I had heard that the Mohammedan troops from Kansu, under the famous general Tung Fu Hsiang, were ordered to Peking immediately after the coup d'etat to support the Empress in her anti-foreign policy. I had heard that they were fanatical, ignorant and intensely hostile to foreigners. But that they would dare to insult the Empress, in the person of a special commissioner appointed by imperial edict, and reveal the purpose of their general in such open language, and that before a foreigner, I would scarcely have believed short of the testimony of my own ears.[3]

It was this deliberate offense given to a representative of the empress dowager that pricked at Coltman's senses. Even worse, General Zhang Xun, commander of the troublemaking troops, sent a servant to accompany Hu and his retinue back to the train to Beijing, when the appropriate action was to accompany them himself. By failing in this, Zhang showed "as great a lack of courtesy and positive insult as he could give to the Empress Dowager's high commissioner," noted Coltman.[4]

Dong Fuxiang had the last laugh. Through various means he managed to have Governor Hu fired and replaced by a more amenable anti-foreign official, while the position of directorate-general of railways was filled by a corrupt opium addict "already in the pay of Russia." Coltman dated the ascendance of Dong Fuxiang and his "swaggering" soldiers in their red and black uniforms from this time; they were, he believed, responsible for the riots that followed the deposition of the Guangxu emperor, even as they were at the heart of the violence of the Boxer uprising.[5]

However in control Cixi thought she was, or appeared to be, the truth was very different. Whether the incident at the Marco Polo bridge was a "premature explosion" or the first move in the chess game of East against West that was to come in the summer of 1900, these events, Coltman knew, were "intended to shake the civilized world."[6]

✳ ✳ ✳ ✳ ✳

When Sarah returned to China in April 1900, after several months of vacation in America, her excitement to see Edwin and her Bejing home again grew sharper as the steamer approached Tianjin.

She had set forth from San Francisco on February 27, the eldest of a group of six women. Along with Laura Conger and Edwin's niece, Mary Pierce, who were also returning to Beijing, Sarah had guests Mrs. Morgan S. Woodward (Anna) and her daughter Ione, as well as a visitor from Chicago named Cecile Payen, a respected portrait painter who specialized in miniatures. Miss Payen was fascinated by Chinese culture; she planned to spend a year in Beijing to study the "customs and ways of the people from an artistic point of view."[7]

Just before they were within sight of land, everything came to a stop as the ship was becalmed in a fog so thick the captain had to drop anchor and the steamer sat motionless in an undulant white world. "We have been fog-bound for about thirty-six hours," Sarah wrote to a friend. She was worried about Edwin—"He has no way of knowing where we are nor what the matter is. He only knows that we are somewhere in the China Sea"—and she was unfamiliar with such fog, which drenched the ship and everyone who ventured out on deck. The captain did not make matters better when he told her that often ships were trapped in fogs like this for up to five days.[8]

Sarah's new Chinese friends might have warned her that these were hardly the most auspicious circumstances for her homecoming. She was no believer in superstitions, but something had already put her nerves on edge as the ship sailed closer to China, counterbalancing her thrill to be almost "home."

The accent on the positive that was inculcated in the followers of Mary Baker Eddy was one of Sarah's more reliable traits, but on this occasion her impatience to get to Beijing bordered on the frantic, so much so that she actually asked the captain why they could not press on despite the fog. It was not easy for her to be "hands off," as she put it: "I have to watch myself, not to become impatient to go on." In one of those object lessons that occurred at crucial times in Sarah's life, news filtered through the mist two days later that another steamer, taking the full-throttle approach Sarah had advocated, had run onto rocks. As Sarah, shocked, watched and assisted the crew in retrieving and comforting the survivors, she knew she had received another lesson in looking before she leapt. "What strange, wonderful, lamentable, encouraging, joyous experiences come into our lives," she wrote, "as we travel on and on through the many phases of this world's living!" When the fog lifted and the ship began to move, Sarah was out on deck with her spyglass, eagerly seeking Edwin along the harbor and rejoicing in the sight of his launch with its flapping American flag.[9]

There was no comparison between Sarah's unpromising first introduction to the American legation in the summer of 1898 and this joyous homecoming. On stepping over the threshold, she was surprised by rounds of firecrackers let off by the servants, who stood smiling at her in their best clothes, surrounded by masses of flowers they had arranged for her. Now filled with her growing collection of Chinese "productions"—

porcelains, embroideries, scroll paintings, bronzes, jades, and carpets—the poky rooms of the legation truly felt like home. Even more, her separation from China and her Chinese things while she was in the American Midwest had sharpened Sarah's hunger for that land and all it offered. Not surprisingly, during her vacation she had talked about China and the empress dowager almost to the exclusion of anything else, showing the ring Cixi had given her as she explained to her friends and the press that the "bizarre tales" about the dowager and her court did not reflect the happy and hospitable experience she had had there. Now back in Beijing, it was as if she could hardly believe she was home. "I go from room to room rejoicing," she told a friend, "and our beautiful Chinese things speak to me." Best of all, "our family is together again"—a happy thought that was to become a crucial mantra in the summer months ahead.[10]

Sarah does not tell us whether Edwin had already apprised her of the unfolding of events in northern China. Neither does she mention that Cixi had invited the diplomatic wives for another audience, on March 9. Lady MacDonald noted that on this second visit Cixi was, if anything, even friendlier toward her foreign guests than she had been in December. It was an affability that would come to seem, in retrospect, to be either senile unawareness of approaching danger or a coldly calculating two-faced denial of it. No one but Robert Coltman seemed cognizant of the movement growing to the south of Beijing, the participants of which went by the vaguely comical moniker of "the Boxers"—a name which in the parlance of the day conjured not soldiers of the supernatural but performing kangaroos on vaudeville stages, or Irishmen duking it out in shorts and singlets in smoky taverns.[11] Whether they arose in the mists of ancient China or simply as a part of the general chaos of the popular movements that tore China in two during the nineteenth century, the Boxers were no passing fad. The young men and women who joined the "Society of Righteous Fists" were not interested in limiting themselves to public calisthenics and unsubstantiated boasts of immunity to foreign bullets—their influences were broad, owing much to the popular heroes of Beijing Opera (Cixi's favorite entertainment) and the shadow theatre well known to all in which the dramatic and the sacred were united in tales of superhuman adventure. Their agenda was clear-cut. The Boxers, with Prince Duan and the court conservatives at their head, wanted nothing less than to wipe China clean of white men, their religion, and the traitorous Chinese who were their converts and friends.[12]

The troubles in the fall of 1898 had erupted suddenly, as people reacted to the dowager's own response to the plot of the emperor's admirers to dethrone her. The Boxer situation gradually increased in intensity, and the catalysts for it were more wide-ranging. If those who threw stones at foreigners in 1898 were expressing the frustration of the hour, the young men and women joining the roving bands of Boxers were venting centuries of resentment against foreigners and their god. They were also reacting to the immediate threat of famine, which had so often been the root cause of uprisings in the past. For a year, China's breadbasket had been verging on empty as the lack of rain dried the fields, leaving men otherwise occupied by farming with nothing to do but nurse their resentments or sit and listen to the Boxers who inflamed everyone with a fear of missionaries and converts, railroads and telegraph poles. With many starving (except the Chinese Christians, given allotments of rice by the missionaries who had converted them), their pain salved by superstition and fear, it was the most natural thing in the world for people to band together in despair and anger.

A political cartoon published in the foreign press during the Boxer Uprising summed up the situation with a deadly accuracy: it displayed an image of furious hornets streaming out of the Forbidden City to sting a pack of fleeing, yelping dogs, a particularly potent symbol for the European powers. Foreigners outside China seemed aware that their overseas compatriots had unwisely disturbed the nest. But the nest was overdue for an explosion no matter what.[13]

✳ ✳ ✳ ✳ ✳

The social rounds that were the trellis on which the vine of diplomacy was trained to grow and that it needed for support were in full flower the spring of Sarah's return to Beijing. Young women like Cecile Payen or fellow American Polly Condit Smith were in their element in this round of parties and dances—particularly Polly, a plump social butterfly who fluttered about the Legation Quarter flashing her pretty wings. Of prominent family and in her early twenties, Polly (whose full name was

Mary Osborn Condit-Smith) was close to Harriet Squiers, the wife of the American legation's first secretary, the handsome Herbert Squiers. Harriet came from an even more exalted American background, being a descendant of millionaire John Jacob Astor, and was famed for the prodigality of her table long before the Boxer Uprising cast her in the role of Lady Bountiful. Fashionable and brisk, Harriet was the perfect older female companion for flighty Polly, whereas Sarah, past middle age and not of their set, was not part of the Squierses' circle, notwithstanding that Edwin was Herbert's boss at the legation. This gulf would kindle ill will between Sarah and Harriet in the last days before and during the aftermath of the uprising.

Signs of unrest had been developing since late winter, but these were either accepted as normal or beneath the notice of a busy foreigner. Even Sarah, who knew as of May 1 that "the Boxer work . . . comes nearer and nearer and is now within Peking," saw no reason to cancel a trip to the Great Wall. She and Edwin set forth on May 10, along with Laura, Mary, Anna Woodward and Ione, and artist Cecile Payen, who was photographed lunching with Edwin in an arch of a ruined guardhouse, a Chinese servant standing at attention nearby. But perhaps Sarah had a more serious reason for taking such a trip at such a fraught time; as if she believed she might never again see this monument to Chinese glory, Sarah brought a little of it back with her. Still limber at fifty-six, she climbed to a crumbling height with her *mafu* to fetch away a souvenir: a brick, with mortar attached, which would survive both the Boxer siege and the San Francisco earthquake of 1906.[14] "Mafoo told me that people come from all parts of China to get the mortar that has held for so many centuries these bricks together," Sarah wrote later. "Many put it upon afflicted parts of their bodies to heal them. I have with the brick some of this powerful mortar." Sarah seemed to feel that under the prevailing circumstances, there was nothing wrong with adding a little magic to one's arsenal of defenses.[15]

The thrilling journey ended, in retrospect, most inauspiciously, with the Conger party returning on May 12 in a dust storm so blinding that, according to Cecile Payen, everyone held on to their mounts, eyes closed, and "trusted to [their ponies'] instinct to guide us home." These ponies were to serve another important purpose in two months' time, which none of their riders could have imagined.[16]

The Beijing to which they returned was fully on edge. Coltman certainly had much to say about the situation at the Congers' dinner table a little over a week after the Great Wall jaunt. "Dr. Robert Coltman, an American who has practiced here for eighteen years and who counts many high Chinese officials among his patients, told us he had been warned by a special Chinese friend (a prince) that the Boxers really meant to kill or drive all foreigners out of Peking," recalled Cecile. This was also what Monsignor Favier, bishop of Beijing, had been telling French minister Stéphen Pichon for some time. As early as May 19, Favier had written to Pichon that the situation was "becoming daily more and more serious and threatening . . . The Boxers are approaching the capital daily," he warned, the only thing delaying them being their stops to ravage missions and the homes of Chinese Christians. Favier had been told by refugees that the actual day of attack had already been set: "the entire town knows about it." He asked Pichon for "forty or fifty marines." Luckily for him and the refugees, Pichon was able to send them. If Coltman's theory about the breakdown of imperial authority was largely circumstantial, Pichon's was far more concrete—the irony being that he was taken far less seriously than Coltman was.[17]

A week after the Congers' dinner party, on May 25, Sarah was making cryptic notes in her diaries, as if afraid of fleshing out her fears too completely on paper: "There is much uneasiness among the foreigners; threatening words have come to us." And the next day, "The foreign ministers of the different legations meet and consult over these unheard-of conditions." By contrast, one Church of England deaconess, writing that same day, tried to reassure her correspondent about the "wild rumours" that were sure to get back to England, noting that "no real harm can happen" and that if only northern China would get some rain, the troublemakers "would probably go peaceably back to their fields." Sir Claude MacDonald shared the same conviction: a few days of heavy rain "would do more to restore tranquility than any measures either the Chinese Government or foreign Governments could take." But there was no denying that the Boxers wanted something more than a steady rainfall to refresh farmers' crops. On May 28, they attacked Fengtai, not far from the Marco Polo bridge, Coltman's ground zero for the insurrection, and a symbol, with its steel railway trestle—and its missionaries—of all that the anti-foreigner clique at court despised most.[18]

"Two railroad bridges are destroyed on the branch road," Sarah noted in her diary for May 28. "Station, cars, shops, Empress Dowager's private car, all burned!" The ministers cabled for guards for their respective legations, and Edwin was inundated by telegrams, letters, and visitors all asking for his help or advice. "The Boxers are cruel, frenzied!" Sarah wrote in an uncharacteristically frantic tone.[19]

Polly Condit Smith was at the Three Hills Nunnery in the Western Hills, with Lady MacDonald's daughters, and had noted in her diary her amusement at the sight of the Chinese soldiers detailed to guard the temple—"opera-bouffe manikins in a Broadway theatre would frighten one with their martial air compared to these ridiculous apologies for soldiers," scoffed Polly.[20]

When the girls' governess, who had been in Beijing shopping, returned to the temple, she reported seeing armed men being drilled in temple courtyards in the city. The servants, "mostly native Christians," murmured that these people were Boxers and were "preparing for a general uprising when the time shall be ripe." The next day, as Polly looked from the temple's balcony, she watched Fengtai being burned, its steel bridge blown up. The *opéra-bouffe* soldiers fled, and the servants told the household they had seen many farmers from the Western Hills, including some belonging to the temple, disappear across the plains for Beijing.[21]

Journalist George Morrison saved the day. Having gone down to Fengtai to assess the damage, he had wondered if anyone was still in the Western Hills, and had ridden across the plain to see for himself. Discovering Polly and the rest of the household, he and Herbert Squiers, who had also ridden up the hill from Beijing, ordered the servants to prepare defenses against attack in the night. Perceptively, Polly noted that the servants worked like machines, knowing as they did that if they saved the foreigners they saved themselves. It was to be a pattern repeated on a far larger scale in the Legation Quarter in a month's time.[22]

Polly and the others made it safely back to the American legation. A few days later, on May 31, the Zongli Yamen gave their permission for the legations to bring foreign guards into the city. Sarah carefully numbered them, as if they were goods being stored in a root cellar against a storm: French, seventy-five; Japanese, forty; American, fifty-six; Russian, seventy-five; Italian, forty—totaling 361 men. Among the

American officers were Captain John T. Myers and Captain Newt T. Hall. Born in Texas, Captain Hall had seen service in the Philippines before being detailed for duty with the first marine detachment sent to China. Son of a Confederate general, Captain Myers had already seen duty in the Spanish–American War, and would end his career as a counter-intelligence officer in World War I.[23]

This small contingent was considered only a stopgap until more troops arrived. On June 10, and without the permission of the throne, the foreign ministers cabled for more troops to be sent from Tianjin. These were to be commanded by Admiral Sir Edward Seymour, to the tune of almost a thousand men. The plan was that they would take the train to Tongzhou, then march on to Beijing. Despite resistance from the Zongli Yamen and the court, the viceroy of Tianjin gave Seymour permission to proceed—whether in defiance of the court hardliners (other viceroys, especially in the south, were as anti-Boxer as those in the north were pro), or to allow Seymour the better to walk into the Boxer trap that lay waiting, is not known. Totally cut off because of downed telegraph lines, the residents of the legations went on assuming that Seymour would appear any day. The court, similarly cut off from the outside world, and believing the foreigners were intent on invading and occupying first Beijing and then all of China, would eventually convince Cixi to break off diplomatic relations and declare war—which is how imperial troops first joined and then superseded the Boxers besieging the Legation Quarter. Little did anyone guess that, together with the man- and woman-power available within the legations themselves, and the strength of the underfed Chinese trapped within the barricades by circumstance or their Christian faith, the 361 men allowed in on May 31 would be among the few professional soldiers to see several hundred civilians through the coming siege.[24]

✳   ✳   ✳   ✳   ✳

The first few days of June had been quieter than Sarah expected, though she noted in her diary that Edwin was mobbed by missionaries, all urging him "to make the Chinese officials act more quickly and protect them and their native converts. In their distress," Sarah added perceptively, "they forget that they have been here many years and know that the Chinese mode of thought and action is not easily nor rapidly changed." With a fairness toward the imperial government which would come to seem, in a few weeks, almost unthinkable, Sarah pointed out that the converts were Chinese subjects. Regardless of their religious faith, Sarah wrote, "the Chinese Government has a right to protect or punish them according to its law."[25]

But she saw over the next few days, as accounts filtered in from the countryside around the city of attacks on Chinese Christians and the missionaries trying to shield them and preserve their own safety, that protection was increasingly unavailable. "The American involvement in putting down the insurrection might have been miniscule, if not actually nonexistent," writes scholar Jared Kreiner, "were it not for the actions of American missionaries in China." Their first-hand information, sent directly from the field to Edwin and, at times, bypassing him to appeal directly to the US Department of State, "pressured the United States into action." The appeals to Edwin multiplied to the point where even if he had possessed the resources of labor and money required to meet them all, he would never have found enough time to administer the aid. "He bears up bravely under the almost numberless pressures that are brought constantly to bear upon him," Sarah wrote, torn between concern for the missionaries, many of whom she knew personally, and her husband's state of health.[26]

By June 4, with the telegraph wires cut along the railroad, the situation was looking increasingly like something more serious than the disturbances of 1898. "Many servants are leaving [the legations]," observed Sarah. "Ours are staying." Among those staying was Wang, the Congers' cheerful and resourceful Number One Boy whose wife and children lived outside the Legation Quarter in the now-dangerous Chinese City. As Sarah wrote, "Wang . . . is calm in his constant doing." His loyalty even among the steadfast Conger servants was unique and heroic, and his calm was needed just as much as a pair of capable hands.[27]

That same day, Cecile Payen remembered, Sarah told Anna Woodward that now was the time to take Ione and "leave Peking at once." Cecile had been urging the Woodward women to do just that for some weeks, perhaps a consequence of sitting beside Dr. Coltman at too many legation dinner parties. As early as May 30, Edwin had asked Anna to take Ione and go, but was rebuffed by that formidable woman: "Why! I would not be a coward and run away if there is danger. I will stay to do my part." (She was no coward: Dr. W. A. P. Martin later saw her during the Boxer siege "[going] about everywhere, even in places of danger, armed with her camera.") But now the Woodwards did not have to be warned twice, and packed their bags to leave the next Tuesday morning. At 10:30 a.m., with everyone in tears, Anna and her daughter set forth for the train station, "escorted in by 3 US Marines and the 2nd Secretary [Bainbridge]," wrote Dr. Emma Martin, who hoped to catch a ride out of town on the same train. The train never arrived. Anna Woodward waited from eleven in the morning until three in the afternoon, hemmed in on all sides by a "howling mob," against which the loaded pistol she had slipped in her purse would have availed nothing. When it was clear no train was coming that day, she started back for the legation. Though Anna would later point out that none of the Chinese had touched her or made any move to do so, Dr. Emma Martin remembered them "hooting [and] jeering," and she was both heartsick and full of fear as she turned to go back to the city.[28]

Sarah still had hope that she could get Laura and cousin Mary Pierce out of the country to the safety of Japan, though this would mean sending them along the railway to Tianjin—not exactly the safest route at that time, though it was the only one available. She must have been more than usually worried about her daughter to consider allowing her to go. Laura Conger was a sweet-faced woman in her early twenties, with dark hair and blue eyes, bright but of a nervous disposition. Married in 1891 to a wealthy young man, George Landrum, she divorced him when he decimated his inheritance, possibly through gambling.[29]

Laura had witnessed as a child her parents' great grief over her young brother's death. Perhaps feeling the guilt of the living who grow up in the shadow of the beloved dead, and the failure of her unhappy marriage, she seemed content to spend her life with her safe, orderly parents, serving her father as private secretary, and helping her mother through the jungles of diplomatic protocol. As we know from Sarah's later comments and those of others who saw Laura during the Boxer siege, for the first month she did not deal well with the shooting and cannon fire, and would throw herself crying into Edwin's arms. Sarah would surely have weighed her options as to whether it was best to send Laura away to safety, albeit through danger to get there, or to keep her in Beijing, where she was likely to have a nervous breakdown. Lady MacDonald had also considered it, hoping to get her two young girls on the same train. But even a fast engine, stopping nowhere along the way and outpacing any Boxers chasing it, could have been halted and even derailed by a roadblock set up on the tracks. Ultimately, the complete severing of the line to Tianjin would make the decision for everyone who wanted to leave—and it was just as well their trunks were already packed, because they would indeed be going somewhere else.[30]

"Mr. Conger visits the Tsung Li Yamen once or twice each day," Sarah reported on June 8, "as new, urgent matters, come up. By getting an interview with them daily, he forms opinions of the situation at the head of the Chinese Government." Edwin's correct impression was that, far from being in agreement about what was happening with the Boxers, the imperial court was riven by factions. However, on one matter they did all seem to be of a single mind: "It also seems," Sarah wrote, "that the Government is afraid of the Boxers. The army, too, seems to be afraid of them. What can there be in the future for China, or for the foreigners who have the promise of her protection?"[31]

This utter lack of defense put Edwin in a difficult position, because without firm assurances from the Chinese he could not be of much use to the foreigners begging him for the same assurances and demanding that he make the Chinese toe the line of international law. Sarah remembered one prominent missionary, Dr. William Ament, requesting a guard to travel with him to the Tongzhou missions to rescue missionaries, their families, and their converts, and bring them back to Beijing. Thinking no doubt of how displays of foreign military might had inflamed the Beijing populace on prior occasions, "Mr. Conger thought it would only enrage the Boxers to see foreign soldiers." Besides which, sending away even a small portion of the forty-five American marines guarding the United States compound would weaken the legations' defenses; and even if Edwin sent all the marines he had on hand, what were they against hundreds of native militants? Edwin did suggest to Ament, in a foreshadowing of events of a much larger scale that would occur in the days ahead, that the missionary might quietly bring the Tongzhou people to Beijing in carts as if nothing were amiss, nonchalantly enter the city, and then get them to Ament's Methodist mission as soon as possible. Ament took the advice and in sixteen carts brought everyone to the temporary refuge of the Methodist mission just north of the legations. Unable at that point to refuse Ament some sort of guard, Edwin spared ten marines, with Captain Newt Hall in command.[32]

The young ladies of the American legation might have been disappointed in their effort to get away from Beijing, but this did not keep them from enjoying themselves. While Sarah was making a careful assessment of their stores—flour, cornmeal, beans, rice, sugar—and of the poultry, livestock, and the contents of the coal bin and water barrels, Cecile, Mary Pierce, Ione Woodward, Laura, and other young women were expending their excess energy in dancing and having fun. On the evening of June 8, they were doing just that when Dr. Coltman, his wife, and their six children arrived at the compound and asked to stay.[33]

As Coltman wrote in his diary for June 7, "I have overwhelming evidence that government officials are the real causes of the Boxer movement, acting under the direction of the Empress . . . The senile cabinet has persuaded the Empress [of the possibility of exterminating all foreigners and Christian converts], and they are quite willing to face the inevitable foreign war that their policy entails." Whether Cixi was really in control, however, would seem to be cast in some doubt by other information Coltman had heard—that Prince Qing would "guarantee the restoration of the interrupted railway in two days" if the foreign ministers desisted from asking for an audience with the dowager. Was she completely a tool of Duan and the conservatives by this time? W. A. P. Martin claimed that "Prince Ching undoubtedly exerted a powerful, though secret, influence in our favor . . . Though he lacked the courage to remonstrate with the tyrant Empress, he had the power and tact to restrain the fury of his soldiers." But did Qing or any other member of the imperial family who was not gung-ho on the Boxers have any power by this time, especially if Cixi's was compromised as well?[34]

Whatever the case, Coltman's information network must have also clarified the risk he and his family ran by remaining at their home— hence the move to the relative safety of the American legation where, as the worried wife entered the room carrying one of her children, Cecile and the other women were laughing and singing. It was, for Cecile, a sobering wake-up call. "While helping Mrs. Coltman to settle her little family," wrote Cecile, who had given up her bedroom to the Coltmans to move in with Laura and Mary, "I fully realized the extreme danger that is closing in on us. Poor little woman, as she entered the house with her sleeping baby in her arms, how disgusted she looked to see us amusing ourselves." If tired Mrs. Coltman appeared disgusted, we can only imagine the look on her husband's face.[35]

What made the move especially hard for Coltman was his scorn for Edwin as US minister as well as for most of the rest of the foreign ministers. Despite the warnings from Minister Pichon, "all the other ministers are greatly to blame for their tardy recognition of the impending trouble," he opined, neglecting to take into account the fact that Pichon had worn out his welcome as the self-appointed Cassandra of the Legation Quarter. That there was proof he was correct meant little as there was nothing that could be done to change the situation everyone was now in. Coltman shared what he described as a "general contempt" for the leadership of Sir Claude MacDonald, and he blamed Edwin for delaying sending for troops because his small compound could not spare more room for them (Edwin was happy enough to give space to the Coltmans, who represented in just one family a little over one-fifth of the marines who arrived from Tianjin on May 31).[36]

Polly Condit Smith was well tuned to the tense air of early June, finding it, as ever, more bracing than alarming. "The atmosphere of the compound is distinctly exciting," she wrote. "The quintessence of American interests are discussed right here in the open air, under a few scattered big trees, by people walking about gesticulating or standing on scorching hot flagstones . . . arguing with one another as to how soon the *coup d'état* will take place . . ."[37]

No wonder, then, that just a few days away from the first explosion of violence, Cecile Payen was to shrug her shoulders and write: "We may as well keep cheerful as long as we can." Sarah tried to do so, but the stories filtering in made it a challenge. She recorded having heard the rumor on June 9 that the empress dowager and the Guangxu emperor had returned from the Summer Palace to the Forbidden City. "The Empress Dowager issues edicts," she noted, "but they do no good." She wanted to believe that this return of the woman, dubbed by one male foreign admirer "the only man in China," meant that the troubles would be cleared up, the Boxers stopped and sent away. But the less visible side of Sarah Conger, the one that gazed into the same abyss her more cheerful public self denied existed, moved her to write somberly: "We have tried to fill our lamps that they may be ready in our hour of need."[38]

That same day, as if testing Cecile Payen's hopeful attitude and affirming Coltman's pessimistic one, diplomatic property was torched and diplomatic blood was shed for the first time since the troubles began.

On the morning of June 9, the legations received word that the newly restored summer residence of the British minister, situated in the Western Hills, had been raided by Boxers and burned to the ground. This was especially hard for Lady MacDonald, because it was at the British legation's summer home that she had kept—she thought in more safety than in the city—most of her Chinese treasures and many other items of a more sentimental nature. (She was to remember this when the allies seized Beijing and the looting of its citizens' own treasures became possible.) Even sadder was the news, unrecorded and unacknowledged by most foreigners, that the gatekeeper for the summer home, along with his wife and children, had been murdered by the same Boxers who had torched the temple compound.[39]

Everyone was still expecting Admiral Seymour to arrive at any moment. Despite the parlous state of the railways each legation sent transport to the train station to welcome the men—only the train bringing them never appeared. Yet the situation was obviously nothing to worry Chancellor Sugiyama Akira of the Japanese legation. Having requested the honor of going down to the station to meet the Japanese men, he was driven there in a cart, wearing a top hat, only to be attacked en route by stone-throwing Chinese. Undeterred, he still waited for the train, realized it was not coming, and started back for his legation. He never made it beyond the train platform. A Chinese propaganda artist quickly released a print showing Sugiyama being formally sentenced to execution in the presences of court hardliner Kangyi and General Dong himself, but such was not the untidy reality. Sugiyama was set upon by Dong Fuxiang's Gansu soldiers and hacked to pieces, his mutilated corpse left to dogs and flies in the street. Sad to say, this killing did not exercise the fury of the foreign community as much as that of a European diplomat not long after.[40]

With this murder in the air came waves of early, unnerving summer heat. "It is dreadfully hot," Cecile Payen wrote on June 12, "the air being absolutely scorching." It was also intense within the American legation. Sarah had already had "an anxious night," she recorded. "Many foreigners are fleeing for safety to the legations, to the Methodist Mission, the Catholic Peitang and Nantang," referring to the two most prominent cathedrals in Beijing. "Guards watch day and night on Legation Street." There had been "much noise" that night in the Chinese City, with what Sarah took to be cannon fire (possibly celebratory firecrackers). There were now another eighteen people crammed into the American compound, so that even Sarah's easy nature was stretched to the snapping point.[41]

Then, on the sultry evening of June 13, Dr. Coltman rushed in, "calling out to us that the streets were full of Boxers and an attack was to be made on the Legation."[42] Interpreter Cheshire had been at the Zongli Yamen that day where, when he told a group of officials of seeing Boxers running through the street, he was greeted with nervous smiles—the face-saving device of a government losing its grip. "Oh, there are thousands of Boxers all over the city by now," Cheshire was told, as if he might take comfort in knowing that there were thousands of Boxers in town and he, a foreigner, was still alive—what was there to worry about? Even more unsettling, these officials offered no remedy for the situation, except to smile as if it were not of much consequence.

In the meantime, Baron von Ketteler was taking out his frustrations more directly. Shortly after Cheshire had left the Zongli Yamen, he saw some soldiers from the German legation drag a pair of suspected Boxers out of a passing cart and haul them into the German compound. There they were interrogated while Ketteler struck them over the head with his walking-stick. Ketteler then sent a message to the Zongli Yamen which would not have helped matters: the ministers were to come to *him*, and until they did he was holding the "Boxers" hostage. This act of aggression, which up to then no other foreigner had attempted, resulted in Legation Street being crowded soon after with "a great mob of Chinese," as Cecile recalled, "soldiers and citizens." Polly Condit Smith also observed this crowd and, serious for once, accurately connected it to Ketteler's violent and pointless theatrics. It is easy to understand his fury. Some of Ketteler's frustration even seemed to have rubbed off on Sarah, because after hearing of a dispute between the United States guard and "Boxers" in Legation Street, Sarah wrote in a letter she feared might never reach her sister: "How *dare* China touch the Legations?"[43]

Sarah watched Edwin and Cheshire as they "went fearlessly" to talk to the Chinese officers meant to be guarding Legation Street. Part of the Americans' fear was that their legation, small as it was, was locked in to the north, east, and west by Legation Street and a series of buildings, and by the Tartar City wall to the south. If the Boxers should reach the Tartar wall and train guns on the legation, there was not much hope for any of the foreigners, let alone the residents of the American legation. What Edwin expected to accomplish with this parley is unknown. "Mr. Conger told them," recalled Sarah, "that if they would keep their people away from us none would be fired upon and none would be harmed. But just as soon as they pressed down the streets they would be fired upon and great harm would come to them." If the Chinese government could not protect the foreigners in the legations, Edwin reasoned, then he and the other ministers would have to take matters into their own hands—a bit like the honest sheriff who comes to the corrupt Old West town to neutralize the local thugs through talk rather than bullets.[44]

Sarah felt her husband was doing what was best for everyone. "He does not accept all the dreadful rumors as facts," she noted. "If men in their extreme anxiety think he should do more for them and say unkind things, he does not let it hurt him, and replies kindly but firmly." But as Polly noted in her diary, speaking for several of the Americans, "The white dazzling star of optimism is blinding him to the facts."[45]

✳   ✳   ✳   ✳   ✳

Not even the Conger optimism could deny, however, that calamity stalked the *hutong* of Beijing. "Last night [June 12–13]," wrote Sarah, "the Boxers have kept the gates open between the Native [Chinese] City and [the Imperial] city and entered in force. Our foreign guards cleared Legation Street and Wall Street [to the south of the American compound] and stationed their guns and men to guard this locality."[46]

The Boxers came in via the Hatamen Gate, at the southeast corner of the Tartar City wall. Rather than going west along Wall Street, which would have brought them to the inner parts of the Legation Quarter but also would have trapped them between the city wall on one side and houses on the other, they headed north up Hatamen Street. As they progressed, one Manchu eyewitness reported, shopkeepers tried to shut down their businesses, knowing full well what was coming. But the Boxers—and Prince Duan—had specific targets. Princess Der Ling, whose family home was destroyed in the mayhem, heard that Prince Duan himself ordered most of the burning of foreign properties and anything belonging to foreign-friendly or converted Chinese in the city. They set fire to buildings—Christian hospitals and missions, shops catering to foreigners, foreign-style houses, churches, and the residences of professors of the Western-friendly Imperial College. They did this while at the same time performing the sort of conjuring tricks with which they managed to dupe the crowds who looked on. "The way in which the Boxers burnt the churches was that they only used a bundle of incense, read charms, and told all the bystanders to cry 'Burn' loudly," recalled a witness, "and then they threw the incense into buildings which caught at once, but all those houses next the churches were left in safety." The Boxers also took the opportunity to paste up placards bearing pornographic anti-foreign verses and exhortations to kill all foreigners. They even pasted one over the sign leading into Legation Street. It was now "Cut Up Foreigners Crowing" Street. Polly Condit Smith grimly noted in her diary: "All last night the sky was bright from the many fires in the Tartar City."[47]

W. A. P. Martin claimed to have heard that Cixi had ordered all buildings around the legations pulled down or burned, "by way of clearing the ground for their operations." But the swath of Duan's operations was so wide, and his intentions toward specifically foreign or Chinese Christian properties so clear, no matter where they were, we can safely discount this among the many rumors that Dr. Martin so easily believed. What good did it do to help their "operations" when, also on June 14, the Boxers torched the seventeenth century Nantang or Southern Cathedral, the oldest Catholic structure in Beijing, dating back to the reign of the Wanli emperor of the Ming? Located far from the Legation Quarter, to the southwest of the Forbidden City complex, the cathedral was not in the way of planned missile launches, but it was a symbol of how closely tied the Ming and early Qing dynasties had been to the faith of the foreigners. As such, along with the houses of English-speaking diplomats like Yu Keng, the missions of different Christian denominations, and the merchants' shops serving the foreign clientele, the Nantang was a foreign symbol to be obliterated.[48]

The fate of the Beitang or Northern Cathedral, controlled by Bishop Favier, was not so clear-cut. Located, as its name implies, in the northern part of the city—technically in the northwest quadrant of the Imperial City—near Cixi's pleasure grounds at the Sea Palaces, the church had originally sat on land given to the Jesuits by the Kangxi emperor, in thanks for having been healed of illness by two fathers of the order. Because the Guangxu emperor (more likely, Cixi herself) wanted to redevelop its site as a park, the cathedral was moved west of the imperial lakes and rebuilt in a stolid grey and a Gothic style by Bishop Favier (with his pointed gray beard and thickset frame, he bore a striking resemblance to it). Luckily both Favier and his church were built to last. When the mobs that had destroyed the Nantang and other churches in Beijing came knocking at his door, he resisted—not just because the Beitang was Favier's church, but because by the middle of June the cathedral had become a refuge for thousands of Chinese Christians, both from the city and the surrounding countryside. It was to become the last line of defense (with far fewer defenders than the legations had) for native Christians from the first days of the Boxer Uprising until allied troops entered the city in the middle of August.

While no one can know just how many Boxers or other militants spent those two months attacking the Beitang—estimates are in excess of 10,000 men—we do know just how many defenders there were and we have it on the authority of Bishop Favier how many Chinese Christians took shelter within its walls. Forty-one French and Italian marines and only two officers saved the lives of almost four thousand refugees, one hundred of whom were foreigners (mostly women and children, with Chinese children in much higher numbers). While these numbers alone lend support to W. A. P. Martin's assertion that it took a miracle of God to achieve their salvation, in fact Bishop Favier himself can take as much credit as the French and Italian marines. He had prepared in advance for the siege, which he had predicted would occur. The residents of the legations thought they had it rough after June 20, the day on which everyone crammed into the British legation to endure their own siege, until their liberation on August 14. And they did watch as colleagues and loved ones died from gunfire and disease. But the besieged in the Beitang lived through several more hells. In one instance eighty were killed by a single explosion, at other times whole groups of children were blown to bits too minute to appear human. According to Favier, the numbers were even worse for others of his flock. He believed that by the end of the Boxer madness, upwards of 20,000 Chinese Christians had been killed or died as a result of deprivation.[49]

Sarah could not help observing the fecklessness of the Chinese imperial troops with whom Edwin had tried to reason. "Chinese soldiers do little if anything to prevent [the Boxers' destruction of foreign property]," Sarah noted in her diary. "In fact they stand by and let the Boxers do their worst without any sign of resistance, and too they will stand by and let foreigners cut down, kill and put to flight the 'Boxers' without a sign of resistance."[50]

"Between you and me," Sarah wrote this same day to a nephew, "I am inclined to think [the Chinese] an abused people. I cannot see that they are any better off for having this foreign element in upon them"—and by "foreign" she could have meant the hapless Manchus, long seen as alien usurpers, as much as she meant the Western foreigners themselves. She could see, perhaps better than other members of the foreign community did, that both residents of the legations and the Boxers were, ironically, becoming more the victims of imperial governmental ineptitude than of each other. Or was this, actually, the plan of Duan and the conservatives all along? They did nothing to prevent the destruction of the Nantang, Sarah noted; Pichon did what he could against the mobs with the small force at hand, finally concentrating them at the Beitang. It was already obvious there was nothing anyone could do to stop the attacks against Chinese Christians who lived around the churches. According to Robert Coltman, "poor mutilated children" from the *hutong* around the Nantang fled to the legations, telling of the massacres taking place at the cathedral. This moved the residents of the legations to organize a relief party.[51]

Sarah wrote to her sister,

> The devilish work done [at the Nantang] I have no desire to try
> to describe . . . Twenty Russians and ten American marines, with
> Mr. Pethick . . . and others, who speak the Chinese language, went
> out as a guard to rescue the people at the Nantang. The Boxers
> fled and the guards worked. Four of our men brought over four
> hundred refugees past this Legation. As these people of all ages
> and conditions in life—many hungry, burned, wounded, and
> slashed—marched by, it was a pitiful sight. The strongest among
> them were carrying the aged and helpless. Later, the Russians
> came in with large numbers, and still later our six men came
> with wounded and burned refugees. They stopped in front of the
> American Legation, and our doctor and a Russian doctor cared
> for them. They were in a sorrowful plight. Such fortitude I never
> beheld, as these people manifested during the dressing of their
> wounds. No shrinking, nor cry of suffering was expressed.[52]

Polly Condit Smith heard even worse. "Babies were seen being torn
in two," she wrote in her diary, after talking with some of the Americans
who had gone on the rescue mission. At the American legation, she saw
for herself the people "half-starved, covered with soot and ashes from the
fires, women carrying on their breasts horribly sick and diseased babies,
and in one case a woman who held a dead baby." Like Sarah, she could
not fathom how these Chinese people, torn by "great spear-thrusts that
made jagged wounds, scalp cuts and gashes," never cried out as they were
being treated by the foreign doctors. Among these was Dr. Coltman, who
marveled at how a ten-year-old girl, who had guided younger siblings
to safety, "patiently endured" the pain of having a sword cut to the head
stitched up, calmly describing for Coltman how the Boxers had hacked
her parents to death.[53]

Several witnesses, including Polly, Sarah, Cecile Payen (who burst
into tears at the sight), and Dr. Coltman, seem to have watched the same
middle-aged man carrying his aged mother on his back. "She looked so
withered and wrinkled," Polly recalled, "one had to think of the burning
of Troy and Aeneas." It was as if the only way she, a protected woman of
wealth, could understand what she was seeing was to relate it to legends

of past sieges, even as her stock response to the soldiers detailed to guard the Americans' Western Hills nunnery was to liken them to comical figures from the Broadway stage. Yet she knew, as did all the foreigners in the Legation Quarter who were paying the slightest attention to the unfolding events, that they were living in a very different reality now, one they did not know, the dangers of which they might not survive. "Our world," Polly noted somberly, "is this dangerous Peking."[54]

11
Siege

There were only two ramps to the top of the Tartar City wall, both open to the sky. But Sarah's dislike of walls that restrained her view of the world outweighed, for the moment, the very real danger of exposing herself atop them. Late on the night of June 18, when it was dark enough for them to be safely concealed, she and Edwin, accompanied by guards, went up to the wall behind the US legation for a midnight view of the destruction.

Looking out across the city, the air filled with the acrid bite of charred wood, they could only imagine the ruins concealed by smoke, flames, and darkness. "Large shops and many of China's most beautiful things were burned," Sarah recalled. "There is no way whatever for people to fight fire." Hoping to damage foreign properties, the Boxers instead had dealt a blow to one of Beijing's architectural treasures: fires set in the Dutch legation were shifted by prevailing winds from the real target, the American legation, and soon had the Qianmen (Zhengyangmen), the grand southern gateway leading into the Tartar City, exploding in flame. "It made an appalling sight," Sarah wrote. The Chinese told Sarah the burning of this gate, first constructed in the early fifteenth century, was a "very bad omen; some great misfortune is coming to the Throne." Yet the misfortune Sarah most worried about was what had happened to an ice coolie from the American legation, who had bravely offered to cross the barricades to find out what news was to be had about the approaching Admiral Seymour. He had already left the compound twice on this errand, and this time had been gone over a day. "Poor old man," Sarah wondered, "where is he?" Her world had already receded to a point where such things loomed large: "We have been fenced in a little more and a little more," she admitted to her diary.[1]

In the related realms of film and legend, one encounters the image of the empress dowager herself up on the ramparts of the Forbidden City palaces, looking out over the same field of destruction as lay burning before the Congers. It is easy to paint such scenes in the imagination for such behavior would have been characteristic of this woman who loved spectacle, but there is little solid evidence to show just what any of Cixi's actions were at this stage of the troubles. Of one thing can we can be reasonably sure, however: through the smoke of burning Beijing, she had an eye trained on the American legation.

We can only speculate about Cixi's apparent impression of the Americans as being especially sympathetic to the Chinese. As early as June 11, two ministers from the Zongli Yamen approached Edwin specifically to ask him to stop Admiral Seymour from marching to Beijing, for doing so would make it easier for Prince Qing to solve the Boxer problem. Whether Qing was actually in a position to do anything about the Boxer juggernaut is questionable, and Edwin evidently thought so too: he told them no. Not long afterward, four more ministers from the Zongli Yamen asked and were granted permission to meet with Edwin. They told him they were under orders from the empress dowager (as they had probably been the first time) "to come to the American Legation, as it was friendly to China, and to say that [she regrets] what has happened through the fires and other disturbances"—an apology she never extended directly to the other ministers at this or any other time. What was Cixi up to? Had word got back to her, from the various levels of Chinese guards up through the Zongli Yamen ministers and thence to court insiders, that Edwin was taking pains to treat the Chinese with a respect lacking in the attitudes of the other legations? Did Cixi or her cabinet consider this an opportunity for dialogue, or a chance to take advantage of an inexperienced naïf? Cixi must have known that Edwin's predecessor, Charles Denby, was an admirer who, moreover, held a "jaundiced view of missionary conduct," and perhaps considering this a common trait of Americans, citizens of the one nation that had not (yet) tried to dismember China, she might have felt a similar trust in Edwin. Or had she heard of Sarah's social activities with Chinese women of rank from Li Hongzhang and his family?[2]

Cixi's biographers all try to divine her actual role in the Boxer Uprising. Aside from the dowager's first biographer, Phillip Sergeant (1909), and her more recent one, Sterling Seagrave (1992), consensus has toed the party line drawn by Kang Youwei's calumnies and George E. Morrison's biased dispatches to the *Times*—that she encouraged the Boxers to attack foreigners and kill them or drive them away. No more able than subsequent writers to discover what was happening with the dowager between her return to Beijing in June and her flight from it in August, Sergeant believed Cixi went from initial enthusiasm for the Boxers to panicked opposition, but found herself unable to jump down from the tiger she had heedlessly chosen to ride. Seagrave takes the view that Cixi intended to protect the residents of the legations, and that Ronglu, far from being their opponent, created a buffer zone of troops around the British legation to hold back and neutralize the attacks by militants, in a complex game of passive-aggressive chess. Seagrave also asserts that the siege was really not much more than a standoff, with shooting deaths resulting more from stray bullets and unwise exposure than from any deliberate intent of the Chinese to kill the foreigners. Both theories have truth in them, depending on where weight is placed in the body of evidence.

Cixi claimed to her lady-in-waiting, Der Ling, that while she identified with the empire she had ruled from behind her curtain for almost half a century—she was, after all, its "mother"—she still could not make independent decisions about what she considered to be in the nation's best interest: "I am not my own boss, but have to consult with my Ministers." In the person of Duan and his cohorts, she also faced threats of a more personal nature, threats as critical, for her, as Duan's threats to the residents of the legations were for them. Reconstructing her actions and policies through the edicts issued under her name before and during the siege gives no proof of any sort of coherent policy—it only shows how many cooks were stirring the pot, swaying events one way and then the other, now protecting the foreigners and now the Boxers. The edicts give a picture of a court and a nation in crisis that lacked a sure (or any) hand on the rudder; and they also suggest a setting in which, had Cixi made a wrong move, she might well have found herself put out of the way, ironically just as the Guangxu emperor's supporters had intended in 1898. Knowing her past methods of reinforcing her control, it is not impossible that rather than belonging to one camp or the other, she played for time—and power—in the noncommittal but perilous no man's land in between.[3]

The *New York Times* published a dispatch claimed to have been issued from Tianjin on July 2, 1900. Although a mixture of fact and fiction, its details show that whoever shared the information had access to a more positive, and possibly more truthful, view of Cixi than most in the West or than any of the foreigners in the British legation. Its negative portrayal of Prince Duan suggests that it did not emerge from his propaganda machine. Cixi is also described as being a mediator between the conservatives and the moderates at court:

> The Empress Dowager, so far from being dead, is actively striving to prevent the factions fighting. Prince Ching has informed her that he would rather lose his head than be constantly obliged to warn her of the consequence of the prolongation of the present anarchy. Prince Tuan is quite willing that Ching should be decapitated, but the Dowager Empress will not allow this. Prince Tuan has decided that he will take full responsibility.[4]

If this account is true, what power Cixi did have was concentrated in her authority over members of the imperial clan, living up to the "motherly" character of her lengthy title. But her power ended where Duan's terrorist tactics began. He was taking more than just responsibility—and surely Cixi knew that his failure to succeed in his wild scheme would deprive her of a lot more than her clan authority. Cixi had had everything taken away from her before, when she fled to Jehol with the Xianfeng emperor in 1860. Then she had been merely a concubine raised up a few imperial notches, but she had returned to Beijing an empress dowager, and now in that role she was watching it all slip away again like dust off Beijing's roof tiles. A leader would have been in charge of Duan and the conservatives from the beginning, not allowing them rogue powers—but she had never been a leader, and now she was a figurehead and pawn all in one.

As Robert Coltman pointed out, the tarnishing of Cixi's authority (perhaps through orders given to General Dong behind her back) had begun as early as autumn 1898, and perhaps even earlier. Duan probably deferred to her as to an elder family authority figure and obeyed her refusal to have moderates like Prince Qing beheaded, against his own preference. This did not save other moderates who were not related to the imperial family later in August. But by then even Cixi's traditional ceremonial role of matriarch was pointless and powerless, and her game, if it can be called that, was even more critical to her survival.

It is known that she faced threats not just from inside China but from reformers outside it who had never forgotten or forgiven Kang Youwei's and the emperor's explosive efforts to alter the imperial landscape. Illustrative of this is an article in the *New York Times* of July 30, 1900. The paper published an exclusive from Ho Yow, Chinese consul-general in San Francisco and friend of the Congers, in which Ho claimed that a Stanford-educated Chinese named Lee had traveled from Honolulu with Liang Qichao, Kang Youwei's partner in reform, to "raise an army of 40,000 malcontents in the southern treaty ports of the empire and march on Peking," the object being to overthrow Cixi and the Guangxu emperor. Ho noted "the absurdity of the claims that this is purely a patriotic reform movement" when it was reported that anyone contributing to the reform coffers would receive military and even imperial titles in return, based on how much they paid out. Absurd this plot may have been, but Ho would have been quick to report it to the throne. As part of the swirling atmosphere of equal parts rumor and fact, it further underscores the instability of the ground beneath Cixi's feet, and explains, if it does not excuse, her grasping at the nearest firm hand-grip on the swaying runaway train that was China.[5]

If Cixi or the Zongli Yamen (or Duan and his coterie) thought Edwin could stop Admiral Seymour, even if he wanted to do so, on the basis of his and Sarah's known sympathy for the Chinese, they were wrong. "Mr. Conger told [the court ministers] that they were repeating the same old story," Sarah recalled. "Their people have been murdering our people, destroying and burning property, and danger threatens everywhere." Taking another tack, the ministers asked Edwin to assure them that the troops, when they arrived, would be kept outside the city walls, in a camp. Edwin told them no again, adding that they would come straight to the legations, "and if they are not enough, more will come . . . All we desire is peace, protection, and a harmonious relation with your people," Sarah heard him tell the men through interpreter F. D. Cheshire. "You do not give it to us and we foreign nations are obliged to call upon our countries for the protection you should give . . . Your own people are so afraid of the Boxers that it is with difficulty that we can send a messenger, even to the Tsung Li Yamen."[6]

Von Ketteler had none of the patience of his American colleague. He seems to have believed that his legation (by no means as close to the action as the French or Austrian compounds), was the leading edge in the fight against the Boxers, and had ordered his guards to shoot "Boxers" on sight, without ascertaining whether the targets were Boxers or just ordinary civilians. He himself took potshots at passing groups of men he assumed were the militants—any Chinese male wearing red, for example—"killing several." This was followed by a night like June 13, with "terrific din" and cries of "*Sha!*" Death was in the air.[7]

※　※　※　※　※

As if to mock the theory that only a good rain was needed to send the Boxers back to their fields, it showered for the first time since the troubles began. Yet things not only did not get better, they got much, much worse.

The next day, June 19, the Zongli Yamen sent a letter to Edwin, copies of which were delivered to the other foreign ministers. In it, the Zongli Yamen ministers stated that as foreign troops were firing on Tianjin (news of which the diplomatic corps had no way of corroborating), all diplomatic relations were to be broken off and the foreign ministers would have to leave Beijing within twenty-four hours, adding that there would be "no further protection." Each foreign minister received the same letter. But no one went to the Zongli Yamen. After meeting, the ministers sent word that they could not safely leave their legations or Beijing, and asked for an audience in the Legation Quarter. They only received silence.

By morning of the twentieth, there was still no response from the Zongli Yamen. This enraged Ketteler, who, against the advice of everyone, ordered two chairs and with his interpreter, Cordes (who had been at the Zongli Yamen and returned safely the day before), and two *mafu* headed for the Foreign Office. Barely a block beyond the Legation Quarter, a Boxer or an imperial soldier—the story varies—stepped from the side of the street and shot Ketteler, either through the head or in the back. Although also shot, Cordes was able to escape; his brief last glance made it clear to him that the baron was dead.[8]

The news, when it reached them, electrified the people of the legations. Polly Condit Smith saw the soldiers and officers of the German legation march out to find the baron or recover his body, but the danger was too great and they returned. This is when the severity of the situation seemed to sink in. "When the story of Von Ketteler's murder had been confirmed," she recalled, "a shiver of horror shook each and every foreigner then in Peking; and we realized, perhaps for the first time, the horror of our position."[9]

This horror was doubled for Ketteler's young widow. An American who had married a handsome and titled European who was old enough to be her father, and probably served her as father figure as much as husband, Maud Ledyard von Ketteler had apparently already feared for her husband's safety, since she seems to have induced him to take a revolver to the Zongli Yamen. But even under the circumstances, it would probably not have occurred to her to plead with him to stay home—what was there to be afraid of from these cowardly Chinese? Cordes had come back safely the previous day, as has been pointed out, and as has also been noted, Ketteler was probably more motivated to give the Zongli Yamen ministers a lesson in how to keep appointments than to accomplish anything serious. When Ketteler was hectoring on such matters, there was no stopping him.[10]

Now that Ketteler was dead, nobody wanted to be the one to tell Maud. Sarah volunteered or, as she put it, "it fell upon me to state to the wife of the German Minister what had happened. She is a young, sweet,

American woman. How my heart ached for her. I did so wish that I could blot the whole thing out of her life, instead of taking it into it." The young baroness refused to believe the news she brought, and Sarah stayed with Maud some three hours, convincing her to come to grips with the truth. She probably would have remained longer, but Ketteler's death had shaken all the foreign ministers to their foundations (as Sugiyama's had not). It was decided that as the British legation was the biggest compound and the easiest to defend, everyone should move into it that day. So on top of having broken the news of Ketteler's death to his wife, Sarah had to persuade her to pack up and leave the German legation, which she finally did, with the help of Maud's maid. Sarah's task was to be shouldered by other women over the coming months as they helped Maud von Ketteler regain the will to live. (Polly Condit Smith even took credit, on one memorable occasion, for saving the suicidal Maud from enemy gunfire.)[11]

The British legation was comprised of some seven acres, with numerous buildings, including a chapel, scattered around a court (which served for tennis) at the southern end of the rectangular site. Because the British had staked their claim so early, they had the advantage of securing a much larger compound than any of the subsequent European or American powers. Originally the palace of a Duke of Liang, who was descended from one of the many sons of the Kangxi emperor, the property was located at what could only be described as the center of official Beijing: to the northwest was the main gate of the Forbidden City, to the west the Imperial Carriage Park (a sort of Qing royal garage), beyond which were the Boards of War, Works, State Ceremonies, Astronomy, and Medicine, with the Boards of Revenue, Rites, and Civil and Imperial Clan Affairs the next block over. The British had restored the many pavilions of the Liang palace to make it habitable, constructing only a few buildings that were not in Chinese style and largely maintaining the integrity of the original buildings. They paid the imperial government a rent of five hundred pounds per year, delivered as silver ingots stacked in a cart and accompanied by a top hat-wearing emissary from the legation.[12]

With its broad entrance gate, "the British Legation is a large place," judged Cecile Payen, "with fine trees, a tennis-court in the center, and with about ten houses about the court . . . It has two wells of good drinking water [and it] is easiest to fortify" with its fifteen foot walls. But as the Americans had felt that the United States legation had been overfilled with guests, despite its greater size and numerous buildings, the British legation was to replicate that crowded situation. The Americans— the families of Conger, Squiers, Bainbridge, and Coltman—along with single people like Cecile Payen, the Woodwards, and Polly Condit Smith, plus their servants—were given the bungalow that had recently been the home of legation physician Dr. Wordsworth Poole. Its six rooms had been adequate for him but they were hardly so for this many people, who now brought with them not only their trunks and silver chests but many containers of tinned fruit and meat. These would come in very handy over the next several weeks but they still crowded the edges of the rooms, making them seem even smaller.[13]

Life in the bungalow began with challenges for the Americans. None of them had ever been acquainted with real want or such crowded conditions—and it was worse for the Squiers' governesses, who according to Polly were given pallets to sleep on "in the ends of small halls." The kitchen stove did not function properly, which meant that the families had to take their meals at different times, eating dishes which according to Polly were not often hot. The Coltmans, well-versed in Chinese ways, had their meals cooked in the courtyard, but the others coaxed Dr. Poole's recalcitrant range. Polly would have us believe that she hardly had much appetite anyway, given where her room, which she shared with Harriet, was situated: it opened "directly on the filthy, dirty Chinese servants' quarters," sniffed Polly. A broken sewer made having to breathe "the servants' air" even more difficult. She probably meant their outdoor toilet; before long the entire compound would smell of more than a Chinese latrine. All in all, it could have been much worse, as was recognized by Cecile Payen. "We Americans in this house are about as well off as anybody in this compound," she noted. "We six ladies [Cecile, Sarah, Laura, Anna and Ione Woodward, and Mary Pierce] sleep on the floor (on mattresses which we roll up against the wall in the daytime), surrounded by trunks, boxes, canned fruit, etc. The other room we use as an eating- and living-room, and at night two mattresses are laid on the floor for Mr. Conger and Dr. [W. A. P.] Martin."[14]

"When I went to South America," Sarah wrote her nephew, "and first realized that I was a 'foreigner,' it was a strange feeling that came over me—and *now* to be a *'foreigner'* and a *'refugee'—it is no joke*. What next?" (emphasis in original).[15]

If this depressed any of them, all they had to do was contemplate the fate of the Chinese Christians. When the Methodist mission was threatened, and then word came that all who would seek protection should come to the British legation, Edwin was approached by one of the missionaries and asked what was to be done with the Chinese in their care. Though he had earlier expressed solidarity with Sir Claude MacDonald, "the most backward of any in taking measures against the Boxers," in the view that "foreign soldiers could only protect foreigners," for reasons we can only guess at he had changed his mind. Without hesitation, Edwin said, "Bring them. I do not know how they will be fed, but it is sure death to leave them behind. Bring them."[16]

That same day (June 20), George Morrison and Dr. F. Huberty James, a British scholar fluent in Chinese, had made a "deal" with Prince Su, a conservative Manchu who owned a palace, known in Chinese as the Suwangfu, located across the Jade Canal from the British legation's main entrance. Su, a relative of the imperial family, was probably not keen on dwelling in what he must have known was soon to become a battle zone. As the foreigners were not about to take no for an answer, he departed, "leaving all of his treasure and half his harem," according to Polly, and the estate was turned over to the supremely competent Japanese military attaché, Colonel Shiba Gorō, a samurai's son, whose cool head and brilliant tactics greatly assisted the defense not just of the British legation but of the Suwangfu, where the Chinese Christians were housed and became special targets. Always amused by such strange ironies, Polly Condit Smith wrote, "How queerly things happen! These poor wretches, who had been tortured and hounded to death only two hours before by Imperial troops, were now housed in the palace of a mighty prince, and almost within the shadow of the Empress-Dowager's palace."[17]

Unfortunately for Professor Huberty James, he extended his trust of the Chinese with whom he had lived for so many years to include those firing on the legation. "On the afternoon of that first day of the siege," remembered Robert Coltman, who had known the professor since

1885, "F. Huberty James, professor of English in the Imperial University, noticed several Chinese soldiers upon the bridge, a few hundred yards north of the legation gate." Without telling anyone what he was doing, Huberty James was seen by the sentry at the gate of the British legation walking toward the soldiers. He made his way along the canal and to the bridge, when other soldiers, whom Coltman imagined were hidden in a wall of the Suwangfu, shot him—perhaps word of his protection of the Chinese Christians had made its way to the snipers hidden among the bullet-pocked masonry. "The sentry saw him hold up his hands, then heard a report and saw him fall. He was seen to partly raise himself, when several of the ruffian soldiers hurriedly ran out, picked him up, and carried him behind the corner of the wall and beyond the reach of rescue. His fate was probably a hasty death at their hands, if, indeed, he was not already mortally wounded."[18]

Everyone hoped the troops were not far away, but with the deaths first of Ketteler and so soon after Huberty James at Chinese hands, the danger grew sharper and hopes thinner as each new claim of hearing Seymour's guns or seeing his signal flares evaporated as mere hearsay. "There are rumors that the troops are getting near," wrote Cecile Payen, "but we are getting tired of these false rumors." To Sarah it was plain that only the arrival of Admiral Seymour—known now as "Admiral See-No-More"—could save them, because in tandem with the murders of Ketteler and Huberty James, she quickly saw that the harassment of noise, the occasional firing of guns, and arson attacks on the part of the Boxers, were hardening into a fully armed offensive—not just courtesy of the Gansu soldiers of General Dong, but also the soldiers of the imperial forces. Cixi's declaration of war meant that whether they were firing alongside the Boxers they were supposed to be holding back, or had sent them out of the way, her troops were deploying the full complement of European armaments purchased from the same powers they were now attacking.[19]

"The Chinese placed a big gun near the Chi'enmen," Sarah recalled, "and opened fire on our men. If the [Tartar City wall] were to be forsaken, the Chinese could come from the East and West and throw their shells right into the British Legation." Everybody knew what that would mean.[20]

According to the official report filed after the siege by Captain John T. Myers, the firing by the Chinese began at 6 p.m. on June 20, before the refugees had even settled into the British compound and before the Chinese Christians had been conducted into the Suwangfu. A barricade was erected across the wall, just over the Water Gate and behind the Temple of Three Officials at the back of the American legation. American and Russian marines held this crucial point of the wall, but not without difficulty. Cecile Payen wrote how everyone stayed inside their various buildings because "bullets are flying in all directions and whizzing by our windows," some of them fired by what she was told were Boxers concealed in trees near the legation walls. The next day, on the bell tower located between the tennis court and the chapel, and to the east of the Americans' bungalow, was placed one of the first bulletins of the siege, one of many that would be tacked to its painted pillars over the next month and a half:

> June 21st
>
> 10 a.m. Methodist mission burning.
>
> Afternoon. Sixty Boxers killed. Late report that Chinese troops are firing on the Boxers who are attacking the Customs legation.
>
> 6 p.m. Austrians have not given up.
>
> 9 p.m. Yung-lu's troops are firing on us, and Prince Ching's men are fighting the Boxers.[21]

Again that internecine combat assumed to be occurring between the progressive Prince Qing and the conservative Ronglu at the court of Cixi—the reality of whose allegiances was probably far more complicated and fluid than the foreigners could possibly understand.

Barricades were being fashioned out of anything the men could find, and had to be built at night to avoid the worst of the gunfire: it was a struggle to get the Chinese, who were pressed into much of the hard labor, to risk their lives raising walls in daylight under increasingly accurate gunfire. By June 22, all women and children who were able to do so were working alongside the men in the legation's defense. When not helping put out fires or tend to the wounded who were filling up the makeshift hospital in the chancery, the American women joined their international sisters in sewing sandbags for the barricades. As with Dr. Poole's uncooperative stove, there was sewing machine malfunction to contend with, and not enough machines to go around. But with what they had, the ladies worked miracles. "We have made several hundred [sandbags] in this room today," Cecile wrote, "out of table-linen, sheeting, everything we can get hold of, including beautiful silks and satins."[22]

Much of this table and bed linen came from the supplies Sarah had brought with her from America, as replacements for the linens in the American legation, while yards of it came from the stores of the British legation and from shops, Chinese and foreign, near the compound. The silks and satins were taken from abandoned Chinese buildings around the British legation; bolts of imperial silks given to the foreign ministers' wives during their first audience with Cixi in late 1898 were added to the stockpile. The silk curtains of both Sarah and Lady MacDonald were also pulled down and put to use. One woman later wrote that from fears that this colorful mélange would attract enemy fire, the women tried dying the gorgeous fabrics with a stew of coal dust and water. They gave up the effort as impracticable, and Cecile Payen was pleased: she thought these bags, stacked up with those of sheeting, sackcloth, and coarser materials in the embrasures of windows, on porches, and along rooflines made a striking mosaic worthy of her paint-box, actually executing a *plein-air* watercolor of the scene (with protective marine guard standing by). Under some of the worst of the fire, Cecile would paint a view of Dr. Poole's bungalow as a gift for Sarah's fifty-seventh birthday in July.[23]

As for Sarah, who rejoiced in any proof that underneath their social class, education, experience, clothes, race, and language, men and women were brothers and sisters in the great human family, the constant work that started soon after the removal to the British compound inspired and consoled her: "We have worked diligently making thousands and thousands of sand bags," she recorded in her diary. "The walls, housetops, windows, doorways, gateways and other places of danger have been fortified with these bags. All have done coolies' work, with Coolies, or Barons, Sirs, Ministers, ladies or Priests. All have most willingly worked for a common cause," even as in the barricades, silk did duty beside sackcloth. Yet as she would discover, just as some of the fancier silks would not take the black dye, there were those working for the common cause who nevertheless drew the line at sisterhood.[24]

✳ ✳ ✳ ✳ ✳

The fear many women felt was increased by the fact that they had their children with them; the possibility of a repeat of the 1857 Cawnpore massacre was terrifying. The Victorian method of raising offspring in a controlled cocoon would have ensured that the children were shielded from knowing the full danger of their circumstances, though from what Polly Condit Smith saw, most of them understood the situation all too well. Growing increasingly stir-crazy as they were made to stay indoors, the children were already echoing the siege in their games. Polly noted that "the younger ones are forced into being the attacking Chinese, and I am afraid when the big ones repulse them, they occasionally get very real bumps on their heads." They even built little barricades (often using carved Chinese printing blocks), made their own sandbags, and fashioned cannon out of bamboo. Polly joined in the fun but with a heavy heart, hoping "that relief will come before they lose their spirit and before they know."[25]

The dangers to the children in the Poole bungalow were far more real than any of the Americans wanted to imagine. Polly recalled a singular example of this on June 23. She was with Mrs. Coltman in the Coltmans' room; the baby Mrs. Coltman had carried into the American legation earlier in the month was sleeping in "a funny, old-fashioned, high-backed crib," Polly wrote. "Although the sound of exploding bullets was to be heard outside the house, we were much startled to feel one . . . enter the room, hit the headpiece of the baby's crib, detaching itself from the main part, and bury itself in the opposite wall." Had the bullet been a mere inch lower, it would have struck the infant's head. Mrs. Coltman grabbed the child and with Polly ran to another part of the house. At that point they were joined by Sarah, who does not seem to have been in the room where the shot had entered. And here is where one of the enduring legends of Sarah Pike Conger begins—one that has clung to her through numerous accounts of the Boxer Uprising, and is accepted by many as the truth of who the woman was.[26]

According to Polly, as she, Mrs. Coltman, and the wailing baby hurried to a safer place, Sarah, dismissively described by Polly as "an open follower of Mrs. Eddy," advised the startled women "that it was ourselves, and not the times, which were troublous and out of tune, and insisted that while there was an appearance of warlike hostilities, it was really in our own brains." Polly claims Sarah took this notion too far by stating unequivocally that a bullet had not actually pierced the room, that "our receptive minds . . . falsely [led] us to believe such to be the case."[27]

W. A. P. Martin, while he felt a friendliness toward Sarah for her hospitality—"Had I been her brother I could not have been treated with more affectionate kindness," he noted later of his stay in the Poole bungalow—even had a few comments to share on this subject in his account of the siege. Though she was "Calm, resolute, hopeful and, as Pope says, 'Mistress of herself, *though China fall,*' " Sarah's views that "all those events [were] as nothing more than a horrid nightmare" were hard for Martin to take seriously. "The round shot by which our walls were pierced," he wrote, "was too tangible to be resolved into fanciful ideas."[28]

The problem with this characterization of Sarah—as party to a cult so weird it moved its followers to deny the hard reality of a bullet—is that none of Sarah's own diaries, those published and those not, bear proof that this is the way she thought or spoke. Nor do any of the extant letters she wrote to Mary Baker Eddy about the Boxer Uprising. All through the siege, Sarah's writings are full of her detailed accounts of near misses by bullets and small gauge cannonballs, of her gathering and measuring the numbers of bullets to be melted down for the defense, and of her actually holding bullets still warm from being fired and showing them to Laura and the girls. Sarah also took note of the damage caused by bullets, as when, in July, a six-inch ball flew through the dining room of the British legation. "Fortunately, it passed near the ceiling," Sarah noted, "so it did no damage aside from knocking off a corner of the frame of Queen Victoria's portrait."[29]

Sarah can be counted among several perceptive witnesses who recorded how the Chinese in fact seemed to habitually fire too high—compelling evidence that some kind of control was being exercised over the Boxers by the government, or over the troops who replaced them, on the foreigners' behalf. "The Chinese have been remarkably bad marksmen," insisted Dr. Coltman. Instead of aiming they fired over the barricades willy-nilly, "having never ventured their lives in the least." Given their access to German-made munitions and their superior advantage, had the Chinese intended to really smash down the walls of the British legation and massacre everyone inside, as many feared and others insisted was the plan, they could have done so within the first few days. But most of their bullets went astray. This constant fire over their heads even moved Sarah to write in her diary, with wry humor, that "the air is musical with these whistling missives. But I cannot say that I love the music"—not the comment of someone deluding herself as to the realities of the dangerous situation she was in.[30]

Sarah was attempting to calm the frightened women as best she could, using the only method she knew, the language and precepts of Christian Science. While perhaps appropriate for life's more meditative moments, metaphysics was not designed to flatten stormy seas, not least because few people frightened for their lives are receptive to philosophical thinking. In the hallways of Dr. Poole's bungalow, Sarah's Christian Science mind-over-matter approach would have been distorted by Polly's fear of the moment and what appears to be Polly's bias toward the teachings of Mary Baker Eddy. Dr. Martin had his own bias—his religious background was of the old-fashioned hortatory sort, full of Biblical quotation but short on the what-ifs that made up Sarah's approach to faith and life.

In any case, whatever Sarah said, it was uttered under stress and not likely to be as subtle as she intended; but it did not end there. Polly probably told Harriet Squiers, or perhaps Dr. Martin jokingly mentioned Sarah's comment to someone, and the story took on a life of its own: Mrs. Conger denies the Chinese are really shooting us, she claims that the bullets are not real—it's all in our heads! Of course she would come off as seeming slightly crazy. And the process by which she came to be seen in this light was curiously not unlike that which had, by the time Sarah saw her again in January 1902, and on a larger scale, eroded the credibility and dignity of the Empress Dowager Cixi.

✳ ✳ ✳ ✳ ✳

"Mr. Conger counts the night of the second and the morning of the third of July as the most anxious and trying period of his life," Sarah wrote.[31]

The last part of June had been bad enough. In the week of June 23–30, the residents of the legations had had fires to put out and gunfire to avoid, and sometimes both simultaneously, as when a blaze broke out in part of the Hanlin Library located on the other side of the north wall of the British legation. A repository for the *Yongle Dadian,* a massive encyclopedia of over eleven thousand volumes, ordered by the Yongle emperor and completed in 1408, the Hanlin Library was what one of those trapped in the legation called the Chinese equivalent of "Oxford and Cambridge, Heidelberg and the Sorbonne of the eighteen Chinese provinces rolled into one." That the Boxers, or General Dong's men, would set fire to this treasure-house just to achieve what, depending on the wind, was a questionable short-term goal of burning out the foreigners, was unthinkable to many of the cultured who were besieged in the legation. But that imperial troops did nothing to assist the foreigners in putting out the blaze by at least scattering the militants (who were shooting at the residents of the legations from behind a screen of smoke), or help them douse the flames, has begged the question of how the fire really got started. It was an early test for the women of the compound, many of whom may have never before hoisted a bucket in their lives, to find themselves in a pail chain stretching from the nearest well to the burning buildings, bullets whizzing overhead. The closest well was the "sweet" one just north of the Poole bungalow; the water they used was potable, which the residents of the legations could ill afford to toss away.[32]

The south wall, on the other side of Wall Street from the United States and German legations, continued to be a thorny patch. The attackers, who recognized this as a superb vantage point for breaking the legation's defense, refused to give up the effort to take it. German and American marines tried to hold the wall, while increasingly larger shells were being lobbed directly into the British compound; the worst fusillades were saved for the middle of the night which, with the terrible wail of the conch shell horns the Chinese blew before and during attacks, made for a constant assault on the ears as well as on the body. When the coast was clear, bomb shelters of trenches covered with boards and sandbags were built in safer areas of the property, but there was not much hope for anyone inside should a shelter take a direct hit. The wounded and the dead filled respectively the siege hospital and the little burial ground in a corner of the compound, and the need for sandbags began to be superseded by a dire shortage of sheets, pajamas, bandages, and other supplies. Cecile Payen recalled sitting with Sarah, Anna and Ione Woodward, Mary Pierce, and Laura as on any given day they turned out dozens of sheets, aprons, pajamas, devising bandages, and other materials useful to the doctors and nurses. Anna also nursed in the hospital, "where our wounded boys affectionately called her by the name 'Mamma.'" The women had all given up their mosquito nets to the men, right at the time when the insects were adding stinging misery to the shot and shell of night. "At the hospital they call Mrs. Conger their fairy godmother," Cecile wrote, "for whenever they need anything she finds the means to provide it." This included risking frequent returns for more supplies to the war zone that had once been the American legation.[33]

On June 27, there was a heady rejoicing when the Americans on the wall surprised "a crowd of greenhorn Boxers," as Robert Coltman described them, and mowed down several dozen with their Colt gun as the men scrambled at the base of the wall. But the triumph did not last. Snipers had found the ruined Chinese houses around the American legation perfect concealment for picking off American marines, so that nobody in their right mind risked crossing Legation Street. And in a sort of crazed climax to the month, in which the weather seemed to conspire to drive the residents of the legations out of their wits, on June 30 there was a crashing thunderstorm, during which "the Chinese started a terrific fusillade from all quarters," recalled Coltman. "The hideous noise, with vivid flashes of lightning, produced an effect on the minds of all who witnessed it that they will probably never forget."[34]

Chinese shelling at the south wall proved too heavy and at one point both the Americans and Germans had to abandon it. According to Deaconess Jessie Ransome, who was nursing at the hospital almost without sleep for days at a time, "some blunder" on the part of the Germans had led them to evacuate their position; and by agreement the Americans evacuated theirs as well. "As soon as the blunder was discovered," she recalled, "the Yankees most pluckily retook their positions, and are holding it but at a fearful cost." She added that the

Germans had yet to return to their own barricade, and the Americans' position was little more than tenuous at best.[35]

Day after day, the attackers were raising their barricade, so that it overtopped the American one some forty yards away. The Americans would not be able to hold out if fired down upon. "This was an exceedingly dangerous position for us," Sarah wrote. "It was too near and must be taken, or the wall abandoned." Because this section was under the Americans' jurisdiction, Edwin had to figure out how the Chinese barricade was to be seized. He conferred with the other ministers, then with Sir Claude, and discussed practical options with Captain Myers. The decision was then made to take sixty men—American, Russian, and British marines—to storm the attackers' defenses. Sarah was well aware of the odds. Sixty men, she meditated in her diary, "to meet hundreds of Chinese."[36]

On July 3 at three o'clock in the morning, Captain Myers gathered his men and gave them a do-or-die speech which both Coltman and Sarah recorded for posterity, but in widely different versions (neither was likely present). Where the two accounts sing in unison they agree on the vivid image Myers summoned to exhort his marines. "Remember there are three hundred women and children whose lives depend on our success tonight," he said. "If we succeed, they live; if we fail, not only are our lives sacrificed, but their lives, too. Now go!" It was a reminder Edwin did not need; he wore his responsibility for the sortie and the men carrying it out very heavily indeed.[37]

Hugging the walls on either side of the open space atop the wall, which was wide enough, it was said, for four Chinese carriages to be driven abreast at top speed, at Myers' signal the men whooped and swarmed over the startled Chinese, driving them as far back as their barricade near the ruined Qianmen Gate. Two men died, several were wounded, and Myers took a spear cut to the leg that laid him up in the hospital (where he contracted typhus and nearly died). But for the time being, the Chinese threat to this important section of the south wall was abated. As many recognized, this single action was the turning point in the siege, giving the residents of the legations the leverage—such as it was—that they needed.[38]

At least the successful sortie made for a less bleak Fourth of July than it might otherwise have been. According to Cecile Payen, there was no celebration of the American holiday as "firecrackers will be rather tame to us after this." And nobody had the energy or will to celebrate anything. She added that it was hard to overcome their disappointment "as we had based our hopes on [Seymour and his troops] getting here on this date." Yet Edwin and Sarah wore small American flags on their lapels, and now that it was relatively safe to do so, they both went to the American legation to retrieve a silk flag, which they laid over the graves of the six American marines (located in the Russian legation compound) who had died thus far in the siege.[39]

"Many of the foreigners and all of the Diplomats called and congratulated us upon our Independence Day," Sarah wrote rather sadly. "They are always very prompt about these things." Spanish Minister de Cologan may have risked breaching the boundaries of tact when he wrote in the guest book, "At least today's firing will remind you of your happy home," but his intentions were sincere, while Dutch Minister Knobel shared the sober but inspiring thought that "Our virtue under these circumstances, is perseverance, our glory: patience."[40]

But Sarah did not really want to be around people. She made her rounds at the hospital—she had offered to nurse but was told she was already "doing [her] duty in [her] present capacity," which kept her busy enough. Finished there, she found some rare quiet place to sit with her Bible, a precious copy in which she had inscribed the date of her first meeting with Mary Baker Eddy. Like a Chinese shaking fortune sticks out of a jar, she opened the volume at a random spot, looking "for what lesson was there for me," and turned to II Corinthians I. The eighth, ninth and tenth verses jumped out at her:

> For we would not, brethren, have you ignorant of our trouble which came to us in Asia, that we were pressed out of measure, above strength, insomuch that we despaired even of life:
>
> But we had the sentence of death in ourselves, that we should not trust in ourselves, but in God which raiseth the dead: Who delivered us from so great a death, and doth deliver: in whom we trust that he will yet deliver us . . .

So struck was Sarah by the appositeness of the verses and the jolt of hope they seemed to offer that she went in search of Anna Woodward, sat her down, and showed her the passage. "I read aloud to Mrs. W[oodward]," she recorded. "We looked at each other and wept together." Dr. Martin was similarly impressed. He copied the verses and tacked them to the bell tower, like a bulletin not from Sir Claude MacDonald but direct from the Almighty. [41]

Edwin had his own epiphany that day. As Cecile, who recounts the anecdote, recalled, Edwin came to her with something he wanted her to see. While he and Sarah had been at the American legation to retrieve the flag for the marines' graves, he had taken from his office wall his copy of the Declaration of Independence. Cecile looked at the framed document, "through which a bullet had passed, embedding itself in the wall back of the frame." Not only had Edwin taken down the Declaration, "as one of the relics of the war," but had similarly preserved the bullet, which he had dug out of the plaster. [42]

Not unlike Sarah's happenstance discovery of the verses in her Bible, the part of the Declaration where the bullet had pierced the text was strangely apropos to the circumstances. When Mary Gamewell, wife of American engineer Frank Gamewell, saw it, she recalled that the bullet had struck "that portion wherein the revolutionary fathers had expressed themselves in somewhat disparaging terms concerning King George." The "repeated injuries and usurpations" of which the English monarch was accused by the Founding Fathers were not far from those of which the Chinese had long accused the foreigner in the Middle Kingdom. [43]

12
Survival

The risks Sarah ran to bring supplies back from the American compound were not slight. Sarah and Edwin went together one morning to gather what they could from the legation. An intrepid photographer, Sarah was walking around the ruined courtyard taking pictures, when "a shell from the big gun on the wall to the west end of [the gateway]," which she had just been snapping with her camera, hit the building "with a thud," puncturing the roof. "We looked around a little more," she wrote, "then ducked our heads & passed out & across the street."[1]

"Not an hour later," Sarah wrote in her diary, "a friend came in and said, 'Mrs. Conger, here are the pieces of a shell that went through the roof and into the room where you and Mr. Conger were working this morning." Shrapnel from the explosion had damaged several other rooms. Had the Congers worked a little longer that morning, they might have been killed.[2]

Yet she kept going back. To get to there, Sarah had to go either along the Jade Canal side of the legation, exposing herself to sniper fire, or west and south through the congeries of shattered Chinese houses between the British and Russian legations, through the latter, across barricaded Legation Street, and finally into the courtyard of the American compound—not an easy trip for a fit young man like Wang, let alone a fifty-seven-year-old woman. And once there, she would have been greeted by a depressing sight. "[Edwin] says it is the most desolate place imaginable," Cecile Payen recorded. While barricades were being built up, existing buildings themselves were being blasted to pieces, so that by mid-July, the United States compound was rendered hardly fit to be lived in. Not only had the little compound's exterior suffered under the constant barrage of shells and bullets, but its use as a billet for the United States Marines was damaging its interiors. Sarah could not help noticing that "our dear home and the beautiful trees are a wreck. The dining-room has been turned into a drying-room for the hospital laundry and our other rooms into sleeping quarters for the marines."[3]

There is evidence that not all the Congers' belongings were destroyed in bombings; many survived, but simply disappeared in the frenzy of looting that overtook Beijing. As Sarah wrote to Laura a year later, with cooler perspective, "I do not grieve over anything—Let them go—no grieving will bring them back—I am thankful." It probably gave her pause, however, to consider that a fair amount of the looting that was going on was, according to Mary Pierce, not committed by Chinese. Many Chinese families had abandoned their homes in the areas around the fighting, leaving everything behind. "Since then," Mary noted, "the foreigners (including some missionaries) have been as unnecessarily destructive as the Chinese and have looted these Chinese houses, many of which were full of beautiful curios and Chinese comforts of all kinds."[4] Had the American legation been similarly pilfered? "Fill your house with gold and jade," warned the *Daodejing*, "and it can no longer be guarded."[5]

The danger that her parents were in, and her own precarious situation, did not improve Laura Conger's already fragile state of nerves. Sarah and Edwin were worried, and they were not the only ones. Wang, too, was disturbed by her worsening condition. When he saw she was about to lose the one thing that still gave her pleasure, her pony, he acted, though in doing so he broke that cardinal rule of any siege— whatever could be used for food had to shared out equally to everyone, with no one made a favorite.

When the last of the sheep had been eaten, the first pony was killed and butchered to serve as food—a turning point that was as much of a shock to people in 1900 as it would be today. "We are now really eating the horse-meat," Robert Coltman recorded on July 7. "A number of people who were using it assured us it was very good, but our prejudices prevailed some time." They tried cooking and preparing the meat in various ways, mostly to disguise its strong flavor or tenderize the toughness. It was fried with bacon (of which the Americans seem to have had a more than ample stash), or it was curried, or rendered into sausages.[6]

In her published diary entries, Sarah is careful to show that she was grateful for the meat, even if it was hard for her to adjust to eating it—after all, for a woman raised on a farm, pigs and chickens, not horses or mules, were the animals one thought of as food. Now both were on the menu, with no alternative proteins (eggs were reserved for the weakest in the hospital and for sick children). "Our family has had horse meat once," Sarah writes delicately, "and it was not bad. We also had mule meat once; I did not like it as well as the horse meat, still many people find it better."[7]

As her private comments show, however, Sarah disliked both mule and horse, and Wang began to make risky trips outside the legation to search for other kinds of meat for her, Laura, and the other ladies. On one occasion, Sarah records, Wang told her he had found a cache of one hundred pigeons. He said he had discovered them in an aviary in an abandoned "Mandarin's house" and that he could only bring six, but if Edwin helped him they could bring all of them. Without a word, Edwin went out with Wang and sixty of the birds were brought back. Wang also "found" chickens, ducks, and other birds for the makeshift dinner table, often, as Sarah learned, by bartering goods from Sarah's larder for them. At any other time, Sarah would have asked for more details, but she accepted Wang's gifts without further comment.[8]

Wang's special attentions were reserved for Laura. She was neither sleeping nor eating enough. "Our boy Wang is always trying to prepare something delicate for 'Miss Laura,'" Sarah wrote in mid-July. He obtained for her a cup of milk a day (through barter)—"what is being taken from our stores for this milk I neither know nor care," Sarah noted firmly. Wang's co-conspirator was First Cook, who took the food items Wang procured, through accident or theft, and made something edible out of them. At supper time one evening, Sarah noticed that on the little table there was a plate "with two small rice birds on it." Wang told her the birds were for Laura. "I put rice on floor," he explained; "small bird come. I shut door and window; catch bird. Cook make 'em Miss Laura." At least Sarah could rejoice that this time, Wang was not breaking the eighth commandment.[9]

That he found time to do this as well as doing the Conger's laundry (not only washing and drying but ironing also), which he took on without complaint after a so-called "washing committee" made a "fearful" mess of the laundry; preparing rice-water for the wounded in the hospital; and carrying out enough other daily jobs to make a Figaro's head spin, was remarkable indeed. It was the tender feeling behind it, however, that most moved Sarah. "This," Sarah noted glowingly, "is only an illustration of his thoughtfulness for [Laura]." He was, she added, a *"jewel* of a First Boy . . . the very best of *the best"* (emphasis in original).[10]

As the ponies that were kept in the American compound began to be used in the feeding of the residents of the legation (the increasingly starving Chinese Christians in the Suwangfu received the offal and whatever else the foreigners would not eat), Edwin's own pony fell to the butcher's cleaver. Not many tears were shed over this black pony, which Sarah claimed "hated foreigners." Edwin's pony, per Sarah, had to be mounted by him while Chinese *mafu* stood at either side of its head, blocking its view—if it saw Edwin, it reacted with bites and kicks. Laura's little white pony was completely different. A photograph of Laura seated on the pony is a sort of portrait of the sympathy that can arise between beast and human—Laura's gentle smile matches the sweet turn of the pony's head.[11]

Quite early one morning, Sarah recalled, she heard the door into the hall open and close, then open again. It was Wang, checking to see if she was awake. "Butcher take Miss Laura's pony," he told Sarah. "I think more better he take mafoo pony." Sarah told him, "All right, Wang, you go and tell the butcher that we wish you to choose from our ponies." Wang evidently interpreted Sarah's order in his own way, because later he came back to confess what he had done. As Sarah wrote later,

> He said, "Miss Laura's pony save to the last. I told mafoo lock
> stables, and told guard let no one get ponies." I said, "Wang!

Our ponies are common property now. We are just taking care
of them."[12]

But her protests were too late. Wang had done what she could not bring
herself to do: he had found a reprieve for Laura's beloved pony for the
duration of the siege. As Sarah would later write to a niece, "These
servants are not all Christians; some are called 'heathen,' but in justice
and truth, I must say that I never saw the Christ-spirit manifested more
beautifully than these so-called heathen manifest it."[13]

"Laura, dear girl, was physically weak when we went into the siege,"
Sarah recalled. "At first when the severe attacks came upon us, she was
almost frantic, and she grew weaker and weaker"—hence Wang's own
often frantic efforts to provide delicacies for her. But after another bout
of "yells and howls" from the attackers, the hoarse cawing of their horns
and the boom and rattle of bullets and shells, Laura was so low Sarah
knew she had to take control of the situation. She knew that if Laura's
health and, even more, her faith in rescue were not restored, she might
have no chance of surviving the harder times that were surely coming.
Sitting with her daughter, Sarah made her memorize a mantra which, she
assured her, would help her conquer her fear. "When you are becoming
frightened," she told Laura, "turn your thoughts to some blessing and
give thanks to God with your whole heart," echoing a famous passage
from Mrs. Eddy's book *Science and Health,* with which Sarah would have
been most familiar:

> Let neither fear nor doubt overshadow your clear sense and calm
> trust, that the recognition of life harmonious—as Life eternally
> is—can destroy any painful sense of, or belief in, that which Life
> is not.[14]

Gradually, the prayer worked. After a week, Laura began to improve.
"She has been getting stronger, eating more, sleeping more," Sarah
noted on July 15. Dr. Martin noticed this, too. "As the siege went on,"
he recalled, "the daily fusillades appeared to act on her nerves like a
necessary tonic. She grew stronger from day to day," to such an extent
that she began to take charge of the food larder, so that portions were
doled out equitably, and was back to helping her father, becoming an
expert decipherer of coded messages. Laura was, Sarah wrote gratefully,

now "working all the time." It was the only way to remain sane in an atmosphere which, according to Cecile Payen, was filled with nights of flying bullets and screams of "*Sha!*," the plaintive distant wailing of traumatized infants in the chapel, and the names of more dead and wounded friends on the lists tacked to the pillars of the bell tower. Yet a bright spot was forcing its way through the gloom, in the form of a red envelope bearing a strange message in a code only Edwin knew, straight from the hands of Ronglu himself.[15]

✳ ✳ ✳ ✳ ✳

On July 9 (the second anniversary of Edwin presenting of his credentials to the Guangxu emperor), Cecile Payen had a talk with Cheshire, the interpreter for the American legation.

He had spent all he had, he told her, on feeding a Chinese man and his family who had taken shelter in the legation. Offering to continue the support if the man would venture into the Chinese City and bring back news, Herbert Squiers succeeded in getting him to retrieve some significant information. The man reported that "there were no Chinese troops in the native or outer city," Cecile heard, and that Ronglu's troops were in charge of the main gate into the Imperial City. However, many soldiers of General Dong's army (whom Cecile erroneously calls Boxers) were roaming about. Cixi and the emperor were still at the palace, and the Beitang was still under bombardment. The man also picked up copies of the *Peking Gazette*, which were quickly read over for details of what was going on. When he was given food and coal for his efforts, he cried for joy, recalled Cecile; but at hearing his report that there were no foreign troops yet in sight and that nobody could tell where they were, the residents of the legations felt like crying. Ronglu being in charge of the main gate was not surprising, as he was believed by most of the residents of the legations to be at the head of the assault against them—it was easy to imagine him watching the door in case any foreign military came into view. But the absence of imperial troops and the presence of the red and black-clad Gansu soldiers was not encouraging. The fact that the emperor and his aunt were still in residence only seemed to further shore up the story that Cixi, like Ronglu and Prince Duan, was one of the ringleaders of the uprising, and that the Boxers were very much in control of the city.[16]

Two days later, and after two nights of heavy fire from both attacked and attackers, with the heat speeding the decay of dead Chinese and horses and sending up clouds of flies to join the mosquitoes, Sarah wrote that she could "hear distant cannonading, and there are not so many soldiers and Boxers fighting us as usual," which she put down to another rumor, that Prince Qing and Prince Duan were having a military showdown of their own. Thus did Prince Qing continue to live on in the minds of the residents of the legations as their only friend, although a letter that arrived on July 14 seemed to offer a decidedly equivocal side to his character.

The letter, signed "From Prince Qing and others," was addressed to Sir Claude MacDonald. "For the last ten days [since July 4, the night of Captain Myers' sortie on the south wall]," it began, "the soldiers and militia have been fighting, and, to our great anxiety, there has been no communication between us." This sounded as if the soldiers, to the contrary of what people in the legation suspected, were actually fighting the Boxer militia, although the legation troops on the wall could attest that plenty of bullets were being aimed at them. Sarah remembered how the Chinese would "send up signal rockets, which give orders to fire and to cease firing [which] seem to be promptly obeyed," not the sort of organization of effort one would expect from impromptu attacks from an undisciplined militia. Through the *Peking Gazette* brought into the legation, they now knew that edicts had been issued from the throne calling for the protection and support of the Boxers—not the first or last contradiction of the uprising.[17]

"The reinforcements of foreign troops were ever so long ago stopped and turned back by the Boxers," the letter went on,

> . . . and if in accordance with the previous agreement we were to guard Your Excellencies out of the City, there are so many Boxers in the Tientsin Dagu road that we should be very apprehensive of misadventure. We now request Your Excellencies to first take your families and the various members of your staffs and leave your Legations in detachments. We would select trustworthy officers to give you close and strict protection and you should temporarily

reside in the Tsung Li Yamen, pending future arrangements for your return home . . .[18]

They were to do this without armed guards of any kind. The deadline for their answer was noon of the following day. If none was given, "even our affection will not enable us to help you."[19]

To Edwin and the other ministers, this was preposterous to the point of being laughable. What good was the protection offered by a government whose own troops had been firing on those they proposed now to guard? What were the chances any of the "detachments" of foreign ministers and staff would make it to the Zongli Yamen, or out of it, alive, given the circumstances of the past month? And what would happen to the Chinese Christians and the marines they would have to leave behind? Dr. Coltman wrote that the message "is thought by everyone to be a rank fraud. It is supposed to come not from Prince Ching, but from the leader of the Kansu troops," whose sole object, he believed, was "to lure some of the foreigners outside the legation and then to shoot them."[20]

Sir Claude sent a short reply, stating that if the marines were shooting at Chinese troops it was because they were shot at first, and that if the government really desired to negotiate it should send a responsible official bearing a white flag to the British legation. There was no response, and the firing continued.

The funerals seemed to come daily, sometimes for more than one person at a time. On July 16, while they waited for a response from the Zongli Yamen, Edwin, Sarah, several missionaries, and other Americans attended a service for a young American marine. Because there was no wood to spare for coffins, the body was wrapped in an American flag. This was followed by another funeral, this time for Captain Ben Strouts, one of the best leaders in the international forces, who had been in the Suwangfu with George Morrison and Colonel Shiba when all three came under sniper fire. With him in the same grave was buried a British student interpreter attached to Customs, Warren, whose death pained everyone, not least Polly Condit Smith. He had been carried through the compound to the hospital the night before, "his face almost entirely shot off," Polly wrote. "I knew him quite well—had danced with him often; he was a charming fellow." With a grim appositeness, during the funeral "two shells went whizzing over our heads," Sarah wrote, "and burst just beyond us."[21]

Edwin was called away before the service was over. A messenger had arrived with a red envelope, said to have come from Ronglu's headquarters. In it was, among other things, a cryptic message in a U.S. State Department code: "Communicate tidings bearer." As in their records of Captain Myers' speech on the night of July 3, the accounts of Sarah and Dr. Coltman differ about this message. Coltman claimed there was an earlier telegram, in the special code, which "had evidently been tampered with in some way by the Chinese," making it impossible to read. Coltman says Edwin sent the telegram back, asking for the entire message as it had been received. On July 17, the original messenger was back with the document Edwin had requested, this time with another telegram from Wu Tingfang, Chinese minister to Washington, and the three-word telegram from Secretary of State John Hay.[22]

Singapore-born Wu was a cosmopolitan who had studied law in England. Always desirous of promoting understanding of China in the West, he lectured widely and wrote a book about his experiences as an Asian diplomat in America. (He was also reported to have devised a plan to rescue Edwin from the British legation and bring him safely to the Dagu Forts, "a proposition . . . so startling it has been kept a profound secret by the State Department"—the fact it was publicized in the press would tend to discount it as either startling or profound.) Wu's missive, the first to reach any minister in the British legation since the siege began, breathed a warm friendliness that felt ironic in Beijing's lurid atmosphere of distrust and mystery, but entirely authentic to his personality: "The United States cheerfully aids China, but it is thinking of Minister Conger. The Honorable Secretary of State inquires after him by cablegram which I beg to be transmitted to him and get his reply" (dated July 15).[23]

Secretary Hay's three jabbing words, however, were the happy signal from the outside world, authenticated by the code in which they were transmitted, which Edwin and everyone else had been longing to hear. In his response, sent back through the same messenger, Edwin put everyone's feeling as well as his own in two sentences: "For one month we have been besieged in British Legation under continued shot and shell from Chinese troops. Quick relief only can prevent general massacre."[24]

Sarah's joy at this sliver of communication from beyond the legations' battered walls was uncontainable. "We are almost paralyzed," she wrote. "We cannot give expression to our pent-up flood of delight . . . Only think, the return message will reach Washington within six days," at which point, it was assumed, even more troops would be sent to march on Beijing. Edwin went to the bell tower, where to those who gathered he explained what had just occurred and answered what questions he could. Both Americans and British came to hear the news. As one Englishman later said to Mary Gamewell, "No other Minister but an American would take the trouble to explain matters to his nation's subjects [*sic*]"— begging the question: Did Sir Claude MacDonald rely a little too often on tacking up bulletins and not enough on personal assurances?[25]

It would have horrified the residents of the legations had they known that in most of the rest of the world, their fate was believed already sealed. While Minister Wu was composing his telegram in Washington, it was assumed from London to Berlin and Tokyo to San Francisco that all the foreigners in the legation were dead. Indeed, certain journalists claimed to know such details as those contained in the especially horrible story in which to save the women and children from certain defilement at the hands of the Boxers, the men had shot them all first. Papers widely distant from one another in geography and as divergent in quality all began publishing obituaries of Edwin, Sarah, Laura, and their guests, along with everyone else known to have been in the Legation Quarter or in missions in Beijing. The *Davenport Republican*, in the Congers' home state of Iowa, was reticent about stating that they were in fact dead, but gave a summary of Edwin's career, dated July 22, which reads a lot like an obituary. A week later, the *Anaconda Standard* in Montana was more blunt: "About two weeks ago, there came from China a message which sent a thrill of horror through all of Christendom. It was to the effect that the Boxer outbreak, marked from the first by the brutal murder of Europeans and Christianized natives, had culminated in the massacre of every foreigner in Pekin," followed by a eulogy of Edwin in everything but name.[26]

The *San Francisco Call*, on July 17, made no pretense at all of hoping for better news: photographs of Edwin, Sarah, Laura, Mary Pierce, and the Woodwards surmounted the words "Died at Peking," with two sword-wielding Boxers drawn on either side like supporters in a ghastly coat of arms. Beside this was a sidebar with the headline "Lost Their Lives In The Massacre," under which were listed all the ministers, their staff and guests known to have been at the foreign legations before June 20.[27]

Far more hopeful, if also desperate, was the activity reported in the *Syracuse Post-Standard* on July 16: "New Hope For The Congers," blared the headline, "Million Christian Scientists Expect to Save Them."

> Through the unaided power of united thoughts, concentrated by nearly 1,000,000 people on a single purpose, representative Christian Scientists of Chicago say they are attempting to influence events and shape destinies in faraway China that the life of a sister in the Scientist faith—Mrs. Edwin H. Conger, wife of the United States Minister in Peking—as well as the lives of the whole Conger family and all Christians in the besieged legations may be spared in the great crisis now imperiling that part of the Asiatic world.[28]

Among Christian Scientists, at least, there seems to have been common knowledge of Sarah's sympathies for the Chinese:

> Holding firmly to the belief that "Love rules all things," the chain of thought of the Christian Science devotee starts with the belief or knowledge that Mrs. Conger entertains for the Chinese people—her supposed deadly enemies—a feeling in which is predominant the true Christian code of sincere and abounding charity and love.[29]

Love and charity aside, at this same time, in the mid-July chaos of false and attempted truces, counter-proposals, hopes of rescue, barrages of bullets, and ominous silences, Sarah was said to have become embroiled in a small battle of her own which would, unfortunately, gain as much publicity after the siege as any of the real warfare that threatened everyone's lives. As it would be easy to blame a woman, the empress dowager, for everything involved with the Boxer Uprising, it would be all too easy for the American press to blame Sarah for a tempest in a teapot that, it was said, not only traduced the service of a brave American officer but cast a shadow over her bright ideal of sisterhood among the besieged residents of the legations.

✳ ✳ ✳ ✳ ✳

"People who in times of peace pass for very nice, sociable individuals, with no particularly mean tendencies," wrote Robert Coltman, "when subjected to deprivation in the food-supply, and their nerves become shattered with the sound of whistling bullets, the shrieking of flying shells, or the dull thud followed by the crashing and grinding of solid shot, show up in their true bedrock character, and are meanness to the core."[30]

During the Boxer Uprising, there were many examples of heroism beyond the call of duty, among men and women both. But there were also examples of frustration, confusion, disagreement, and antagonism. Not everyone was meanness to the core, but there were many real emotions under the slick veneer of late-Victorian manners; and by the middle of July, even the thickest coat of lacquer was wearing thin.

How and when conflict arose between Sarah and Harriet Squiers is not known. Harriet left no account of her experiences during the siege, and Sarah barely mentions Harriet in her own published and unpublished writings. Nor is it clear what it was that would have prompted Edwin to rush to General Adna Chaffee the minute he arrived with the relieving forces on August 14, demanding that charges of cowardice be brought against Captain Newt Hall. Though there are accounts that state he had disputes with both Edwin and Herbert Squiers, and that his men were often drunk, others found Hall an affable man and a resourceful officer. Yet something occurred to spark antipathy between him and Edwin, and between Harriet and Sarah, embarrassingly in the middle of what all understood to be the fight of their lives.

After the July 3 sortie on the south wall, Captain Myers was laid up in the hospital with a spear wound, followed by typhoid fever, and Captain Hall assumed his command. Hall's report of this period, filed in September 1900 in tandem with Captain Myers' report, covers the weeks of July 2 to 21. On July 15, when the letter arrived from "Prince Qing and others," and a few days before receipt of Minister Wu's and Secretary Hay's telegrams from Ronglu, Captain Hall was instructed by Herbert Squiers that the barricade on the south wall was not "far enough along," as Hall stated in his post-uprising report, and began to supervise the building of another one closer to the Chinese barricade. Squiers stayed on the wall until he was sure his directions were being followed. Later that evening, Captain Hall took Private Dan Daly (later awarded two Congressional Medals of Honor) up to the wall to scope out whether snipers were still active from the Chinese side, and if not, to start sending the coolies up with sandbags to fortify the position. When neither the coolies nor the two privates detailed to bring them arrived, Hall reluctantly left the bastion in the charge of Daly to go look for them. On the way he met the secretary of the Belgian legation, who told him there had been a mix-up with the interpreter and he would interpret instead. Captain Hall gathered up the privates and coolies and headed for the bastion, where the sandbagging commenced.[31]

Aside from this irregularity, admitted by Hall and reviewed and accepted by Captain Myers in his report, there does not seem to be any evidence of Hall doing anything that crossed the line beyond which court-martial was called for. George Morrison recorded in his diary on July 10 that Hall's men had "no confidence in his judgment," that he allowed them to get "blind drunk" and insult their officer. Edwin mentions none of this in the charges he later brought against Hall, which were: that he had asked Hall to hold the south wall and was refused; that when asked to perform "certain other military duty," the captain had again refused to obey; and that when Edwin asked two marines to carry out what sounds like a reconnaissance mission, Captain Hall would not let them do it.[32]

Nothing about this is addressed in Captain Myers' official report, nor in Hall's. "[Hall] made no mention of friction with Minister Conger in his report on the defense of the legations," wrote a reporter for the *New York Times* on May 25, 1901. In fact, Hall writes, "The command is very much indebted to Mr. E. H. Conger . . . for his many kindnesses, placing his house at our disposal for shelter, and for doing everything in his power for their health and comfort." We would expect to find at least a mention of some kind of contretemps in Dr. Coltman's published diaries, in which he pulled no punches where Edwin was concerned. Sarah later refers to the Coltmans as people Edwin would rather avoid, so the bad blood from summer 1900 outlived the siege which had brought it to the boil. But Coltman says nothing about Edwin tussling with Captain Hall. There were certainly incidents of military men chafing under the orders of civilians; though Herbert Squiers had left the US Cavalry with the rank of lieutenant and had taught military science in St. John's College (now Fordham University), career soldiers were not thrilled to take the orders he liberally dispensed to them. Hall is said to have been "at odds" with both Squiers and Edwin, who both asked him to move his barricade nearer that of the Chinese, and both were refused.[33]

The real bombshell was a letter sent in January 1901 from "a well-known Naval Commander, serving in the Asiatic Squadron" to the *New York Times*, and the headline says it all: "Women Quarreled and a Man Suffered." According to this anonymous officer, what really caused the rift between Captain Hall and Edwin was a "petticoat feud" between Harriet Squiers and Sarah, which took on an especially ridiculous character as it occurred "at a time when the chances of the Christian refugees in the British compound appeared to be slimmest."[34] As the officer tells the story, it began when a detachment of US Marines obtained a number of tinned goods (from a raid on a foreign-owned shop?) and brought the spoils back to the legation. Sarah, as wife of the head of the American contingent and the person responsible for their food stores, asked Harriet Squiers to set aside some of the tinned food for Captain Hall and his men. Harriet refused, for reasons unexplained, and "thereafter she and Mrs. Conger did not speak."[35] Per this account, the marines sided with Sarah, and to show their gratitude they stood at attention and presented arms every time she passed. Harriet seems to have experimented to see what would happen if she walked past the marines and was chagrined when they showed her "indifference." For all her elegance, Harriet Squiers was no fainting violet. Cecile Payen describes an occasion when Harriet, furious at seeing a Chinese man striking his wife, had the husband tied up and displayed at the bell tower, around his neck a sign inscribed with the Chinese characters for "wife beater." In a similar show of righteous temper, Harriet was said to have confronted Captain Hall and informed him that his men were "loafers and blackguards" for not showing her proper respect (or, rather, the same respect they showed Sarah), and that they must begin doing it. Captain Hall explained that his men were dead-tired and not always able to rise to salute, but that in the future she would receive a salute, too. But when she did, the writer claimed, Hall "incurred the wrath of Mrs. Conger." This was the real reason, concluded the officer, behind why Captain Hall was accused of cowardice by the outraged Edwin.[36]

This letter and the reportage that followed set off a firestorm of indignation. Sarah and Harriet were treated to varying degrees of what would today be seen as egregious sexist criticism in the pages of the *New York Times*. It was implied that any quarrel between women was perforce a petty one and a needless distraction to the important affairs of men (agreeing with the male Chinese attitude: the character for "quarrel" is made up of two of the characters for "woman" placed side by side.) The scandal only died down when Hall was found innocent of the charges, and when the acting secretary of the navy, F. W. Hackett, made it plain in the press that there had been no such quarrel between the women. He emphasized that Edwin's charges against Captain Hall were unconnected to any such event.

The whole scenario begs many questions. Did Edwin, as accused by the unnamed naval officer, trump up the charges against Hall because of his salute to Harriet Squiers? Was Hall a troublemaker whose real machinations are not represented in his or Captain Myers' official reports of the siege? Would Sarah have stooped to such a row with Harriet? There is no evidence to clarify either way. But it is obvious that two disparate groups of people were thrown together in Dr. Poole's bungalow on June 20: the middle-class Congers and Woodwards on one side and the upper-class Squierses, joined by Polly Condit Smith on the other, with the artistic and empathetic Cecile Payen between the two camps.

Certainly in her published writings and comments Polly gives plenty of evidence that she respected neither Sarah nor Edwin. After the siege, when she was safely back home in the United States, Polly regaled newsmen with the story of how Sarah had made her laugh when she told her she feared Edwin more than the Boxers, since he was "in such an overwrought condition she was afraid he might shoot her dead on some false alarm"—a statement it is unlike Sarah to have made. Polly also made hay out of an encounter with Sarah in the last days of the siege, in which, during an especially heavy nighttime barrage from the Chinese, Sarah found Polly lying on her mattress in a fashionable nightgown. In a crisis when most people had not changed their clothes in weeks, nor had a bath in the same time, somehow Polly managed to do both, and her nonchalance in the face of Sarah's fright was ironically a reverse of the incident in which Polly claimed Sarah told her the Boxers' bullets were not real. When Sarah, according to Polly, asked her with a "tragic" manner whether she wanted to be found by the marauding Chinese in such a garment, Polly replied impertinently: "I told her I was going to stay in my bed unless something terrible happened, when I should don my dressing-gown and, with a pink bow of ribbon at my throat, await my massacre." As this is the last time she mentions Sarah in her published memoirs, it was probably the last time they had anything to do with one another.[37]

These comments and others from Polly's pen were clearly not offered in a spirit of lighthearted jest. Given her close connection with Harriet, and the shared exclusivity of their society backgrounds, it is likely that Harriet entertained many of the same prejudices toward the Congers that Polly did. Sarah never mentions Polly, and rarely the Squiers couple, which may mean something or nothing, but does hint that she had deliberately left them out of her otherwise detailed account of the siege. Their absence is all the more striking in that the Congers and Squierses shared the same roof that entire time (though Sarah's frequent trips back to the American legation, sometimes just to sit there, may mean something—or nothing).

If this incident with Harriet and Sarah has to be left unresolved, it provides a rare glimpse behind the high screen of bravery and self-sacrifice which both women, and most of the other foreigners with them, put up around their siege experiences. If Sarah's affableness and Harriet's consciousness of her dignity could be compromised to this degree, what was it like for those less self-controlled? The differences between these groups sharing a single roof could not have been more profound had one set of people come from another culture entirely— say, had a Chinese family come to live with the foreigners. "We are all one now," Sarah had written, more in hope than fact, but this upheaval shows that some divides could not be bridged. Significantly, Sarah would have considerably less difficulty entering the private circles of Chinese princesses than she would have done the drawing rooms of Polly Condit Smith's New York.[38]

* * * * *

Starting on July 18 and for a few days after, a "truce" of sorts, broken by occasional sniper fire, settled over the legation. In the middle of this strange silence came more reason for the besieged to hope for rescue.

The Japanese minister, Baron Nishi, had spirited two messengers out of the legation to bring back whatever news they could from Tianjin. They now returned with the information that the Dagu Forts had fallen to the allied forces on July 14, and most importantly, that foreign troops were to start for Beijing on July 20, pending the arrival of additional men. This was sensational and it was also bittersweet to digest, because everyone had assumed Seymour was already on his way (their hopes of a July 4 arrival having already been dashed). What they did not know was that the "news" of their massacre, trumpeted by the world's press without proof, had had the effect not of hastening the rescue but of delaying it.

That was the biggest problem of the many faced that summer in northern China: without a functioning telegraph, nobody had any information. The residents of the legations did not know what was happening in Tianjin or in the palace; the empress dowager did not know what was happening in the legations or in Tianjin; and the would-be rescuer, Admiral Seymour, did not know what was happening in the legation, the palace, or in the less than a hundred miles of ground between Tianjin and Beijing. The residents of the legations, having had one ray of hope that Seymour was on his way, clung to it long after there was any good reason to do so, while Cixi and the conservatives who controlled her could only assume that the troops rumored to be coming to rescue the residents of the legations also intended to occupy and partition China, as foreigners had shown every indication of wishing to do for the past fifty years. And as if he had had a page of Chinese characters put in front of him to decode, Seymour completely misread the spare, dusty Plain of Zhili. Some of his blunders were unavoidable, but others were the direct result of poor planning and the sort of nineteenth-century thinking that was to die its final death in World War I. Ultimately, the only thing everyone had in common was that they did not know anything and had to guess everything.

The trouble began with trains. On June 10, Seymour took five of them, loaded with 2,100 men and equipment to repair the rails reported to have been damaged by the Boxers. He and the other officers also took their dress uniforms. It is easy to picture the scenario they had in mind: a few hours on the train to Beijing, maybe some skirmishing with the amateur militia the Boxers were believed to be, rescue of the residents of the legations, and a celebration warranting gold buttons and feathers. It did not quite turn out that way. On June 11 and 12, one of the trains had to be sent back from Langfan, where the convoy had stopped for more repair supplies only to encounter Boxer resistance and torn up tracks; it had to return. Seymour decided to retreat to Yangcun, one of the towns further east of Beijing, where his men ran into stiff opposition from both Boxers and imperial troops. Shedding much of their equipment, including the dress uniforms, the men towed their remaining equipment and the wounded along the Beihe River toward Tianjin. In so doing, they stumbled on the Xiku Arsenal, a fortress containing tons of matériel and food stores that was so lightly guarded it was easy to seize. They then hunkered down for their own rescue, which arrived on June 26 in the form of a force of Russian Cossacks.

While all this was going on, the Dagu Forts at the mouth of the Beihe River, the port for Tianjin and Beijing, were taken by allied naval forces navigating outmoded but still-effective ships on June 17 and 18. This led to the siege of Tianjin itself, where a smaller but no less deadly version of the Beijing siege was occurring between Boxers and the foreign and Chinese Christian communities. Tianjin was captured by the allies on July 14, but nothing concerning the push on to Beijing could be organized, or even decided on, until the first week of August. Under the command of General Arthur Gaselee, who chosen by the generals of the coalition, the assembled troops, amounting to some 20,000 men from eight countries, set forth for Beijing on August 4. A view from where the boots met the dust is given by English war journalist George Lynch. Not as well-known during or after his lifetime as was George E. Morrison, and enjoying none of Morrison's glamour, Lynch nonetheless was far more serious, and offered a perspective on the relief march, the freeing of the residents of the legations, and the treatment of Beijing and its citizens afterward that few other correspondents shared—only Sarah would come close to Lynch's openness to the Chinese point of view and his admiration for the empress dowager.

Lynch reached Tongku the day after the relief forces had left, though he noted they were not far outside the suburbs of the city. He caught a train full of "a miscellaneous collection of passengers" which included American soldiers, British sailors, a few reporters like himself, and "some trucks with goats and sheep." They were sent off in a truly international style by a Russian military band.[39]

He was struck, like Sarah and Alicia Little before, by the sheer numbers of graves along the route to Tianjin, which seemed to "pimple" the landscape like the anthills Lynch had seen in South Africa. These were just part of the desolation now: "All the houses on the way lay in ruins," Lynch recalled. There were no signs anywhere of human habitation, just "a palpable breath of blasting desolation that seemed to have passed over the land." He rode through towns where "a sickening, heavy stench hung in the morning air," and carrion dogs were "busy on mysterious heaps of something from which they slunk away at our approach."[40]

Because the Japanese formed the majority of the forces, and by virtue of Chancellor Sugiyama's murder were to be given precedence in punishing the Boxers (the German reinforcements not having arrived yet to do battle in Ketteler's name), Lynch shrewdly attached himself to them. He admired their organizational genius, as did those in the British legation who watched Colonel Shiba and his troops defending the Suwangfu. "It is simply wonderful how quickly they move," Lynch reported. "Nothing can be prettier than to watch them at work . . . Cheery, bright, and intelligent, they are all keenly patriotic from general down to private," an impression shared by the nurses at the siege hospital in the legation, who rated their Japanese patients highest in cheerfulness, gratitude, and courage under stress and pain. (The French and Italians occupied the opposite end of the spectrum.)[41]

Plodding on horseback along the wretched road snaking through the sorghum fields, the plants grown in the hot August sun as high as the tallest Japanese, Lynch saw poetry even in bloodshed. "A few shots were exchanged between the Japs [*sic*] and the enemy," he observed, "and then the Bengal Lancers got a chance, that they gallantly availed themselves of, by sweeping through the high *kowliang*, scrunching and crashing, horses plunging, the tall green-plumed stalks waving and bending, the glitter of their leaves mingling with the bright gleam of the lances, and leaving a track behind like that of a whirlwind, from which they emerge with bloody blades and four captured standards." He had heard that the river was filled with the bodies of Chinese women who had drowned themselves rather than fall into the hands of the foreigner invaders, and would see for himself, when the troops reached the lovely walled city of Tongzhou, that this was no mere rumor. Both Chinese and foreign looters were stripping shops and houses, while others were indulging in another kind of despoiling—Lynch heard shouting Russian soldiers and the screams of Chinese women, and drew the obvious conclusion. He then stumbled on the tragic results of these assaults. At the foot of a cliff below the houses where the rapes were going on, Lynch found two girls, broken and dying in the soggy midday heat. "From their richly embroidered silken tunics and trousers," he recalled, "their elaborate coiffure and their compressed feet, they were evidently ladies." Though prostitutes were as likely to wear this garb as more virtuous women, they would have been no more amenable to the attacks as their married or virginal sisters. Lynch gave the young women some of his water but could do nothing for them except curse the men who had provoked them to leap from the cliff, taking cold comfort in the fact that, contrary to foreign paranoia, Chinese men wanted nothing to do with Western women, their big feet, long noses, and fleshy frames symbolizing all that the Asian male found least enticing. (There are no reports of any rapes of foreign women by Chinese men before, during, or after the Boxer Uprising, though Boxers did readily kill them, especially if they were missionaries.)[42]

Lynch found some peace and quiet in the home of a scholar, who made tea for him and allowed him to use his own paper, ink, and brush to create a sign that he then pasted to the house's front gate, "intimating that this house was the property and Tung-Chou office of the *Daily Express* and *The Sphere*, and that there was no admittance except on business." Yet on returning from an errand a few hours later, Lynch found the quiet house ransacked, its camphorwood furniture and scroll paintings broken and torn, and the scholar sitting in the yard with a sword cut to the arm, "his wife beside him trying to staunch the flow of blood." Again, Lynch suspected the Russians.[43]

The march continued along the uneven stone-paved road, under a blazing sun that even had the Indian troops fainting along the way; and then the Japanese stopped within three miles of Beijing's eastern city gate, the Qihuamen, to rest for the night. As darkness descended, Lynch recalled, "a drizzling rain began to fall, and one of the dogs kept howling dismally" outside the broken temple compound where Lynch had laid himself down to try to sleep. When he did drop off it was not for long. In the middle of the night he was jerked awake by gunfire that seemed to come from every side of the building. The turbulence settled eventually, and the troops and Lynch packed up to move on. They stopped near a ruined house, looted of all its belongings, where Lynch tried resting again, but this sleep was as brief as the first. Back in the saddle, Lynch "saw General Fukushima pass close beside me, with an angry expression on his face, gesticulating to a couple of officers who rode beside him." From another officer, Lynch heard that the firing that night had been the Russians attacking the city wall before the agreed-upon time; their general had sent to Fukushima for reinforcements and been refused, as the Americans and British were to assist, per their agreement, in any such endeavor. Taking the Russian attitude of *nichevo* ("don't worry") a bit too far, the Russians merely shrugged and asked, "Why need we trouble about them if we can do without them?"—a nonchalance that would serve them ill when they touched off and lost the Russo-Japanese War in five years' time.[44]

The Japanese continued their march, "until, rounding a slight bend of the road, the great wall of Pekin and the massive gatehouse came into view." There was no opposition. They entered a street, after crossing the moat bridge and passing under the gate, and their footsteps echoed on the paving stones: "the only thing that broke the stillness was the sound of a racking cough, as if proceeding from some very old man or woman in one of the shuttered houses, and probably too decrepit to get away."[45]

As they drew nearer to the last gatehouse, suddenly "a hellish fire at short range" forced Lynch and several soldiers, including General Fukushima, into what sounds like a sort of public latrine in a narrow, airless *hutong*, where amid "all the dirt and refuse of the neighbourhood" they held their breath as the bullets "were pattering like hail on the wall outside." And there they waited for the next six hours, while the Japanese gunners tried to blow the gate down and the Chinese above fired down on them without cease.[46]

Toward evening, General Fukushima's plan to blow up the city gate was ready to be carried out, but there was some delay; again Lynch's sleep was shattered by two huge explosions which shook his building. He rushed into the moonlit street. While "gusts of bullets stormily swept [into the faces of the Japanese]," they made a final lunge for the gate, which stood unbarred now, its great doors half blown off their hinges. "The deep circular archway of the gateway overhead made an ebony frame for the ivory moonlight picture within," Lynch recalled. As the Japanese struggled in the shifting shadows in hand-to-hand combat with the Chinese, Lynch glimpsed terrible scenes, such as a Japanese soldier bayoneting a Chinese over and over on the ground, where the victim "squirmed and wriggled like a worm" in the gloom. He stumbled over dead and dying men, then was up above the city on the wall, where more dead men lay sprawled. He clambered northwards and reached Sarah's beloved observatory, which he was astonished to find undamaged. He looked out over the city. The devastation was visible even in the uncertain light of the moon. But through a "labyrinth of ruins" between the Hatamen Gate and the British legation, Lynch and the Japanese finally reached the barricades of the residents of the legations. It was two o'clock on the morning of August 14, and the siege was finally broken.[47]

✳   ✳   ✳   ✳   ✳

From the last few weeks of July until the first two weeks of August—the period of muggy, oppressive heat aptly dubbed by the Chinese "give-up-weather"—life in the besieged legation grew harder, seedier, and more desperate. It was even worse for the Chinese Christians cowering in the Suwangfu. Their presence made the palace and its once-lavish gardens a target for gunfire and arson, reducing the fairytale setting—the ponds and pagodas, bridges and ornamental rockeries, moon gates and spirit screens—to a cratered moonscape of shattered tile, torn branches, and ugly ditches. And the people were starving, as Edwin had feared would be the case.

For the first part of the siege, while the ponies lasted, the Chinese Christians were given the offal left over from butchering. They now made do with the occasional dog, cat, or crow shot for them, along with a sort of bread. "It is made in little cakes of millet, black-bean flour, and earth, mixed with the leaves of elm trees," Cecile Payen wrote, having seen some of the "cakes." "The sight of this, and the thought that we may soon come to it, fairly made me sick." It must have made plenty of the Chinese sick as well—some of them, like the wife and family of Manchu mandarin Ching-chang, former minister to France, were used to much the same delicacies as any of the upper-class foreigners in the legation.[48]

More torture than godsend for the residents of the legations were the gifts of fruit, vegetables, and flour that arrived from Cixi and the emperor on July 28. Nobody could feel quite right about accepting such gifts from a woman who was said to be intent on killing everybody in the legation. "We are using all but the flour," Sarah wrote, her lines tinged with regret, adding that as there were questions about whether the flour was poisoned or not, "we are not going to use it until it is badly needed." But the watermelons, cooled in one of the wells, were much enjoyed, and the ice they came with was useful for the wounded and sick in the hospital. The pragmatists (which included Sarah) refused to look the gift horse in the mouth.[49]

Good news arrived via another paid messenger on July 27, which Sarah noted in her diary. "He reports the progress of our coming troops," she wrote, "says that they are fighting their way through a strong force of Chinese." This same day, Sarah went through the ruins of the Hanlin Library with Captain Poole, brother of the doctor who had given up his bungalow to the Congers and Squierses. For Sarah, who had helped put the fires out, this was a mournful visit. "The Chinese themselves burned this wonderful college," she noted, but added that "the destruction of these treasures is not only a calamity to China, but to the whole world"—a world which, she seems to be saying, cannot be absolved of some shared responsibility in the library's destruction. "It made me heartsick," she wrote.[50]

The next day brought even better news. A slender teenaged boy name Liu Wuyuan, aged as young as fourteen (according to one account) but probably closer to sixteen, had volunteered to be sent out of the legation on July 4, posing as a beggar, with a note for the allied command in Tianjin hidden at the bottom of his begging bowl. Now he returned, having had enough adventure along the way to last the rest of his life. The boy spent his first night hiding in the ruins of the Qianmen Gate, then reached as far as Tongzhou before being captured by villagers and made to work on a farm for over a week. Escaping, he had made his way to Tianjin on July 18 and through means of a foreigner who spoke Chinese, had got his note to the British consul, W. R. Carles. The consul gave him a letter to take back, and he turned right around for Beijing. On his return he had slept again in the Qianmen Gate before slipping back through the Water Gate. In a sad commentary on the attitude some foreigners took toward the Chinese, he was relieved of the only money he had, a dollar, by foreign soldiers in Tianjin, who told him they feared he would lose it if they did not keep it safe for him.[51]

Carles' letter was not very clear on details and in fact angered many of the men with its chatty airiness—it was certainly not the weighty communication warranted by the bravery of the boy who had traveled so far to fetch it. But it did furnish the news that Tianjin was being held and that the troops were preparing to march on Beijing any day. Robert Coltman may have thought Edwin a fool, but having marched with Sherman to Atlanta during the Civil War, Edwin knew what the allied forces were up against. "Many say to me, 'Mr. Conger is a strong support to us all,'" Sarah noted. "His judgment we can trust, and his good cheer has power in it." As he pointed out to those frustrated by the delay, there were special difficulties involved. "He often says," Sarah added, "that we must not be impatient for troops to arrive, as there is much to be done to move a large army in a strange land fortified by the enemy." That the enemy was not trying very hard to vanquish the invaders was beside the point; even the men who, like the US Marines, were accustomed to the climate and terrain of the Philippines would have had no way of preparing for the Plain of Zhili or the squads of militia secreted away in the sorghum fields.[52]

Good news came at a premium, because the funerals were now never-ending. Noncombatant men, women, and children were added to the military dead, but the latter were more often the ones buried in an increasingly crowded corner of the Russian legation compound.

Sarah was present at one burial which came a few days after she had attended her first Russian Orthodox church service. At the service, she had been immediately struck by the fact that everyone stood throughout the ritual. There were no special pews demarcating social rank, no place to sit and daydream. Those who came for this service did so because they were prepared to suffer a little, perhaps more than a little, for their faith. Sarah was fascinated also by the absence of musical instruments— the thundering organ that was the staple of hymn-singing Protestant churches of her experience was replaced by a choir's massed voices raised in the plaintive prayer of Orthodox sacred music. "Each listened, looked strictly to the leader, and caught the harmonious key-note, and all sang together in sweet harmony," Sarah wrote.[53]

The funeral Sarah attended afterward was for one of the American marines. He had died defending the hellish south wall, and his burial, like all the others, was held at midnight for reasons of safety, with few lights to attract the attention of snipers. As Sarah stood beside Edwin in the darkness, the dead marine lying nearby, "a Russian marine was passing on his way to his rest." As Sarah wrote,

> He halted, then stepped to the open grave, and jumped into it. With care, he removed every stone, and softened this marine's last resting place by pulverizing the soil. Those about him protested, as he needed sleep. But he said feelingly, "My brother on the wall," and continued his work of tenderness. He helped lower his comrade into the grave, then smoothed the flag winding sheet, tucking it in gently at head and feet, while he continued to repeat, "My brother on the wall."

"These brothers on the wall," Sarah noted, "spoke no common language of the tongue, but they spoke the common language of the heart."[54]

It helped to keep busy, and luckily there was no lack of work for anyone. Not only was Sarah devoting hours each day to the making of sandbags, pajamas and clothing, sheets and bandages, she was also visiting the hospital (she, Wang, and First Cook boiled up gallons of rice-water every day to help the dysentery cases filling the ward), and foraging among the ruins of the American legation. Filling sandbags was work which, a month earlier, would have seemed incredible. She had evidently made a friend of the Russian priest at that first Orthodox service, because she was soon seen laboring with him in the sandpits. "If the demand for bags was not urgent," wrote Mary Gamewell's biographer, Ethel D. Hubbard, "the women would leave their sewing and resort to the ditches." Sarah was often spotted there, standing "in a deep, dusty hole, holding bags open while a long-robed priest of the Greek church filled them" using "a porcelain kettle." To complete the international force, "a little Chinese boy tied the strings [of the bags], and the English chaplain bore away the finished products."[55]

It was on one of these occasions that we have, through Sarah's own admission, one of the few instances of her losing her temper at anyone—in this case a Chinese man who was on the staff of the American legation.

> The other day I said to a scholarly Chinese, "Will you help to fill these sandbags?" He replied, "I am no coolie." Then I in turn said, "I am no coolie either, but we must all work here and now. I will hold the bag and you come and shovel the sand." I took the bag and a Russian-Greek priest stepped forward and filled it. He spoke no English and I no Russian, but we both understood the language of the situation.[56]

The Chinese scholar, still refusing to stoop to assist, was taken aside by Edwin, who seems to have spoken to him rather more sternly than Sarah did, telling the man that if he did not work, he could not expect to be fed. Having lost face, the man hid away for three days, but at last appeared and took up a shovel, his stomach having conquered his pride. Sarah loved many things in traditional Chinese culture, but "face" was not one of them.

✳ ✳ ✳ ✳ ✳

The nights from August 12 to 14 were among the heaviest of the entire siege. Li Pengheng, former governor of the Boxer province of Shandong, had arrived in Beijing on July 26. Said to be a favorite of the empress dowager's, Li had a loathing of foreigners and of those friendly toward them that Cixi certainly cannot be said to have shared, but her counsel mattered to no one now. Once Li got to the palace, he took charge, playing a role in the executions of two liberal ministers who had denounced the Boxers and urged Cixi to protect the foreigners. "[Li's advent] was, effectively, a reign of terror," writes one historian. Even Prince Qing dared not argue.[57]

Legation troops patrolling the wall now began to see banners belonging to troops whose generals' names were new—a sign, did they but know it, that the foreign-hating governor of Shansi, Yuxian, had also joined the fray, along with his troops, to help Li Pengheng blast the foreigners out of their fortifications. Had such an onslaught been in place since the siege began on June 20, the residents of the legations could not have lasted the fifty-five days that they did.[58]

Amid all the ear-shattering shot and shell, Sarah tells us that Edwin had a little cat, of which he was especially fond. It had been coming to the American legation well before the Boxer trouble began. Cats and dogs were being regularly shot for food for the Chinese Christians, and in any case there was no extra food to spare for pets. Edwin, however, seems to have been keeping the cat alive, though whether this could have been done in the precincts of the British legation is unlikely (there was just enough food for the humans there). Was it possible, then, that he made arrangements for the cat to stay at the American compound? He visited the compound regularly and there were always marines at the site resting between shifts, one or two of whom may have agreed to look after the animal. When the shelling was focused on the Suwangfu and the northern part of the British compound, the American section would have actually been safer than other parts of the diplomatic quarter. Perhaps, then, when Edwin was found in the garden of the American legation by the British relief troops, he was looking for the cat—an ironic scenario given the violence and bloodshed in that vicinity over the past weeks.[59]

Sir Claude MacDonald had sent General Gaselee and United States General Adna Chaffee a note and map showing how to make their way into the legation compound via the Water Gate, which ran under the Tartar wall immediately to the east of the American legation. The route was picked out for the generals, just in case they misunderstood the directions, by the planting of three flags atop the wall—British, Russian, and American. At first this precaution nearly ruined the plan, as the wary allied brass thought the flags a ruse by the Chinese, whom they had heard—via another penny dreadful rumor—had overcome and murdered all the foreigners. Then they saw a marine lift himself up on the wall and signal rapidly in Morse code to "Come in quickly by the sluice gate." With bullets flying at them from all quarters, the relief forces cheered and ran for it.[60]

Lieutenant Roger Keyes of the British forces was first to slither his slender frame through the sluice gate's wooden bars, helped by US Marines and Chinese Christians. According to some reports, Keyes waded through sewage and arrived in the British legation to greet Lady MacDonald covered in filth, but Polly Condit Smith describes the Jade Canal as being dried out by the August heat and now filled with choking dust. In any case, the officer who presented himself to a thin and startled Edwin in the American legation's garden was probably as conspicuous for his need of a bath as for his wide grin. To Keyes, Edwin seemed "to be quite calm, and did not strike me as being particularly interested," but he did recover from his surprise enough to show Keyes and the other men the way to the British legation. Robert Coltman somehow was on the scene in time to see "Sikhs come pouring" through the Water Gate— Cecile Payen heard there were four thousand of them, and commented later, "I do not know who was the happier, the relievers or the relieved, for they hurrahed more than we and seemed so proud and happy to find any of us still alive."[61]

Polly had just been asking her maid whether to venture to the American compound for "the cheerful bath which I had been indulging in each day lately," when she sensed that something strange was happening in the center of the British legation, where the long-abandoned tennis court was. Hurrying outside, she found "everybody flying in the same direction," and some two hundred Sikhs, "great, fine-looking Indians, in khaki uniforms and huge picturesque red turbans, strutting about the compound." She looked on, amused and perhaps a bit envious, as one of the Englishwomen latched on to the Sikh nearest to hand and threw her arms around him, to the man's surprise. Ever aware of the ironies, Polly thought it curious that "the word 'relief' should have been personified in these Eastern and heathen-looking Sikhs." Such was in keeping, she concluded, with the *Alice in Wonderland* atmosphere of the past fifty-five days.[62]

Sarah had known about the pending arrival of troops since two o'clock in the morning. "During the entire night," she wrote, "the firing upon us was more fierce, determined and constant than at any time before."[63]

As the night wore on, she sat with the small ledger book that she used for her diary, listing in a feverish rush the many blessings she and the others had to be thankful for, even under this hail of fire. She spent most of her ink in gratefulness to the Chinese trapped in the legation with her, not only Wang and First Cook but the many others who, unlike the scholar who refused to fill sandbags, worked under conditions many of them had never before experienced to save the legation. "We should have been lost without them," she recorded. "They work with a will, and do the part that no foreigner among us could do." And she made careful note in the list of just how courageous the female contingent of the legation had been. "The band of women have not fallen behind in bravery, endurance, good cheer, tenderness, and untiring work . . . The best that men and women put into this siege will remain unwritten." With all the differences of background, languages, and nationality, not to mention political views and religion, the mixed group in the legation had almost always worked as a team in small, unrecorded acts of heroism as well as large, public ones.[64]

Later on the fourteenth, only when it was clear that the legation was truly relieved and that the Congers—including Miss Laura—were safe and secure, did Wang come to see Sarah with his hat in hand. "Madame," he asked her, "I go find my family." For fifty-five days this man, trained in all the graces of a major-domo, had worked as hard as any of the rough coolies. He had helped Sarah and Edwin set up and run their siege household, washed their clothes and hunted down their food, assisted the wounded in the hospital, and, of course, saved Laura's beloved white pony, one of just six to survive the siege. He had done all this faithfully, knowing that his wife and three children were out in the Chinese City, where Boxers, Gansu soldiers, and assorted bandits were still taking potshots at foreign troops. We have no record of how often Wang had to watch the torn and battered Chinese as they stumbled into the safety of the legation, whether he looked at each for the faces of his family. It must have been a constant temptation. But when most of their other servants fled he refused to leave the Congers. Now that it was safe to do so, Sarah's first thought was to return to the American compound and begin making it the home it had been, but there was no way she would stop Wang from what he had to do. She did not know when—or if—he might return.[65]

He was away only two hours. When he came in the gate Wang brought his wife and their three children (his eldest, a son, was safe in Tianjin), worse for wear but alive. Sarah listened to their tale of survival. "Their house was looted, then burned," she wrote, "and for seven weeks they have been wandering beggars . . . The children were naked and the wife poorly covered." They had at least avoided the terrifying experiences of a four-year-old boy named Paul Wang (no relation), member of a Christian family known to Sarah. Sarah heard that not only was Paul stabbed by the Boxers with swords and spears, but had been thrown into a bonfire three times, perhaps in some ritual to determine whether or not he was Christian. "He manifested such tenacity of life that the leading Boxers bowed to him," Sarah learned, "and turned him over to the village elders, saying that Buddha was protecting him." The irony, of course, as Sarah would have seen it, was that quite another spiritual force was behind his immunity to harm.[66]

If the Buddha and the Christian God could have sat in council on the ashes of Beijing, they might not have had much wisdom to share, but been rendered as speechless as mortal men and women by the disaster that had befallen the capital of imperial China. Yet the mayhem had hardly begun. The next chapter in the history of Khublai Khan's old city was about to open, in an orgy of killing and theft that would radiate through China and from it to all parts of what Sarah might describe as the "so-called civilized world." Treasures were to be looted from both the high street and the palace. "What war now means I can now comprehend," Sarah confided sadly. "It is selfish, destructive and cruel."[67]

III

Saving Face

Only simple and quiet words will ripen of themselves.
For a whirlwind does not last a whole morning,
Nor does a sudden shower last a whole day.

— *Tao Teh Ching* 23, Lao Tzu (translated by John C. H. Wu)

13
Loot

The topography that made Beijing prone to miserable dust storms in the spring also left the city vulnerable to biting north winds in the winter. The afternoon of January 7, 1902 was no exception. But chilled air glittering with Gobi Desert grit did little to detract from an occasion that, despite the ravages of weather and war, was nothing less than splendid—the formal return to Beijing of the Guangxu emperor and the Empress Dowager Cixi, after a year and a half of self-imposed exile. While the state coffers had run dry long ago, what remained of imperial officialdom in Beijing was pulling out all the stops—a total of US$9.1 million was spent smoothing the imperial court's way from Xian to Beijing.

On January 7, Sarah was met at the American legation at 11:30 a.m. by officials from the Chinese government, who arranged for a Chinese bodyguard to accompany her to a grandstand on Qianmen Street (which still runs on a north–south axis straight toward the Forbidden City), constructed especially for the comfort of foreign observers. For added security, Yuan Shikai's troops, trained to foreign-style perfection, lined the broad boulevard. The comfort of the emperor and dowager had been considered as well. Over the burnt ruins of the Majiapu train station to the south, where the dowager's private car had been torched by Boxers two years before, a false front had been erected, with awnings of yellow silk and tents for the emperor and dowager to rest in before starting for the city. And just as in the old times, the streets of Beijing were scattered with yellow sand, so that the imperial son and mother need not travel over ordinary brown earth.[1]

Besides the foreign diplomats, invitations were also sent to customs and banking officials. It was a good thing, too, as Sarah wrote to Laura a week later, because most of the diplomatic corps did not show up— British, French, and Russian all stayed away. Edwin was invited but had found some other pressing business, the nature of which Sarah does not explain, to prevent his attending. "[The return] was a brave act on the part of China," she wrote. If others in the foreign community chose to give such an event the brush off, Sarah quickly showed she would not be among them. Given prime seating on the second storey of the building, on the east side of the thoroughfare, right in the front row, Sarah had "plenty of blankets keeping the wind from our feet," she assured Laura. Behind her, should she need it, was a room warmed by a fire, and refreshments were served throughout the event. This lent the highly anticipated imperial parade the flavor of a cross between a country fair and a circus (the *New York Times* characterized it as "a glorified Lord Mayor's show"), in which the dowager, though not swinging down from a trapeze in tights or cradled in an elephant's trunk, was the star attraction.[2]

Sitting on the edge of her balcony and looking down at the golden street below, Sarah would have had much to review from the past year and a half. When allied British and French troops had marched on Beijing in 1860, the focus of anger and vengeance was centered almost totally on the Xianfeng emperor, whose minions had kidnapped, tortured, or killed foreign nationals in abrogation of military etiquette and international diplomatic law. The Yuanmingyuan had been ransacked and burned in part to teach the emperor a lesson, to shake him out of his isolationist somnolence and wake him to the exigencies of foreign trade and foreign hegemony. The people of Beijing, and of China in general, were not thought responsible for one ruler's infirm grasp on the new reality.

The aftermath of August 14, 1900 had offered a different set of lessons to be taught, not just to the emperor per se but also to the people of Beijing, the surrounding towns and villages, and the entire province of Zhili. There was much for the world outside China to be angry about. Armed militants, professional soldiers, and hoodlums eager to vent their anger on foreigners and on Chinese who had accepted the foreign god and foreign ways, had tortured and murdered hundreds in the months before and during the Boxer Uprising. Much property of foreign title was damaged or destroyed—indeed, the attack on the diplomatic body, starting with the murder of Sugiyama Akira, broke the rules of the Hague Convention of 1899 and the tenets of international law, not to mention exceeding the minimum expectations of human decency. But what the conquering Europeans and Japanese presided over during the months of mid-August to November 1900, and continuing beyond in more official form, was an orgy of theft and deliberate defilement, far out of proportion to anything for which most of them could be considered answerable.

How much of this Sarah witnessed—and, more to the point, how many of the items in her own Chinese art collection came to her via these means—remains unclear. Her own record is sketchy for these first few weeks after the liberation. But she had had ample opportunity to witness the process of how Beijing itself was "won," starting with events right after the liberation. On August 15, when allied troops were still flushing out pockets of "Boxers," she and Mary Pierce (a fearless young woman who inspired in a smitten Sir Robert Hart some of his most florid poetry) went to the ruins of the Qianmen Gate, along with several other members of the diplomatic corps, to witness American forces as they shelled the main entrance to the Forbidden City.[3]

As Sarah and Mary watched United States artillery bombard the Meridian Gate, "the yellow tile roofs quaked." Nobody seems to have quaked at the sacrilege of aiming cannon at a world architectural treasure, including Sarah. She heard that the explosion did little but frighten the eunuchs who had been left behind by the fleeing imperial court. But it did a lot for the foreigners watching—like many in the diplomatic community, Sarah admitted she was not sorry to see the crimson gates get blown off their Ming-era hinges. "The sight of these guns bombarding the Forbidden City gate was wonderful to us," she admitted. After all, from these red walls, in the last days of the siege, had come some of the heaviest shelling. And the devastation that lay about the intact palaces was, after all, a ruin "wrought by the Chinese themselves," Sarah observed, though not entirely correctly. She might have had a different opinion of the shelling of the palace had she known that shortly before, US gunners had turned their Maxims on a group of Chinese men running through one of the courtyards (the same eunuchs Sarah had heard were merely frightened?), mowing them down as if they were Navajo braves fleeing over an Arizona ridge.[4]

The Forbidden City was spared the fate of Yuanmingyuan. American Brigadier General A. S. Daggett would not countenance its destruction, because if this most sacred symbol of imperial authority were obliterated, what was left of the emperor's mandate of heaven might disappear in chaos, and the huge indemnities soon to be exacted from the Chinese never paid—not to mention all the foreign investments that would go up in smoke. The Forbidden City also had to be left as the staging ground for ceremonies of foreign military might over the Chinese, which took the form of parades with full military bands filing through the blasted gates and past the most holy of holies, the Dragon Throne (the Americans playing, rather tactlessly, "It'll be a Hot Time in the Old Town Tonight"), and the establishment within the palace itself of supreme commander General Count Alfred von Waldersee.[5]

Amid so much to catch the eye of a discerning journalist already more than half on the side of the conquered Chinese, George Lynch took note of what to a writer is the most unholy of acts, the burning of books. Believing that Buddhism (despite its doctrine of *ahimsa* or "do no harm") was one of the evil forces empowering Boxer violence against Christians, foreign troops and missionaries broke into temples and tossed volumes of sutras into the fires they lit. In the street outside Lynch's lodgings he saw, day after day, "carts passing backwards and forwards laden with books which were brought to be consumed in a huge fire burning in a yard outside the Palace wall." It was a "literary holocaust" of texts "printed with those wooden blocks by which these barbarians practiced the art of printing for centuries before the time of Caxton." He imagined, as he watched the burnt fragments dance in the relentless Beijing winds, the laments of the "long dead authors—priests, hermits and scholars— mourning over the ashes of their life work."[6]

More than literary treasures, too, seemed to fill the very air. The French press, so often sensationalist in its Grand Guignol depictions of the empress dowager, this time produced a tellingly accurate glimpse of what was occurring in Beijing. The cover of the February 1, 1901 issue of *La Vie Illustrée* featured a scene of multinational soldiers layered like a Hieronymus Bosch vision of Hell, all the men grabbing at a rich miscellany of Chinese curios, garments, and temple idols, and carrying bags swollen with mysterious contents. George Lynch watched a much more orderly but just as cynical British military auction of looted goods, noting how the auctioneer, the constable of the British legation, swigged whisky and water as he held up silks and furs, turning them to and fro for an audience of officers that sometimes included members from other nations. One of these, an American war correspondent, called out higher and higher bids that were too grand for his purse but obviously not for that of some American grandee back home. "Every afternoon," Lynch recalled, "except Sunday, these auctions occurred under the colonnade in front of the British Legation." Thus, he declared, was the loot "systematised"—the high color of its pilfered origins was watered down to a more palatable hue of the "spoils of war."[7]

"This China expedition affair," Lynch observed, "has been the biggest looting excursion since the days of Pizarro." And there were many different ways of looting. There was the relatively benign sort wherein one entered an abandoned Chinese home, assumed the owners would never return, and took whatever they had left behind. Polly Condit Smith received a bracelet from an officer via this method. Even Wang, Sarah's impeccably honest Number One Boy, gave her a pearl ring he claimed to have found in the street (which he probably did: American marine Smedley Butler recalled there were "brocades and furs lying in the gutters").[8] The Western powers had had their fifty-five days of misery, like mice cowering in a hole—now the Chinese were the mice, only with no place to hide. From looting, the liberated foreigners moved on to games of field hockey played on the grounds of that most sacred of imperial precincts, the Temple of Heaven, while amused foreigners took turns sitting on the throne in the Qianqing Palace in the Forbidden City. It was important to show who was boss, which included showing off one's knowledge of how much Chinese culture was worth on the antiques market. Unlike in 1860, when so little was understood about China, by 1900 there was considerable foreign knowledge about the porcelains, paintings, silks, and bronzes of China, and many now knew what they stood to gain when they turned over a stolen cup or bowl to see the ideogram beneath.[9]

Lynch had the surprise of discovering that these vengeful diplomatic worthies were not above a bit of kleptomania. Touring the Forbidden City was something like wandering through a series of priceless and unlocked antiques shops which had suffered some dirtying cataclysm— the waters of chaos had ebbed and receded, leaving a dark film over everything. As all foreigners had brought along their own private fantasy of what China was, or should be, many were disappointed. Others found that, if their fantasy was dashed, their biases against the Chinese and their culture were reinforced. Upheavals and Cixi's own avoidance of the Forbidden City had left it looking like a derelict property on an overgrown lot. Weeds sprouted through pavements, making lush meadows in the larger courtyards that were criss-crossed by the wheels of caissons used by the foreign allies. Seed had taken root among the golden roof tiles, which were now growing cascades of incongruous green hair as a result. And the dust which has been Beijing's burden since the city was founded had filtered deep into the heavy eaves, coating the furniture, and mingling with the bird droppings left on silk carpets and cushions.

Those seeing this squalor assumed that the dynasty was in literal decay, the dowager a careless housekeeper as well as a bloodthirsty tyrant, the emperor a drooling idiot incapable of caring for his imperial legacy. George Lynch entered rooms that were "dark and gloomy-looking," in which stood "a tawdry throne coated with dust as thickly as the heavy yellow carpet on which we trod." He could barely see the patterns of the cloisonné vases through the grime. The eagerness for souvenirs was greater than most people's fastidiousness. Lynch soon saw that just about everyone shared this yen, including a foreign minister he does not name who, after examining a jade tablet in the Guangxu emperor's bedroom, put it back, "seemed curious to examine it again . . . Then he put his hands in his pockets, and seemed intent on contemplating the pattern of the ceiling. He apparently got so interested in it that he must have forgotten that he had not put that bit of jade in its stand." It was this kind of acquisitiveness that helped Herbert Squiers, a noted collector of Asian porcelains, leave China in September 1901 with several railway cars filled with Chinese art, some of which he donated to the Metropolitan Museum of Art in New York City. "Knowing this," writes James Hevia, "it should be difficult indeed to look at any piece of Chinese porcelain or Qing imperial regalia in the great museums of France, the United States and Great Britain and not think about the sack of Beijing in 1900."[10]

✳ ✳ ✳ ✳ ✳

Sarah saw the destruction from two very different perspectives. On August 16, the day after she had thrilled at the shelling of the Meridian Gate, she was taken to the palace of a noble family by one of her missionary friends, who hoped to rent the house for "mission work." Unlike her visit to the Li mansion the previous year, this was an experience of a private Chinese house of the upper classes that Sarah could both savor and mourn. She was, at first, delighted, as she wrote to her sister, "to have the opportunity to enter one of these Chinese palaces." She was taken through numerous pavilions, courtyards, and gardens that seemed to have preserved their calm despite the human storms that had passed over them. Then, just when she was least expecting it, Sarah came to a building that contained three coffins. The coffin as such is to the Chinese nothing like the symbol of death and decay that it is to a Western observer. It is often the finest piece of woodwork in the house of a poor family, and is displayed proudly in the open, nothing to be ashamed or afraid of. These three coffins, however, were not put out empty. Inside were "princesses" of the house who, rather than risk rape by the foreign troops entering the city on August 14, had thrown themselves in the compound's well and drowned—a common form of suicide for Chinese women, who after all had no place else to go in the confines of their homes. A fourth sister had been pulled out of the well alive—one day, under happier circumstances, Sarah was to meet her and listen to her story. The "intense sufferings, sorrows, and sacrifices befalling these people no words can depict," Sarah wrote. "They secretly tell their story and help to color the stream of time."[11]

Sarah had another glimpse of the inner life of the Chinese, this time that of the erstwhile enemy. She and Edwin took two ponies lucky to have escaped the dinner menu during the siege, and on August 20 rode the entire fifteen-mile circuit of the Tartar wall—the ultimate freedom for a woman who hated walls. The devastation she saw from above was unforgettable. "The streets and houses are deserted," Sarah recalled. "Not a Chinaman was to be seen except as he wore the colors of some one of the foreign nations," a device too many Chinese thought would protect them from looting and other foreign savagery. "The Boxers first, and then the Chinese soldiers, took what they wished," Sarah added, noting that "the foreign soldiers culled from the remains." Especially chilling was the sight of the British cemetery, where American marines who had died in the smallpox outbreak in fall 1898 had been buried. "Where had that awful tumult gone," Sarah wondered darkly, gazing at the shattered monuments, burnt chapel, and gaping graves, "—and the people who made it?" Even more striking, though, was her discovery of the leavings of Chinese soldiers who had fled their defensive positions on the wall. Many of them had made small living quarters out of stacked bricks and refuse, and some had set up primitive shrines still containing the Buddhist or Daoist figures to whom they had prayed. Though these men had tried to kill her, Edwin, Laura, and everybody else in the legations, Sarah saw that they, too, had been "true to [their] gods" in an endeavor that must have seemed to them as desperate as the fight being offered by the foreigners.[12]

The next several weeks gave opportunities for other "field trips" into what had been, only weeks before, a war zone. On August 24, Sarah, Laura, and Mary Pierce went to the Beitang, which had been relieved two days after the legations, suffered losses which were far greater, and fended off more concentrated attacks with fewer professional troops. When Sarah met Bishop Favier, who had gallantly defended his cathedral, he told her that the first time he caught sight of relief troops was when, through his spyglass, he had glimpsed the American flag. "There is not a room in the whole compound that is not injured," Sarah observed of the battered cathedral. "Thousands of bullet holes are in the fine windows . . . the large organ is shot through and through." As if to get a better view again of a destruction the scope of which she could not grasp, or to make it recede into the distance because she grasped it all too well, Sarah took the girls up to what had been out of bounds to any but the emperor and the empress dowager, Qingshan or Prospect Hill, an artificial eminence to the north of the Forbidden City, studded with exquisite pavilions bearing fairy-tale names. "It was," Sarah noted, "our first visit to this hitherto forbidden spot." From it, she could look right down upon the golden roofs of the Forbidden City itself.[13] It would not be forbidden to her for long. On September 10, Sarah had her greatest wish answered. "With a permit from General Chaffee," Sarah wrote, joyful as a child, "officers took Laura, Mary, and me through the Forbidden City! The real Forbidden City!"[14]

"The officers ordered opened many buildings and private rooms of the Emperor, the Empress Dowager, and Empress [Longyu, Guangxu's primary consort]," Sarah recorded, "and we passed through them," where she saw "objects of beauty that I cannot name." Hoping, as she had done from her first day in China, for a glimpse of how Chinese women and their families really lived in their own homes, Sarah could not believe that she was actually walking through the private spaces of the palace of the Chinese emperor. She overlooked the dirt and grime of the untended palace buildings and their dusty contents, and she optimistically told her diary and herself that these things were being carefully guarded by the Japanese and the Americans, "protecting these treasures from vandalism." She was truly seeing something different from what most foreigners noticed on their tours through the imperial apartments. As one historian has pointed out, by the time Sarah visited the Forbidden City, she had made a diligent effort to understand the many symbols used in Chinese art, architecture, furniture, porcelain, and embroidery—in everything a given artisan had created. She did not comment on the dust and cobwebs in the palace and courtyards because she was more focused on decoding the messages she saw on every pillar, painting, vase, and bedcover, reading the "language" she saw there.[15]

Chinese art, Sarah believed, had "a positive meaning throughout its whole construction; and with these accumulated expressions in thought-symbols it portrays a culture that graces any drawing-room, library, gallery, museum. It has something to say and, in dignity, calmly says it . . . China's art is like a scholarly man, at home everywhere," quite the opposite of much in Western art, which she felt was "like a beautiful person without depth of thought," ornament for its own sake.[16]

Sarah was not the first American woman to find a sense of balance and rightness in Asian decoration that the European variety seemed to lack: one American women's magazine of the early 1890s pointed out that while a Sèvres vase might be "agreeable," there was nothing like a Japanese one to "blend" with a room's décor and even become an element of it unto itself. The difference was that Sarah saw it the other way around—Asian art was no curiosity to fit politely in with one's Western furnishings, but a lexicon of positivity to be emulated by its foreign observers. "Her interest in finding meaning in Oriental splendor," writes James Hevia, "foreshadowed later reactions to the Forbidden City, ones that would reimagine the palace and the city of Beijing as sophisticated works of art."[17]

Sarah's tour of the sacred imperial spaces was one of the few bright spots for her in the dark post-Uprising fall and winter of Beijing. On one of her earliest trips outside the American legation after the end of the siege, she had checked on the Imperial Observatory, fearing that the instruments would have been damaged in the fighting. She was astonished to see that they were intact, echoing George Lynch's amazement that such fragile creations should have escaped bombs and bullets unscathed. Perhaps the altazimuths would be safer in a less conspicuous position, Sarah thought, but could not bear the idea of their being taken from the pedestal they had occupied for several hundred years. "It would seem cruel," she wrote, "for anything to move them from their sentinel watch," from where they had witnessed so many storms, human and natural. The fact that they had done so seemed to guarantee their immunity to any kind of disruption, but Sarah had not reckoned on the French and the Germans. To her dismay, on a return visit to the thirteenth-century platform in mid-November, she saw that the instruments that war could not harm were gone—unbolted and carted away to Paris and Berlin and not to be seen again all together in Beijing until after World War I. This act of incredible theft was, she told a nephew, "one of the most heartrending acts" she had yet seen, more so even than another that had horrified her—the blasting open of the Tartar City wall and the laying of railway track through a Chinese graveyard, all so the British could bring rolling stock right up to the Temple of Heaven. Her joy at surviving the siege was gradually being dampened with each fresh punishment levied on the Chinese. "There is no Chinese government here to hold the Chinese or the foreigner to law and order," she lamented that September. "Poor China! Why cannot foreigners let her alone with her own? China has been wronged, and in her desperation she has striven as best she could to stop the inroads, and to blot out those already made." It was then, for the first time, that Sarah formed an opinion that to most of the diplomatic corps, after what they had been through, would have seemed the height of madness, if not treachery: "My sympathy is with China."[18]

* * * * *

Even as Sarah Conger's appreciation for and understanding of China came to flower among the ruins of Beijing, so in Cixi's flight into the back hills of western China did the dowager's scope widen to embrace the realities of her empire. Witnessing life along the dusty roads also schooled the dowager not only in the state of things in her own country, but brought her face to face with the fact that if anything was to ever bring China to its feet again, it would occur not by avoiding foreign ways but by embracing them.

Cixi may or may not have been thinking of this on January 7, 1902 as she jounced along from the Majiapu train station over a roadway scattered not with dirt but with golden sand. Here was one of the great royal comebacks, a woman who had returned twice to a ruined city she was blamed this time for having brought to destruction, yet who glittered like a serene golden idol, calmly possessing a power that no one could take from her. The woman who had lived on the run for almost two years was coming back to where it had all begun, where it had all ended, and where it all might just begin again. It was a tremendous gamble. And against all the odds, Cixi gazed out from her chair at crowds that—surely to her surprise, but perhaps not—did not abuse her but cheered her.

The rumor started early that Cixi had fled Beijing on August 14, 1900 dressed as a Chinese peasant. She later denied it, but this was how she looked to Huailai magistrate Wu Yung when her exhausted court arrived in his walled city northwest of Beijing a few days later. Before the court's departure, other tales had circulated that carts were loaded and ready to go in mid-July. If true, this does not explain the haphazard state of the people who arrived on Wu Yung's doorstep, lacking a change of clothes or any utensils to eat with. "In going to [Xian]," explained Frederick W. Eddy of the *New York Times,* assuming as many did that the vastness of China was beyond most Americans' comprehension, "the imperial family has made a journey that may be compared to one from Albany to Pittsburg or Cincinnati." Cixi was "dressed in cotton clothes and with her hair done in a simple knot on top of her head," recalled Wu, while the emperor, as if stunned by all that had occurred, slumped silently in a wrinkled black silk coat, with no sash, his face unshaven and dust-smudged. When Guangxu did speak, "the sound of his voice," Wu claimed, "was light and thin like the hum of a mosquito," hardly the authoritative utterance one expected from the earthly embodiment of the heavenly dragon. The imperial pair did not even have chopsticks—Wu gave the dowager his own ivory ones, and soon was giving up his and his family's spare clothing to the refugees.[19]

Rapidly recovering from the huge surprise of the dowager's impromptu arrival, Wu managed to organize food and lodging for her and her numerous court so quickly and so well that Cixi put him in charge of her traveling plans, a dubious honor Wu tried but failed to evade—Cixi later remembered his efforts to calm her demanding eunuchs, "begging them to keep quiet, and promis[ing] them everything."[20]

As all who were in a position to know affirmed, Cixi was both a pleasure and a challenge to serve. Wu's impression of her was that, while charming and given to apt quotations from the Confucian classics and great poets, she sometimes fell into displays of temper which made her frightening. "Her eyes poured out straight rays," he recalled, "her cheekbones were sharp and the veins on her forehead projected." When in this state she tended to hiss through clenched teeth, completing the picture of an enraged cat. But she was often also a person of sense and equanimity, and could even be ingratiating. In her eagerness to show favor toward a lowly cook in Wu's employ whose pulled noodles and fried pork strips she greatly enjoyed, Cixi deprived Wu of his own dinner: while the cook received his sixth grade hat button of rank, Wu went hungry to the local police station, asking his friend the police chief if he could have something to eat there.[21]

British diplomat Sir Ernest Satow, a thoroughgoing orientalist who admired the dowager as much as he distrusted her, heard from one of his contacts who had seen her during her perambulations away from Beijing that Cixi was "the man of the situation," and such was Wu's experience of her. For a woman used to the attendance of thousands of servants, whose every whim was instantly obeyed, on this cross-country trek Cixi was remarkably reasonable in her requirements, content with her water pipe and the simple country specialties of Wu's former cook, and always ready to help set things into perspective with a wise remark or ironic joke. (She had been so hungry on arriving in Huailai that even the leavings of a pot of porridge were received and eaten like a rare feast, though she had then sent Wu on an impossible wild goose chase for eggs which, after he had searched through half the town, were finally procured for her, a precious handful.) She was so engaging a listener, and her travel organizer such a handsome young man, that Wu was soon criticized by jealous court officials for spending hours talking with her. He had a hard time getting away. Often in tears, Cixi told Wu in great detail about the difficulties of the flight from Beijing—how, when she was thirsty and the eunuchs could find her no water, they cut fresh stalks of millet for her and the emperor to chew. One night, in the middle of nowhere, "the Emperor and I had only a bench between us, and we sat shoulder to shoulder watching the sky for morning," a state of misery captured with the hard sparkle of a line of Chinese poetry. The courtiers soon became annoyed with Wu when, after he blatantly answered with the truth when Cixi asked him about the state of the people in his jurisdiction, Cixi would tear into them for lying to her about the suffering of the Chinese people—though had she really wanted to know, there was no one who could have prevented her finding out the truth long before being forced to come to grips with it.[22]

As her "progress" went on, Cixi went from a tired and querulous old lady in plain cotton at Huailai to the smiling silk-and-jade empress dowager, thanks to the tribute payments organized by Wu along the route. This increased his stock with her but added to the number of his enemies. In one of their intimate discussions at this time, Cixi shared with Wu her side of the events leading up to her decision to flee Beijing. She had been, she said, simply carried away by the seeming patriotism of the Boxers. Everyone who watched them perform their rites admired their discipline and strength; she had seen so for herself. She was told they were "one part true and nine parts genuine," men she increasingly felt could be depended on to—what? Wu was not sure what it was Cixi had depended on them for, gallantly blaming her poor judgment on "devil fever." But Cixi is clear on the subject. The Boxers had offered hope for her ideals and kindling for her hatred of meddling Christianity. Because she was told, by the same courtiers who dared not reveal to her the full truth of affairs outside the Forbidden City's walls, that the Boxers were immensely popular with people in and outside Beijing, she opted not to "exterminate" but to support them. Only when the Boxers attacked the legations and burned the Qianmen Gate, she told Wu, did Cixi see that they were not dependable at all—that she had a mob on her hands, a flock of blackbirds that, having descended into her courtyards, could not be shooed away. All she knew was that the palace was suddenly crowded with men in red turbans and sashes, coming and going, flashing their swords and performing their stunts, declaring they could uncover secret Christians just by slapping their foreheads, and strutting about impersonating figures that must surely have recalled to Cixi some of her favorite characters of the stage. Tempers had flared in the summer heat and under the heightened tensions; arguments were rife, even as the small camp of moderates quailed under the pressure of a mob of aggressive radicals. Duke Cailan, a brother of Prince Duan, had flown into a temper while dining with Cixi and nearly overturned her dinner table, an act that could have resulted in his instant beheading at any other time. But Cixi found herself in the middle of a curious and dangerous game. "I had to temporize with them in many respects," she explained, "yield a bit to them in order not to arouse their mob spirit."[23]

Cixi insisted that on August 14 nobody, not even the eunuchs, was aware that foreign troops had entered the city. Her first clue was when she heard the whistling of bullets, that same eerie "music" Sarah had been listening to for the past month and a half, which sounded to Cixi like the wailing of cats—she even made the sound for Wu, a sample of her famed talent for mimicry. Like Sarah, when a bullet actually fell into Cixi's room she had to pick it up and hold it to convince herself that it, and the conflict that brought it there, was real.

When the crisis came, Guangxu was not in the palace but making a sacrifice in one of the temples, and had to be hurried back to Cixi's rooms. On hearing that foreign soldiers were in Beijing he was all for flight, with an alacrity that was to spell doom for his excitable favorite, the Pearl Concubine. In the chaos of their leave-taking a tragic incident occurred which has frequently been used as proof that Cixi was a monstrous tyrant.

According to the traditional account, the Pearl Concubine rushed into the dowager's presence and begged to be taken along with her and the emperor. Cixi had no reason to love this young woman, who had aided and abetted her nephew's avalanche of reforms in 1898 and ever since had shared his fate of seclusion and surveillance. The story goes that Cixi hated the Pearl so much that after refusing her request, she ordered the eunuchs to throw her into a well in the northeast corner of the Forbidden City, a spot still pointed out to gullible tourists and Chinese alike as the scene of her murder. That the well is of a narrowness that would have barely permitted the easy introduction of a child does not seem to register; the story, supported by Chinese and foreign propaganda, has clung burr-like to almost every narrative about the dowager.

According to Cixi's great-nephew, Na Genzheng, whose grandfather was driving the cart in which Cixi escaped, what in fact happened was not murder but suicide. So many members of the imperial family and so many court officials (not to mention hordes of eunuchs) needed to be organized for the flight, and so many more could not be accommodated, it was a waste of precious time for anyone to quarrel with Cixi about who was going and who not. The Pearl did just that, true to the form which had always rubbed Cixi the wrong way. She declared it a disgrace that the Guangxu emperor should be made to flee in this manner, and told Cixi she would rather die than witness or endure such humiliation. Cixi snapped back at her to do as she liked, and to her horror, the Pearl killed herself.[24]

How much of the account Cixi gave to Wu Yung is to be believed is difficult to say. It must be remembered that she was recounting all these adventures to a good-looking and respectful young man, a fresh audience. As she did a few years later, when describing some of the same events to her young and admiring lady-in-waiting, Der Ling, Cixi may have cast herself in a more heroic role than she had in fact played. Like many self-made and ambitious people, she did not like to accept blame. As Wu accurately assessed, "in the past she had encountered too much humiliation," which had made her fiercely proud and apt to fall into denial when cornered. He did, however, believe her when she insisted that she had been poorly informed by her advisors—he had had proof of this himself.[25]

Finally forced out of the dowager's charmed circle by these same jealous officials, Wu was appointed *daodai* in Guangdong and saw the court off for the last time from their temporary palace at remote Kaifeng on the Yellow River, which had once been an imperial capital of China and which Cixi, briefly, threatened to make its seat of power once again. Under a brilliant winter sun and in a respectful silence broken only by the sounds of horses and the cartwheels grinding over sand, the imperial procession made its way to the ferry to cross the milky width of the river known as "China's Sorrow." "A city of silk stretched for miles along the river bank," Wu recalled, "and the accoutrements of a thousand soldiers flashed like fire." He did see a smile on Cixi's face as the flag-draped ship began to move north, and hers was not the only expression of pleasure. "The soldiers and citizens shouted and danced with joy," Wu reminisced.[26]

"It was, indeed, a curious fate for the late patroness of the Boxers, haters of all things foreign, to be coming back to her capital by the aid of the 'fire-carriages,'" wrote Phillip Sergeant—trains were, after all, the chief disturbers of the Earth Dragon, jolting out of place the unseen but potent energy streams of *qi*. "Both she and the emperor, however, were said to have been enchanted by their first railway journey." Perhaps the fact that the engine and the imperial cars had been decorated with yellow silk dragons (a favor on the part of the British railway officials) lessened the fears of the first-time passengers by putting this quintessential foreign gadget to the uses of Chinese imperial pageantry.[27]

One witness to the return to Beijing, a reporter for the *Peking and Tientsin Times,* sourly described the imperial procession as being "of that tawdry, shoddy character that Chinese shows usually present to Occidental eyes," but in fact it was a far more gorgeous spectacle than an impoverished state should have been able to put on: yellow silk, vivid banners, orderly troops, and the urgent cadences of Chinese processional music surrounded the returning imperials. "Two companies of Chinese cavalry mounted on white horses and two companies astride horses from Australia were drawn up at the station," reported the *New York Times*. "Two thousand officials, Princes, Viceroys, and Taotais—a kaleidoscopic field of silks and furs, in which gleamed an occasional yellow jacket—were massed upon the platform" and followed the imperial parade the four miles into the city. As their chairs moved toward and into the city from the train station, all the Chinese along the route knelt; packs of coolies, who would not have dared to do so in former times, gathered to gape at their emperor and Cixi in a "complete effacement of the traditional deification of Chinese royalty." A few foreigners were even seen with hats in hand. Cixi accepted it all with great grace. "She swept on through the Chienmen entrance from the Chinese into the Tartar City," wrote Sergeant, "leaving behind her almost a feeling of good-will."[28]

At the first sight of a foreigner, the woman considered by her subjects to be nine-tenths a goddess drew back her yellow curtains and bowed in respect. "She smiled and nodded to the [foreign] ladies on the wall, and even called out, shook her hands, or pointed a friendly finger to some whom she recognized personally." After the emperor had completed his worship at the Temple of the God of War, Cixi stepped out of her chair, supported by eunuchs, to visit the Temple of Guanyin, goddess of mercy. "She advanced a few steps and bowed . . . in acknowledgement of the salutations of the foreigners," reported the *New York Times*. "She then returned to her chair looking upwards at the semicircle of foreign faces and bowing repeatedly." Not even Europeans had such access to their royals as had been accorded both foreigners and Chinese this January afternoon.[29]

As Sergeant described, when Cixi had returned to Beijing from Jehol forty years earlier there had been damage enough on view, "but now matters were a thousand times worse. Not merely had the outer sections of Peking been used as barracks and encampments and their architecture changed to suit the invaders' needs, but the sanctity of the Imperial and Forbidden Cities had been violated." Sarah's longed-for opportunity to enter the Forbidden City and her tour of the emperor's and dowager's private apartments had been a kind of sacrilege she herself did not intend but which was part of the general plan from the allied command's first days in Beijing. After the allied armies took the city, "actions were staged for the benefit of the camera," writes James Hevia, "transforming punishment into a performance of power, a spectacle for viewers in North America and Europe to share."[30]

Comparing the photograph of Edwin, Sarah, Laura, and guests entering the Forbidden City by the sacred Meridian Gate in September 1900, and the informal image of Cixi waving from a small temple courtyard (taken by one of the foreign ladies watching her from the Tartar wall) in April 1902 makes for an interesting contrast. In the photo of the Congers, a panorama of the yet-to-be-conquered palace lay ahead of them, shot from a great height but at an angle that seems to amplify rather than diminish the Congers' figures. In their straw boaters and leg o'mutton sleeves, and carrying parasols, they proceed vigorously toward the mysterious locus of Chinese power, the American troops lined up on either side of the roadway asserting and justifying their right to make the Forbidden City forbidden no longer. The photograph of Cixi captures an image of the diminutive dowager that shows Cixi already in some part a prisoner, not so much of her own rank now as that of the foreigners who had let her escape and, under conditions, had allowed her to return. Her small, silk-robed figure is held in check on every side by courtyard walls, by the several eunuchs around her, those grinning palace jailers, and by the extreme angle of the photographer looking down directly on the dowager's head, foreshortening her both as person and as potentate.[31]

In a letter to daughter Laura, then living in California as the wife of Lieutenant Fred Buchan,[32] Sarah described the return of the imperial court and the moment she first saw Cixi again:

> The street was cleared of all Chinese except officials, officers and their armies . . . The court left the train at [Majiapu station]— General Ma [Yuekun] & his mounted large guard came first— then, Emperor in a yellow chair carried by many men—He sat upright—not looking to the right nor left. We could see him— Many soldiers & more music followed then came another yellow chair with Empress Dowager. She looked up to us, waved her hand & bowed, then put her face up to window as if she saw some one that she knew & pointed her finger and bowed—I was in the

front . . . People who saw her said to me—She recognized you. Later, through Chinese we learned that she did.[33]

From what Sarah could see, the dowager had never been in better form—the radiance of her goodwill glowed through the dusty winter air. "She seemed to wish to have foreigners feel that she was friendly inclined," Sarah wrote, with a sense of relief and wonder palpable on the page. "This surely was a great day," she continued. "The future will detect more in it than the present understands."[34]

Cixi must have had good eyesight to spy Sarah sitting atop the grandstand with all the other spectators. She had had no means of knowing which of the ladies she had invited to the 1898 audience, if any, had survived the Boxer attacks; those who saw her noticed how carefully she scrutinized the crowds, as if looking for what had been lost. But as Cixi's most admiring biographer, Princess Der Ling, put it, "Old Buddha, fleeing from her capital city, had not lost nearly so much as she herself believed." When she saw Sarah, her happiness was obvious to everyone in the respectful bow that followed. It was a gesture made from across the crowds of soldiers and spectators, the flapping yellow banners, and from across the void of language, custom, race, and rank, which Cixi seems to have intuited that Sarah would receive and understand—the homage of one survivor to another, and a Confucian desideratum that, even if Sarah did not know about it, could be said to characterize both women's experiences that January morning: "To have friends come from afar is happiness, is it not?" Possibly in that moment, Cixi realized that in Beijing, in the heart of a foreign woman who had every reason to hate her, she still had a friend.[35]

14
Reconciliation

Cixi began her new lease on the throne by keeping her word. Before returning to Beijing, she had issued an edict stating her intention to invite not just the foreign ministers but their wives to audiences at the palace, and so she did. A few days after the court's return to Beijing, the Guangxu emperor received the credentials of six foreign ministers, among them Edwin; and as Sarah points out, they were shown especial favor by being permitted to enter the Forbidden City through the Meridian Gate, "for the first time in China's history"—certainly a less violent means of paying a visit than were used by the United States Marines and their cannon on August 15, 1900.[1]

There was another first that day: after their audience with the emperor, the ministers were received face to face by Cixi herself. It was not her first time to meet with a male foreigner—in 1898 she had granted an audience to the Kaiser's brother, Prince Henry—but it was a first for these ministers. Sarah was told the meeting was "formal, dignified, and most respectful." It was all those things, and it was remarkable for something else: that it was held in the Forbidden City, and in a most sacred building.[2]

The Palace of Heavenly Purity (Qianqing gong) is a sprawling audience hall within the Inner Court toward the northern edge of the Forbidden City, which had been used as a residence by the Ming emperors and as a meeting place by Qing rulers for the Grand Council. From January 1902 onward, foreigners were no more to be shunted off to some small pavilion outside the precincts of the imperial palace. Sir Ernest Satow was present for the audience. "The Emperor was seated at a table draped in black and yellow on a slightly elevated dais in the middle of the floor," he recalled, "while the Empress-Dowager occupied the throne on the higher dais behind." The Austrian minister, Baron Moritz Czikann von Wahlborn, made a speech, duly translated for and transmitted by Prince Qing to the emperor and dowager, via means of a francophone Chinese courtier whose linguistic abilities Satow did not hold in high esteem. Nor was Satow particularly impressed by the emperor, clearly considering him— as did almost everyone else in the foreign community—an unfortunate victim and mere figurehead. But on meeting Cixi, Satow noted what to him seemed in her manner an excess of feeling—perhaps withheld tears? The actress rebelling against an unseemly script that forced on her too much humiliation? Cixi "appeared to me to be under the influence of strong emotion," Satow observed. Then she recovered her equilibrium before she spoke calmly to the ministers "in set phrases." Perhaps they seemed commonplace to Satow, but they were significant for just how far they went toward apology. While the emperor had contented himself with a few polite greetings, Cixi "added an expression of regret for the events of 1900, and an assurance that they should not happen again."[3]

That this was no mere placating statement was proven when the ladies of the diplomatic corps were received on February 1, 1902 by both Guangxu and the dowager. As wife of the dean of the corps, Sarah had prepared a speech which among the men caused ripples of concern and disapproval before she had even spoken a word. Ernest Satow came to hear of it through the German minister, Baron Dr. Alfons Mumm von Schwartzenstein, a cautious and careful gentleman for whom this posting was his first time in China. "[Mumm] says that Mrs. Conger has drafted a sort of political speech to be addressed to the Empress-Dowager," Satow confided to his diary, "and as it will probably have to be sent to the Chinese thro' the Doyen [Czikann, standing in for Edwin] we shall in a measure become responsible for it. Expressed my opinion against ladies mixing in political matters." He noted he would speak to Edwin about it, though if he thought Edwin shared his opinion about "ladies mixing in political matters" he was mistaken. After Sarah had begun holding regular entertainments for Chinese ladies, an American admiral opined to Edwin that these cross-cultural meetings could not be of much use, since all women ever talked about when they got together was clothing and jewelry. "Quite the contrary," Edwin corrected him. "They talk about the Manchurian troubles, political questions, and many things pertaining to their government."[4]

Whatever the men thought, Sarah forged ahead with her speech and her plans for the audience, inviting the other ladies of the corps over to the legation for a bit of rehearsal in the intricate rules of the Chinese imperial court. As the only foreign woman left who had attended the 1898 audience and the one who had lived longest in Beijing, Sarah took her responsibilities seriously—she wanted to make the best possible impression on Cixi. But not all the diplomatic wives were interested in Sarah's prudent preparations. A daughter of the seventh Earl of Albemarle and wife of Sir Walter Townley (Sir Claude MacDonald's replacement), Lady Susan Townley was an observer of crisp, cool wit and she described Sarah's rehearsals for the audience with a deliberately bored socialite air.

"She was a funny old lady, a Christian Scientist," explained Lady Susan, "spoken of as a possible successor to 'Mother Eddy,' and great was her excitement at the prospect of the morrow. She bade us all curtsy to Her Majesty, and strongly recommended that we should all wear white embroidered under-petticoats, so that, in the event of our tripping over our feet in the performance of these curtsys, no undue display of stockinged leg should offend the susceptibility of the surrounding Chinese dignitaries!" Sarah could have informed Lady Susan that Chinese women had been wearing some form of pants for hundreds of years, displaying more leg than a tripping foreign lady in petticoats could ever divulge. She was probably more concerned with the women appearing ungraceful, given her admiration for the smooth manners of the Chinese, from children to adults, and having read reports in the foreign press that the diplomats had shown poor manners at their audience.[5]

The trip from the legations to the Forbidden City was similar in most respects to that taken by the ministers' wives in 1898. The ladies left in their official green sedan chairs, which were switched at the palace for red satin ones. The big difference for Sarah lay in the fact that while her earlier audience had taken place in the lesser Sea Palaces when she had been the least of the diplomatic ladies, she now entered the Forbidden City itself as the first of them, and she and her ladies were heading not for some vast impersonal place like the Palace of Heavenly Purity but for the part of the Forbidden City which even now has about it the refined eighteenth-century perfume of the reign of the Qianlong emperor. She could not hide the fact that she was as dazzled as if this were her first time meeting the dowager. "Never have I more greatly desired the power of innate and cultured art of word and pencil," Sarah recorded, "to express what I felt and saw . . . It stood for far more than extreme beauty."[6]

Lady Susan had heard all of the stories about the evil old lady she was about to meet, envisioning her "urging on her fiendish soldiers to destroy the 'foreign devils,'" or, in repose, as a "sort of Buddha sitting on the floor with crossed legs and hands . . . receiving the homage of her worshipping subjects." Never to be second-guessed, Cixi took her by surprise. Though Lady Susan did wonder why the revered dowager was wearing a "kind of paper-cutter of beautiful green jade" atop her head, and thought she resembled nothing so much as a "kindly Italian peasant," she saw in her none of the characteristics of a woman accustomed to urging on fiends. "Her piercing brown eyes, when not looking benignly on the foreign ladies (she seemed most anxious to impress us with the friendliness of her feelings towards us, though she would willingly have eaten us up the year before!) roved enquiringly about among her surroundings, an angry gleam appearing in them if her attendants did not instantly appreciate the significance of an order or even of a gesture." If Lady Susan is to be believed, all through the audience Guangxu presented himself with lips parted and eyes sadly glazed, all due to what she had been told afterward was his "opium-sodden condition," an addiction enforced by the dowager's own order.[7]

"At the door of the throne room we halted," Sarah wrote, "fell into our rightful places, and entered, bowing three times at intervals as we approached the throne of Her Majesty." As the ladies drew nearer, "the

Empress Dowager smiled a recognition to me." It was at this point that Sarah took out her speech and, with Edward T. Williams, Chinese secretary to the American legation, interpreting for her, read three extraordinary paragraphs in which reconciliation, forgiveness, and an undercurrent of feminism all ran together in the same cleansing stream:

> Your Majesty, the ladies of the Diplomatic Corps have responded with pleasure to your kind invitation for this audience; and we most heartily congratulate you and all the Imperial Court that the unfortunate situation which led you to abandon your beautiful capital has been so happily resolved, and that you are now permitted to return to it in freedom and in peace. Your safe return to Peking and to this undestroyed palace will furnish pages to future history little comprehended at this time.
>
> The events of the past two years must be as painful to you as they are to the rest of the world; but the sting of the sad experience may be eliminated, and we sincerely hope that it will be, through the establishment of better, franker, more trustful, and friendlier relations between China and the other peoples of the earth. The world is moving forward. The tide of progress cannot be stayed, and it is to be hoped that China will join the great sisterhood of nations in the grand march. May all the nations, united, manifest forbearance, respect, and good will, moving on to the mutual good of all.
>
> The recent Imperial Edicts give promise of great good to your people and to your vast empire, and it is our earnest prayer that God may preserve Your Majesty and the Emperor and guide you to the fullest fruition of this promise.[8]

When Sarah had finished, Prince Qing took Cixi's reply from her and it was translated for the ladies:

> Last year the dissensions in the palace caused a revolution which compelled our hasty departure, but it is a great gratification to us that our return to the capital has caused such rejoicing in China and abroad.[9]

This brief and rather perfunctory message was obviously not everything that Cixi needed to say. After greeting the other ladies and the children they had brought along, Cixi moved to the adjoining room, where refreshments were being served. Sarah came in, and at once Cixi asked for *"Kang taitai"* (Mrs. Kang [Conger]).

"She took my hands in both of hers," Sarah recalled, "and her feelings overcame her. When she was able to control her voice, she said, 'I regret, and grieve over the late troubles. It was a grave mistake, and China will hereafter be a friend to foreigners. No such affair will again happen . . . we hope to be friends in the future.'" Holding Cixi's hands, Sarah replied, "We believe that you are sincere. By knowing each other better we believe we shall become friends." Cixi took from her finger "a heavy, carved gold ring set with an elegant pearl" and placed it on Sarah's hand; "then from her wrists she took choice bracelets and placed them upon my wrists." The other ladies were given souvenirs of their visit, but none had been accorded this gesture of respect. When all were gathered for tea and biscuits, Cixi "placed her glass in my left hand, gracefully pressed my two hands together, so that the glasses touched," Sarah recalled, "and said, 'United.'" Cixi served Sarah's tea, lifting the cup to her lips, then broke a biscuit and placed a fragment of it in Sarah's mouth—for the other ladies she merely placed pieces on their plates. "Her manner was thoughtful, serious in every way," Sarah wrote. "Her eyes are bright, keen, and watchful that nothing may escape her observation." Above all, "her touch is gentle and kind." And before Sarah left, Cixi said to her, "I hope that we shall meet oftener and become friends by knowing one another better."[10]

✳ ✳ ✳ ✳ ✳

A cynic might assume that something other than friendship—namely politics—motivated Sarah and the empress dowager when they reunited in the winter of 1902. But their motives were clearly concerned with higher matters than the political chess games that were beloved by the men in their lives. For all their shared diplomatic acumen, both Cixi and Sarah were essentially fascinated with the way the other lived, learning what made the other and her culture tick. Both also loved with a mutual passion the art, history, and beauty of China. Whoever loved these was Cixi's friend, though whether she was able to match Sarah's capacity for compassion is debatable—few had Sarah's gift for that. "We cannot love too much with unselfish love," she wrote to daughter Laura just before her audience with the empress dowager, "it is the lack of it which causes trouble."[11]

"There were sharp and bitter criticisms of the ladies' acceptance of the Imperial invitation," Sarah told Laura, who had no doubt already read them in the American press. In later years, Dr. Headland noted that by showing Cixi "the honour due her position," Sarah had done "more than any other person ever did, or ever can do, towards the opening up of the Chinese court to the people of the West." But at the time few appreciated her efforts. One of the more vigorous complaints about the audience came from John Otway Percy Bland, an English journalist working out of Shanghai (whose 1911 biography of Cixi, co-authored with Sir Edmund Trelawny Backhouse, set the standard for anti-dowager propaganda but is now entirely discredited given Backhouse's forging of key documents supporting their theories about her). "The address which Mrs. Conger incongruously read," Bland wrote to George Morrison, "strikes on the mind like a cold douche of imbecile fatuity." He went on to say that while he did not object to the women accepting the invitation, in so doing they had failed to comport themselves "as the representatives of that civilisation which the Chinese Court and Govt. so lately flouted and bombarded! . . . there is no excuse for Mother Conger." A few women chimed in. Alicia Little wrote, "The American Minister's wife speaks of 'my friend the Empress Dowager' or 'Her Majesty.' But at each fresh foreign visit to the Old Buddha . . . Chinese Christian women weep and protest bitterly thinking of their murdered relations, whom they esteem *martyrs*" (emphasis in original).[12]

As reported in the *New York Times*, the *London Globe* blamed the male members of the diplomatic corps for allowing their women "to be degraded by bowing to this infamous woman and receiving decorations from her blood-stained hands," as if adult females had no proper ability to make considered judgments or decisions of their own. Sarah was singled out as having failed to "spurn the gift of murderers chargeable with the torture and death of American Christian women." Disapproving letters to the *New York Times* and other newspapers would continue for the next year, most calling for a swift rejection of any overtures Cixi might make, a few hinting that Sarah had been sorely duped, and all picturing her as having kowtowed complaisantly to a bloodthirsty ogress. Soon after the audience, a story began making the rounds that Cixi had actually sobbed on Sarah's shoulder during their meeting, shedding what were assumed to be particularly cynical crocodile tears.[13]

Sarah felt it necessary to address the rumor herself, and did so directly to a female journalist who had sent a series of questions about the audience to Dr. Maud Mackey, a Presbyterian missionary, who gave them to Sarah. The journalist's questions were the same ones that would dog Sarah even after she left China, all circling her friendship with the empress dowager. "What is the foundation for the newspaper reports that Dowager wept on neck of Mrs. Conger?" and "Can you get for me a copy of Mrs. Conger's speech on that occasion?" The journalist confessed that she found herself "half inclined to write in advocacy of Mrs. Conger's cause, though when I first heard of it, I was of quite another opinion." Sarah answered with a barely concealed impatience which was unusual for her but was evidence of how frustrated she was by the "scandal" her audience had created. As she stated flatly,

> The Empress Dowager did not weep upon my neck. There was nothing said by either of us about forgiving and forgetting . . . I have been living among these Chinese people for nearly four years, and have tried to learn about them and from them . . . My feelings and actions toward Her Majesty and her people I have reason to believe are well taken.

She rejected the notion that she was asking the impossible when she insisted on seeing the Chinese side of the Boxer affair. Should the Chinese not be asked whether they would easily forgive the foreigners for their many trespasses in China and elsewhere? "Can the foreigner 'throw the first stone'? Surely this is not a one-sided relationship," Sarah went on. "All the nations will have to repent, forgive and labor patiently if they would become friends with China."[14]

Sarah spoke of her reasons to another American, Bailey Willis, the young engineer whom the Congers had invited to their (and his) first Christmas Eve dinner in China and later employed to locate potable water in the American compound. Willis had suggested that perhaps it was too soon to extend so strongly the hand of friendship to a woman who had not proven herself worthy of trust. Sarah told him she had been unable to resist when Cixi had made such a sincere and humble effort. "When the door opened a little way," she told him, "I had either to close it or to go in and see where it might lead . . . It is not for me to say what the influence might be." Sarah cited the personal evidence that, to her, was the only proof she needed: "If you could meet her," she said, "and she should take your hand and look in your eye and speak to you as she has to me, you would think her sincere." Sarah felt that "pressing the thorns of sorrow and revenge deeper into our hearts will never lessen the sting of the horrible past nor permit us to rest in peace." Only with "much patient work and forbearance" would the Chinese and foreigners come to an understanding and mutual appreciation beneficial to both. The way to begin that process was by approaching the empress dowager herself, even as, later on, she was to be convinced that the only way the world could appreciate the dowager was to see her image face to face. "When the battle is fought and the smoke clears away," she wrote, "the good is still there and at times is revealed in all men."[15]

Regardless of the negative press, Sarah achieved a coup of diplomacy that none of the gentlemen of the foreign legations could claim. She also may have had a direct effect on imperial state policies on reform, one of the thorniest issues for even a Chinese to meddle in. Shortly before her audience with Cixi, Sarah had visited a school for Chinese boys run by American missionaries. During her face-to-face talk with the dowager, Sarah had told her about the school "and of the deep interest I felt in those bright boys." Off hand, she mentioned that with such intelligent young men learning so diligently, they would in future serve as "a power in their honorable country. If some of your ablest youth could be educated abroad as well as at home," she went on, "would it not enable them to meet and understand the incoming ideas?" The irony of this suggestion was that the notion of sending young Chinese men abroad to study, the better to reform China's outdated ways, had been one of the programs dear to the Guangxu emperor and his mentor, Kang Youwei. Four years earlier, such an innovation, coming on the flood of similar reforms, had cost the emperor control of his throne. Now, sitting in her palace with this pleasant older lady from America, Cixi thought it over.

That same day, she issued an edict that young men be selected from each of the eight Manchu banners to be sent overseas to "familiarize themselves with foreign methods and enlarge their experience, that they may assist the Court in its purpose to cultivate talent for the services of the Government." Whether Sarah was the catalyst for this edict or not, she did not care, nor did she take credit. What mattered to her was one thing: "the edict has gone forth," and reform could finally begin.[16]

While the men of the diplomatic corps could not prevent Sarah and the other ladies from participating in a second audience with Cixi on February 27, they did all they could to put a damper on the proceedings. "The foreign ministers requested that no presents be given to the ladies by the Court," Sarah wrote to Laura. It was an insult to both Cixi, as if she were trying to purchase favors, and to Sarah, as if her favors were to be bought, and a sad comment on how women were seen from within the male enclave of foreign diplomacy. In any event this new rule had no effect on the tone of Cixi's audience—if anything, it clearly made both Sarah and the dowager more determined than ever to carry on as though nothing were amiss. This second meeting was not as formal as the first one. "Our visit was delightful," Sarah reported, "and full of womanly significance." Cixi felt enough at ease to confide in Sarah that she was learning English, a language in which, however, she never betrayed competency beyond a few set phrases. This was immaterial to Sarah; it was that Cixi was trying that delighted her. Cixi did something else she had never done before: she invited Sarah and the other ladies into her private rooms for a tour and more talk. As she had done at the first audience, Cixi took Sarah aside and asked her to sit with her on her bed, where they conversed. Behind this *kang* were shelves filled with ornaments, including seven clocks all ticking and chiming the hour. Cixi "took a small jade baby boy from the shelf," recalled Sarah, "tucked it into my hand, and with actions interpreted her unspoken words, 'Don't tell.' I took the dear little thing home, and I prize it." Sarah does not say what she and the dowager had discussed at this more intimate meeting, but perhaps the little jade boy gives a clue. Had Cixi, whose curiosity was insatiable, discovered that, like herself, Sarah had lost her only son? Had Sarah, in that talk of "womanly significance," told Cixi that they had this sad loss in common? Or was the gift just to show that while men might make rules, women were free to disregard them?[17]

Sarah was charmed. "I was truly grateful," she wrote later, "that I could see the good spirit manifested in that woman whom the whole world has so bitterly condemned." We can get some idea of the "womanly significance" of the conversations between Sarah and Cixi during these meetings from a letter Sarah later sent to Laura, summing up her relationship with Cixi. First of all, she maintained, she had been careful never to do two things: to carry to Cixi any requests from other people (she was swamped with them, to her distress), and not to discuss under any circumstances her or Cixi's religions. As Sarah wrote to Mary Baker Eddy, she had to live her faith, not proselytize about it. On a later occasion, she was moved to respond to Mrs. Eddy with a degree of sharpness rarely used with her revered "Mother" by this most loving of "daughters." Newspapers printed worrying tales of Sarah speaking of Christian Science to the empress dowager, alongside accounts of Cixi assuring Sarah that nothing would supplant Confucian teachings and that she planned to spread the word using missionary-style lectures—an interesting insight into her thinking, if true. These accounts prompted Mrs. Eddy to sternly advise Sarah that "[s]ilent prayer in and for a heathen nation is just what is needed," and that any attempt to convert the dowager would lead to more violence in what she regarded as a benighted country. Sarah, who could not countenance the terms "benighted" or "heathen" being applied to the Chinese, even from Mrs. Eddy, quickly answered: How could she proselytize in China when she was not a missionary, nor knew the required languages? She was not in China to teach but to learn, and there was much of that to do, for herself and other foreigners. "In a degree," she explained, "[I] found the inner heart of the *so-called* 'heathen Chinese' . . . I touched the chords of Sisterhood and we joined hands" (emphasis in original). And any fear Mrs. Eddy might have that speaking of Christian Science to the dowager would touch off what she called "a war on religion" was groundless, Sarah insisted, because it was the last thing she would ever do. Her credo in China was simple. "It was my earnest prayer," she wrote, "that Her Majesty—the Empress Dowager of China—the Princesses and the

Chinese Ladies should realize the tender touch of the true friendship of
a foreign lady." That had nothing to do with Christian Science, or any
religion, and everything to do with the capacity for sympathy shared by
all people, regardless of religion.[18]

In her letter to Laura about her meetings with Cixi, Sarah used more
direct language to explain what she was trying to do:

> Never have I tried to bear to the Imperial Court personal ideas . . .
> Questions of my own I did take to [the empress dowager]. She
> never avoided nor refused to answer and act favorably upon any
> question I laid before her.
>
> Whenever I found that we had customs at all in common
> with theirs I would speak of the Chinese customs then state that
> our country has similar ones . . . In speaking [for example] of
> cemeteries I told her that we too had beautiful burying grounds
> with monuments and tablets, grass, flowers, shrubs, trees, lakes
> and bridged streams. I said that we often visited these beautiful
> much-loved spots, and carried fresh flowers in loving memory of
> our dear departed ones.[19]

Even on so universal a subject as the respect of the living for the dead
and the holding sacred of their place of burial, Sarah found Cixi deceived
by stories that foreigners forgot about their ancestors and never bothered
to honor their graves. Having come of age during the Civil War, even as
Cixi had come of age during the Taiping Rebellion, Sarah was part of a
generation uniquely qualified to discuss the honoring of the dead and the
sacrifices made by them, as well as the shaping of rituals around funerals
and burial. Perhaps she told Cixi about these rituals. Her surprise and joy
was to thus find herself instructing the woman from whose culture she
herself felt she had so much to learn.

And this audience gave her an idea. While it was out of the question,
given the many hurdles of protocol, to ask the dowager to tea at the
American legation, what about inviting the ladies of the court—the
princesses and high-born ladies-in-waiting? Sarah put the question to
Edwin, who "said it would do no harm to try"—the court could always
say that custom forbade acceptance. So Sarah presented her plan to
Prince Qing, who consulted with Cixi. They agreed that the idea was an

excellent one. Sarah next asked that the dowager select which ladies were to come. Finally the day was set—March 14, 1902—for the first of a series of what were to become Sarah Conger's famous tiffins.[20]

Eleven princesses were expected, among them Cixi's adopted daughter, a daughter of Prince Gong, known as the Imperial Princess; Youlan, the second Princess Chun, who was Cixi's niece and future mother of Puyi, the last emperor of China; Prince Qing's two wives and three of his daughters, and several other ladies of rank. Sarah had asked Wang to fill the house with flowers, and he outdid himself. "The little potted trees filled full of red and white buds and blossoms [probably camellias, an auspicious flower] came into the compound in processions." On the wall of the reception room, Wang hung a special scroll painting which had been rendered for Sarah by the empress dowager; he filled the room with Chinese embroidery, vases, objets d'art, and other pieces from Sarah's collection so that the princesses might know how much their hostess valued and understood their art. Before the guests arrived, Sarah ran her ten American lady friends (missionaries and wives of diplomats) through a brief rehearsal, so that each "knew how to receive the Chinese ladies and how to go to the table; each had her number and knew just where to fall in line."[21]

At half-past noon, a long and colorful procession began to file through the modest entrance gate of the American legation, all eleven princesses—and nearly five hundred servants. First came a yellow silk imperial chair topped with a golden knob—this was the Imperial Princess, the dowager's adopted daughter. Next came the red satin chairs of the princesses, followed by the green ones of the ladies of lesser rank. Each princess brought with her eight eunuchs; beside these were accompanying court officials, crowding the street and the courtyard. "What a sight!" Sarah wrote. "The compound was full."[22]

"Some of these first ladies of China had never seen foreign ladies before," Sarah reported to Laura. Sarah first received the Imperial Princess; then the others followed them into the house, where introductions were made and Sarah was satisfied that each lady was in the care of one of her American friends. When everyone had been brought into the dining room, with its table decorated with red flowers and inscribed red place cards, Sarah raised her teacup in a toast:

> Let us lift our glasses filled to the brim with the best of good
> wishes for the health and happiness of the Emperor, the Empress
> Dowager, and Empress of China and to the prosperity of their
> people. May China and America continue in their friendly
> relations![23]

In reply, the Imperial Princess read a statement from Cixi: "She hopes that the pleasant relations that now exist between America and China will always continue as they now are."[24]

After tiffin, the women retired to the drawing room where, as might have been done in Des Moines or a suburb of Paris, the American ladies "served tea, played duets on the piano, sang, and looked at pictures." When it came time to go, "the grand procession passed from under the American flag and into the streets of the Dragon flag," Sarah recorded. Orders had gone out from the palace that no one was to stand in the streets to look at the princesses, but Sarah witnessed "thousands . . . enjoying the sight," yet another new chapter written in the old book of Chinese imperial customs. As the last of the princesses departed, Wang turned to Sarah, beaming, and said, "Might stay hundred year, never see like this." Servants from the other legations had come to ask him about the imperial ladies, expressing their awe and envy of him. As Sarah was later told by Sir Chentung Liangcheng, the baseball-loving Chinese minister to Washington, D.C., he had been an official at the Summer Palace for several years and had never once seen these ladies but from a distance. At the palace, only carefully selected eunuchs were allowed to wait on such ladies. And here Wang, the mere butler of the American minister, had been accorded the honor. "They think very great," Wang told Sarah with pride.[25]

Wang and the five houseboys, all neatly uniformed "were delighted over their unheard-of privilege," she told Laura. But the greatest privilege, she felt, was hers. "My dear girl," she wrote, "I bow my head low in most earnest prayer that love and love's wisdom may be revealed to me in all my intercourse with the Chinese, as well as with the other nationalities, and with my own dear people."[26]

⁂ ⁂ ⁂ ⁂ ⁂

One thing had to follow another. Soon Sarah and the American ladies who had feted the princesses were sent an invitation to tiffin with them. Sarah accepted, but now she had the anxiety of needing to prepare for the occasion so as not, as she put it, "to merit [the] ridicule" of the Chinese she so wanted to please. Even as he had been her saving grace during the Boxer Uprising, Wang was so again in these forays through the mysterious byways of Manchu and Chinese aristocracy.[27]

Before his death in late 1901, William Pethick, Li Hongzhang's American-born secretary and advisor, had been Sarah's advisor in all things Chinese, helping her comprehend the culture and its symbols. It would have been hard to replace Pethick had Wang, the Congers' Number One Boy, not been so eager to assist. He became another kind of teacher for Sarah—not only did he advise her on what colors of clothing and which flowers were appropriate for which season, but he drew Sarah's attention to that inner life of the Chinese she was so eager to explore.[28]

"The Chinese are very systematic in all they do," Sarah wrote a friend in America. "Twice a year an edict is issued by the Emperor indicating the day when his subjects shall change to winter or summer clothing." It also applied to one's daily conveyance. While out making calls in her official cart, Sarah remarked to Wang that it seemed warm enough to remove the padded panels and replace the glass windows of the cart with summer screens. She asked him to speak to the *mafu*, her chief stableman, about it. Wang did as she requested, only to return with the stableman's reply: "Madame, Mafoo say, 'No proper time put summer dress on cart. Mafoo and carter wear winter clothes, cart wear winter clothes.'" It is all too easy to imagine how most foreign mistresses would react to such advice. But Sarah listened. "All right," she said to Wang, "wait for proper time."[29]

Even without imperial edicts, the Chinese seemed to operate according to an unspoken plan that changed as ineffably as the seasons. Sarah never had to tell her servants that in winter she and Edwin dined at seven-thirty, at eight o'clock in summer—they just knew when the proper moment had come to make the transition. Wang's involvement in helping Sarah went beyond refitting the legation cart as the weather warmed. "[Wang] watches me very closely," Sarah observed, "and I encourage him to do so." This encouragement brought with it incidents which in the typical master-servant relationship would have been unthinkable. On the occasion of preparing for an audience with Cixi, Sarah had carefully selected a pearl and coral ornament the dowager had given her, thinking it might please Cixi to see her wearing it. But Wang stopped her before she reached the door. "No proper time wear that summer ornament," Wang told her, polite but grave in his mission to save his mistress from certain embarrassment. Sarah put the ornament back in its box, in exchange for another that passed Wang's judgment. On another evening, just as Sarah was leaving for a Chinese dinner wearing a long, fur-lined black satin coat, Wang approached her with that look. "More better," he advised, "you wear light, long, foreign coat." "Off it went," Sarah wrote, "and my own 'lady's coat' was donned." Far from being annoyed, she loved this advice, not just because she valued every opportunity to learn but also because, like the Chinese, Sarah shared a sense of everything being in its rightful place, as foreordained as the motions of the stars. "I am quite methodical myself," she noted, "and it appeals to me."[30]

At Autumn Moon Festival, Wang felt confident enough to help Sarah step into his world, if only for an hour. He asked her if she would like to see the servants' Moon Festival celebration. Pleased to be invited, Sarah followed Wang to an outer courtyard that the servants used, where in most foreign households in China the lady of the house rarely ventured. There she saw all of her houseboys sitting at a round table, its top crowded with dishes and teacups, all the men as neat as if ready for tiffin with the imperial princesses. The Moon Festival was another of those Chinese holidays in which Sarah would have noted resemblances to holidays in the West. The Moon Feast's celebration of the summer harvest gave it the flavor of the harvest festivals of New England and the American Midwest; its emphasis on the gathering together of people to eat and celebrate friendship under the full moon, and to speak of loved ones far away yet lighted by the same moon, and the showing of curios and children's toys, had something in it of Thanksgiving and Christmas. The colored lanterns hung in the garden, the music and singing, and the eating of special moon cakes imprinted with auspicious symbols, would have completed the resemblance. Perhaps, too, Sarah knew by now the story of the rabbit in the moon. Buddhist legend told of how the animals in a celestial garden each brought a gift to the Buddha. The rabbit, however, appeared with nothing to give but itself, so leapt into a fire for the Buddha's food. The Buddha said, "He who forgets self, be he the humblest of earthly creatures, will reach the Ocean of Eternal Peace." In Brazil, Sarah had made the vow to forget herself in order to learn about the people around her. Her enjoyment of the Moon Feast in the servants' courtyard, the young men smiling as they drank their tea, perhaps offering Sarah a moon cake, was all the proof she or the Buddha might need that she had come very close to her desired goal. As she wrote to her sister of this night, "I just wish you could realize what lovely, valuable things come my way, now that I know them and with delight recognize them." Born herself in the Year of the Rabbit, like that animal she had reached her own version of the peaceful ocean.[31]

✳ ✳ ✳ ✳ ✳

For the princesses' tiffin, held in a palace of the Forbidden City, Sarah and her ten American ladies were joined by the slender and elegant Madame Uchida, wife of Japan's foreign minister in Beijing, Viscount Uchida Yasuya, and all headed for the palace in a parade of "chairs, carts and ponies," their servants numbering a mere one hundred. This was a far cry from the army of 481 servants the princesses had brought to the American legation, but as Sarah pointed out, "Well, we got there!" On their arrival, the ladies were met by the princesses, who escorted them in to tea. "The feast was delicious," Sarah wrote her daughter. "[The] table looked beautiful in the white linen, flowers, candies, fruits, etc. We had plate cards and menus," all foreign details that they had learned from Sarah's tiffin. The princesses themselves were Sarah's chief delight. "They were beautiful in their bright, rich garments and decorations," she told Laura, "and no people could have been more hospitable or gracious."[32]

Sarah had barely finished sipping her tea when "two eunuchs entered, each with a pretty new basket with red satin pad," and on each "a beautiful little dog." Sarah's puppy was "like a little puffball" and "her imperial trappings of harness and ornaments were wonderful . . . a yellow silk collar with gold bells . . . a harness of heavy yellow silk braid fastened with gold buckles," and for a leash a silk cord attached to the collar with a golden hook. One of the ladies who read Chinese looked at the yellow silk label on the collar and told Sarah the puppy's name was

Sherza. Possibly the label simply explained that the breed of dog was a *shizi* [*gou*]—"lion dog"—as Sherza certainly was, but Sarah concluded that this was her name. "Lion dog" certainly had an ironic charm, as Sherza was a mere fluff of a creature, her collar and leash heavier than she was. "The little one looked right into my face with her big, round, black eyes," Sarah wrote approvingly, "without one thought of fear." The other puppy was given to Madame Uchida, whom Cixi also liked—as she told her lady-in-waiting, "She is always very nice and doesn't ask any silly questions." Both were gifts from the dowager, who was clearly pushing the diplomatic restrictions on gift-giving with delight.[33]

Sarah had wanted a "palace dog" since first arriving in Beijing. "If Father can have a cat," she wrote to Laura, "I can have a dog." But none were to be found in Beijing that were not gifts directly from the palace, or stolen—many *shizi* and Pekingese had left the Forbidden City when stolen during the post-Boxer looting. The dowager had special kennels for her dogs, each animal with its exotic name expressive of temperament or color; and several witnesses left accounts of how obedient they were to her, running or stopping at her command, and greeting her joyfully when she visited their kennels. Cixi was as jealous of their affections as she was of those of people she cared for, disliking anyone but herself to pet or caress them. Thus she had to really like someone to give them one of her precious palace dogs. She was to send Sarah another of her animals, a white and fawn Pekingese named Lao Hu ("Tiger"), who would accompany the Congers back to America.[34]

Each of the ladies was taken into the dining hall by one of the princesses, where the Imperial Princess offered a toast, "and good cheer, lively conversation, the Princesses in their rich clothing, their dainty ways and graces, made the day glow with enjoyable beauty." When Sarah and her ladies took their leave, the princesses surprised them by smilingly saying "good-bye" in English. This visit was of great significance to the project Sarah had in mind for Cixi's rehabilitation; without it, it is not certain her plan could have had the success that came. "I am truly grateful," Sarah wrote Laura, "to have this little knowledge of the inner lives of this strange yet attractive people." Referring as much to herself as to other foreign people, she added, "It is best to pause before we condemn people of whom we know little." Spending an afternoon with kind and gentle Chinese women, in their palace and her legation temple, "removes much of the ignorant prejudice I had against them."[35]

It would take several months and more meetings with Cixi before Sarah knew exactly what tack to take to address the many prejudices against the dowager in the Legation Quarter and beyond.

15
Sisterhood

It was obvious to Sarah, if not to many others in her circle, that the dowager was a hapless victim of gossip and sensationalist journalism created by people who knew nothing about her. She concluded that if people could just see Cixi as she did, they would feel about her as Sarah did. Sitting with Cixi and holding her hand, Sarah detected in "her strong character the golden threads of kindness and tenderness. I do not proclaim this on the housetops as the wise world would call me mad," she assured Laura, "and it would do no good." Along with her steadfast tactic of living in accordance with her beliefs, "striving all the while to bring out the best thoughts in people with our sayings and doings," a portrait to challenge the world's misapprehension of the dowager was tailor made to augment Sarah's form of passive edification.[1]

The only way Sarah could think of to represent what she saw as the truth of the empress dowager of China was to co-opt a uniquely European art form, the portrait, and offer the world an image of Cixi as she really was, not as illustrated papers and biased journalists depicted her. In so doing she was also borrowing a leaf from the public relations handbook of Queen Victoria—incidentally Cixi's favorite European monarch—whose photograph was to be found in ready abundance all over the world and whose family never shied from a camera lens. Thanks to this exposure, Victoria was seen as in some way belonging to the nation—her minatory nose, crisp mouth and blue eyes beneath coronet and mantilla became the very personification of Britain. Perhaps the same was possible for China, whose female ruler was, like Victoria, as much mother figure as monarch.

Sarah may have had another reason for insisting on the portrait, one closer to home. Everywhere she lived, Sarah hung up a portrait of her son Lorentus—it can be seen on a wall of her Pasadena parlor in a photograph taken after she and Edwin removed to the United States in 1905. The nearly life-size image of the boy, dressed in jacket, short pants, and the horizontal-striped stockings of the 1870s, sits looking out thoughtfully into a future he would never know. Through this picture, however, his mother would never forget him and would, in a way, keep him always near her. Sarah thus knew the power of an image, politically and sentimentally; and clearly she believed that if people could have such a picture of the empress dowager as she really looked, they would see the false caricatures for what they were.

Sarah first began to realize this on a trip to the fabled Summer Palace—Yiheyuan—that place of exotic mystery to which none of the diplomatic corps had yet been. When Alicia Little visited the then-abandoned spot in 1901, she judged it something of a Chinese "Rosherville," referring to a low-brow public pleasure garden in England, and was especially censorious of the so-called Marble Boat. Built in the eighteenth century, the Marble Boat was popularly believed to have been constructed for Cixi's pleasure using funds earmarked for the Chinese imperial navy. What actually happened was that Prince Chun, currying favor with the dowager, added to the low slung elegance of Qianlong's barge a Victorian superstructure resplendent with stained-glass windows and wall mirrors that reminded Mrs. Little of a restaurant, along with marble paddle wheels to show Cixi how up to date Chun was. Cixi ordered none of this, though she did enjoy it. If anything, it is the Summer Palace of today, crowded with tourists, some of its historic buildings shared out to the highest bidders in the pin-striped business world and others staffed by young people in ersatz Manchu court regalia, that most resembles Mrs. Little's Rosherville.[2]

The Summer Palace offered highlights not just of Chinese but of world architecture: the Tower of the Fragrance of the Buddha; two of the most perfect marble camelback bridges in China; and islands in Kunming Lake studded with delicate temples and pavilions, like some enchanted vision of the Eight Immortals painted on a scroll. The eastern lakeshore was adorned with the Qianlong-era Bronze Ox, while to the west was the Long Gallery, the longest covered walkway in China, every beam and lintel awash in bright scenes from Chinese opera and legend. As in 1860, in 1900 this dream-like setting was damaged by foreign troops. It was nothing like the all-out annihilation of Yuanmingyuan, but perhaps the symbolic mistreatment was worse. One hopes Cixi never saw the proofs of violation that left no record save for photographs later reproduced by the travel photographer Burton Holmes: British troops laughing in the Marble Boat, cooling lotus leaves on their head, or skinny-dipping in Kunming Lake. By the summer of 1902, much of the damage had been repaired, but here lay another minefield of calumny for the dowager. Blamed for robbing the treasury to make these repairs, Cixi in fact had little to do with them: it was mostly subscription funds from the Chinese people that helped erase the vandalism of what was, after all, a national treasure.[3]

Early one summer morning, Sarah, ladies of the corps, and the ministers started out in sedan chairs and carts over the road from Beijing. The surface was still covered in yellow sand from an earlier imperial progress, its crunchy golden grit lending a certain glamour to the travelers' journey. In villages along the route, the inhabitants had obviously been ordered to keep quiet, but this did not prevent them staring at the passing cavalcade—this many foreigners coming out to the Summer Palace in peace instead of war was surely something none had ever seen before. Parting the curtains of her chair, Sarah looked back at them wistfully, "as I pass on alone in my little house, shut away from their touch."[4]

After a two-hour journey, the party stopped for rest and refreshments in what Sarah calls a temple, likely one of the pavilions in the Garden of Harmonious Interests, an enclave of courtyards intersected by bridge-covered canals, its pavilions reflected in pools thick with lotus. From there the guests were taken to a series of houseboats, at the head of which was Cixi's private steam launch. "The Ministers' wives and those highest in rank were asked to enter Her Majesty's private boat," Sarah recorded. This boat took the lead, giving Sarah a dramatic view aft "as these many boats with their brilliant colorings, flags and streamers waving, passed in and out of the many turnings of the watercourses."[5]

Sarah's flotilla passed through shaded waterways, past Suzhou Street, a replica of a southern China merchant bazaar, and more temples and outbuildings. Floating under the high marble arch of the Bridge of Embroidered Ripples, the party was suddenly bobbing on the shimmering jade waves of Kunming Lake. Sarah felt she had entered "fairy scenes of dreamland": "We saw the island, with its high rocks, glistening yellow tiled roofs, grottoes, marble terraces, with their white, carved marble balustrades, large bronze statues, and gardens with flowering shrubs and spreading trees."[6]

The launch drew up to the palace's dock; marble steps rose to a courtyard where officials conducted everyone to an audience with Cixi, followed by refreshments, and then a promenade along the Long Gallery and through the many secluded gardens and pavilions of this "dreamland." The schedule gave Sarah little time with the dowager, and when she next saw her, she was in the steam launch sailing across to South Lake Island, where there was a temple to the Dragon King.[7]

Sarah and the ladies were taken out to the island. On reaching the double staircase below the temple, Sarah climbed to the top, where a broad verandah and a wide-angle view of the Summer Palace unfolded before her. Cixi stood waiting for her. "The Empress Dowager stepped to the marble balustrade," Sarah recalled, "and looking out upon the wonderful scene stretched out before her, spoke my name. I went to her and she took my hand in both of hers. Looking at the scenes about us and beyond us, she said in a tender, thoughtful way, 'Is it not beautiful?'" As they stood holding hands, wordlessly looking across the lake to the golden-roofs and crimson pillars among the trees on the opposite shore, both women clearly felt, even if they did not speak it, that they were sisters in appreciation. When it was time to return to Beijing, Sarah stepped aboard the steam launch with the other ladies and so began their chug back across the lake, "taking with us the remembrance of a happy day." She turned in time to see Cixi walk out to the terrace and the balustrade again, to watch as the vessels sailed around the Marble Boat and away from view.[8]

Sarah already cherished an affection for the dowager that she had shared with many people, and been accused of by others, an affection ribbed with the defensive conviction that if Cixi was lovable, surely she was not also terrible. Of the dowager's feelings about Sarah we have little evidence—in fact it would appear she was as puzzled as she was pleased by Sarah's attachment to her. Yet it would seem that on this day, standing on the terrace of the Dragon King Temple, she had reached that point in their relationship where, knowing Sarah better, seeing her passion for the same things she loved, Cixi was able to trust her—something Cixi never did lightly. The impression Sarah left, watching the thoughtful Cixi studying her as she sailed away across the lake, seems to imply that the bond between people who are tied by fate—that thin red thread of the Chinese proverb—was indeed there. Both women had felt its tug.[9]

✳ ✳ ✳ ✳ ✳

June 1903 began with a telegram from Fred and Laura reading simply: "Girl." The birth of Sarah Conger Buchan on June 3 brought "a joyous promise into your life and into ours," Sarah wrote to her daughter. When a packet containing locks of the baby's hair arrived in the diplomatic pouch, Sarah showed them to the servants, who were thrilled that "Miss Laura" had a baby and was doing well, but were concerned that her hair had been cut—such was never done to Chinese baby girls. But Sarah reassured them, observing that "they do not quite understand how unselfishly generous our American babies are."[10]

Shortly after receiving the news of little Sarah's birth, Sarah received permission from Cixi for an audience at the Summer Palace requested for June 15. Sarah had asked for this audience ostensibly to present her friend, Charlotte Evans, wife of the commander-in-chief of the Asiatic Fleet, to the emperor and dowager, but she also had another motive related to her plan for rehabilitating Cixi's reputation. "For many months," Sarah wrote, "I had been indignant over the horrible, unjust caricatures of Her Imperial Majesty in illustrated papers, and with a growing desire that the world might see her more as she really is, I had conceived the idea of asking her Majesty's permission to speak with her upon the subject of having her portrait painted." Sarah had written to a Paris-trained American artist, Katherine Carl, who was living in Shanghai but whom the Congers had met in Macao, and asked her if she would do the honors. "Mrs. Conger hoped, if the project should materialize," recalled Kate, "that her Majesty might later consent to send the portrait to the [1904] Exposition at St. Louis. She thought such a portrait would be of great interest to the American people . . . She also felt, as she had had an opportunity of seeing a great deal of the Empress Dowager, that if the world could see a true likeness of her, it might modify the generally accepted idea which prevailed as to Her Majesty's character." This was a tall order for an artist who had not yet painted anyone so high on the totem pole of world celebrity.[11]

The day of the audience, an eighteen-year-old Manchu girl, Der Ling, was standing beside Cixi's throne chair when the dowager spied figures being conducted toward the hall. Der Ling's teenaged eyes quickly recognized Sarah, who had had her family to dinner at the legation, and determined that the other was Charlotte Evans. Cixi was relieved, but scowled as a third figure appeared: it was another of the missionary translators Sarah brought with her, despite the fact, Cixi grumbled to Der Ling, that "I have your mother, your sister and yourself, which should be sufficient," and the missionary ladies seldom spoke a Chinese Cixi could understand.[12]

Pretty, ambitious, and bright, Der Ling—later known by the title of "Princess"—was the daughter of Yu Keng, a cosmopolitan Manchu aristocrat who favored reform, and his wife, Louisa, daughter of a Boston merchant established in Shanghai. Der Ling and her sister, Rong Ling, spoke English and French, played the piano, had studied dance in Paris with Isadora Duncan, and had taken acting tips from Sarah Bernhardt. Cixi had expressed interest in Yu Keng's daughters coming to court after hearing about them from Prince Qing's playboy son, Zaizhen, who had danced with them in Paris when their father was Chinese minister there. Given that Sarah knew the family before this, it is certainly possible that she, too, put in a word of recommendation. What Cixi wanted were ladies-in-waiting who would fit in as Chinese women but be able to speak the languages of the foreign ladies she entertained—who were, significantly, American. She also wanted to be seen by her foreign guests as *au courant* with their fashions and manners, hence requesting that Der

Ling, her sister, and their mother wear their French gowns and hats while they served at court, and even trying on their high-heeled Paris shoes. Like Sarah, Der Ling had naïvely but sincerely come to court with the hope of effecting Western-style reform by encouraging the dowager to model herself along the lines of a European monarch. While this was a huge task for anyone, let alone a teenage socialite, it was part of the trend of Cixi's own thought: to embrace rather than reject foreign ways, through foreign women rather than foreign men.[13]

Cixi had not only gone to a great deal of trouble to plan this audience but, as Der Ling relates, had put her court ladies through more rehearsals and run-throughs than a hard-driving Broadway director. Besides being Cixi's interpreter, Der Ling was put in charge of the dowager's vast collection of jewels and ornaments, and so was privy to much of the planning that took place behind the scenes. Not unlike Sarah with the ladies of the diplomatic corps, Cixi demanded perfection from her court ladies when entertaining guests, so that "they had grown to hate the very mention of a foreign audience." Cixi's gown, per Der Ling, was a gorgeous creation worthy of a goddess, embroidered all over with one hundred butterflies and fringed with pearls. Her *tianzi* was adorned with butterflies of jade, and the rest of her jewelry all bore butterflies in its design. Since the butterfly was a symbol of longevity, Cixi was wholeheartedly declaring to her guests that she hoped and intended to be around for a very long time to come.[14]

Termagant though she might sometimes be, Cixi was not without humor as Sarah, Mrs. Evans, and the interpreter approached her throne. "I think [the missionary woman] must like to see me," she quipped sarcastically to Der Ling. "I will tell her that I am glad to see her always, and see if she understands what I mean."[15]

Introducing Mrs. Evans to the dowager, Sarah sat in a chair brought by eunuchs. After some polite small talk, Cixi surprised Sarah by warmly congratulating her on the birth of Sarah Buchan, whose advent she had heard about through Der Ling's mother. Cixi was not merely obeying a foreign convention here. While a Han Chinese family might regard a daughter as a misfortune, Manchu families felt quite differently, according their unmarried daughters rank fully equal to their sons. As Kate Carl was once told by a Chinese diplomat posted to the United States, "the only unmarried woman in the world whose position is analogous to that of the 'American Girl,' in her own family, is the Manchu girl." Cixi's interest in Sarah Buchan, including showering her with clothes and jewelry, much of it purchased by Der Ling at the dowager's express order, was to continue until the dowager's death in 1908.[16]

The ladies were conducted into a dining room and seated at a table arranged by Der Ling with white linen, gold menu holders, and silverware augmented by chopsticks. Clearly the court princesses had been closely questioned by Cixi on their return from the American legation about how things were arranged at Sarah's tiffin, and she had ordered her table to be laid in conformity with the standard Sarah used. Der Ling, her sister, mother, and the other princesses dined with Sarah and Mrs. Evans and were served the best champagne. After all, "I know that foreign ladies like to drink," Cixi explained knowingly to Der Ling. Afterward, Cixi invited the ladies to come see her in her private apartments, where she flattered Mrs. Evans by telling her that China had "not such fine buildings as there are in America," and that she longed to travel so that she could see the United States for herself—the polite, self-deprecating small talk of a well brought up Chinese lady (she did often say that the United States was her favorite foreign country).[17]

Amid the conversation, Der Ling, who was with Cixi all the time translating, noticed Sarah asking the missionary translator to tell Cixi she had a question for her. Der Ling heard the words "the portrait" and, guessing what Sarah had in mind, was about to tell Cixi when the missionary blurted out: "Mrs. Conger has come with the special object of asking permission to have Her Majesty's portrait painted by an American lady artist, Miss Carl, as she is desirous of sending it to the St. Louis Exhibition, in order that the American people may form some idea of what a beautiful lady the Empress Dowager of China is."[18]

In her letter to Laura, Sarah couched this request in a good deal more ceremony and dignity. "With intense love for womankind," she wrote, "and in justice to this Imperial woman, I presented my subject without doubt or fear. Her Majesty listened, was interested, and with a woman's heart conversed with me." Cixi had at first reacted with complete silence. "I kept very calm, most respectful," Sarah recalled, "as I talked with her, telling my reasons why I greatly desired that Her Imperial

Majesty's portrait should be placed with the portraits of the Rulers of other nations." As the result of this conversation, "the Empress Dowager gave consent to allow her Imperial portrait to be painted." Yet Cixi was actually more confused than convinced, as Der Ling reports, because what Sarah had made was, in the Chinese tradition, a very strange request. In China, portraits were only ever painted of the deceased. However many longevity-ensuring butterflies Cixi had on her gown and *tianzi*, Sarah's petition to have a portrait painted of the still-living dowager unwittingly threw a shadow of the tomb over the happy gathering.[19]

Der Ling says that in fact it took the better part of the next two days for her to help the dowager understand what it was that Sarah wanted and to agree to it. Even then, there were doubts, especially after Der Ling showed Cixi a portrait of herself painted by Kate Carl in Paris. Besides the use of oil paints, Cixi's greatest objection was one that she would hold on to until her last portrait was painted by a foreigner in 1905: she hated the shadows used in Western art to render perspective. "Do you think this Artist lady will paint my picture to look black also?" Cixi enquired with concern. And of course, Cixi's final worry had to do with what this new project would do to interrupt her busy schedule. "When I explained to her that it would be necessary for her to sit for several hours each day, she was excited," Der Ling reported, "and afraid she would never have the patience to see it through." As it happened, Der Ling herself and her younger sister, Rong Ling, would end up sitting in for the dowager more often than not over the next several months.[20]

"Only think of it!" Sarah exclaimed to Laura, having departed the Summer Palace in a haze of happiness. "That this portrait may present to the outside world even a little of the true expression and character of this misrepresented woman, is my earnest wish . . . Her intuitive ability to perceive and conceive is not easy to surpass, nor even equal, by man or woman." But perhaps even she began to wonder whether Cixi really intended to follow through with the project. That she later had doubts is clear from Der Ling's account. Sarah wrote a letter to Der Ling that very night, "begging me not to prejudice Her Majesty against Miss Carl in any way." She had seen Der Ling pull at Cixi's sleeve as the missionary translator explained what Sarah wanted the dowager to agree to, and thought it might have been in criticism of Kate—it was actually to keep

Cixi from saying anything embarrassingly uninformed. Cixi was incensed when Der Ling naïvely showed her the letter. How did anyone dare, she exclaimed, to try to influence her through one of her ladies-in-waiting? This is the one record we have of her being angry with Sarah, but it may not have been so much that Sarah had tried to enlist Der Ling in the cause as that Cixi would have preferred that Sarah communicate with her directly—a method Sarah had always used until now. As possessive of her friends as she was of her palace dogs, Cixi would not have liked that her favorite Sarah was writing notes to her favorite Der Ling.[21]

Cixi soon recovered her equanimity toward Sarah and her project though she continued to be wary of Sarah's future requests (due, it must be said, to her habit of bringing missionary friends to audiences). Of one thing she could be certain. She now knew just how much the portrait meant to Sarah and, thanks to Der Ling, how significant it could be for her own legacy to agree to participate in this the most modern and foreign project of any she had undertaken in her reign. After all the fuss and delay, Cixi finally gave her gracious assent, "If you know all about this artist lady, and think she is quite all right to come here to the palace," she placidly told Der Ling, "of course she may come, and I will tell Prince Ching to reply to Mrs. Conger to that effect."[22]

16
Portrait of a woman

Katherine Augusta Carl was born in New Orleans in 1865, the daughter of Captain Augustus Carl, who had died in the Civil War. Her mother, a relative by marriage of Sir Robert Hart, became president of the Tennessee State Female College in Memphis, and it was there that Kate received her education. Not content with becoming a teacher, Kate went to Paris to study at the famed Académie Julian, an art school which, unlike the École des Beaux Arts, allowed women to enroll and participate in life drawing classes using nude male models. It was in Paris that Kate had met Lady Yu and her daughter Der Ling, and painted the portrait of the latter which had helped convince Cixi to allow Kate to paint her own portrait. Kate was in China because her brother, Francis, was commissioner of customs in Chefoo (now Yantai), and future co-commissioner for China to the 1904 St. Louis Exposition. Their mother had wanted to see him one last time before she died; Kate brought her to China across Siberia, she saw her son, and passed away soon after, leaving Kate in Shanghai.[1]

For the start date for the portrait, Cixi had chosen August 5 after consulting with her court astrologers. She evidently also chose the hour, eleven o'clock, on the same basis. It was the hour of the horse, a favorable sign in the Chinese zodiac for profitable undertakings but one which perhaps should have given Kate pause as well, since the horse is not known to like being tied to any one place.

"The day was a bright one," Sarah recalled, and Kate concurred: "The distant hills, where lay the Summer Palace, were delicately limned against a soft blue-gray sky, and the whole made an entrancing picture." The ladies were received at the palace entrance by Chief Eunuch Li Lianying, and escorted to the Hall of Benevolence in Longevity, Cixi's official audience hall, with its bronze lions snarling at malefic spirits and giddy American visitors.[2]

Kate, too, had heard all the stories about the empress dowager, and was as shocked as Lady Susan Townley to see "a charming little lady, with a brilliant smile," who stepped forward to greet Sarah. Kate was so overcome that she made a gesture of homage, a breach of custom unthinkable to any Chinese, which would characterize her adoring relationship with Cixi over the next nine months: she took the hand Cixi extended in greeting and kissed it. Stunned breaths may have been taken by the ladies and eunuchs standing by, for kissing just among ordinary Chinese people was not done, let alone in the protocol-choked atmosphere of the palace. But Cixi did not seem to mind—pleasantly surprising changes of routine never displeased her. "Her Majesty's first impression of Miss Carl was a good one," Der Ling recorded. Cixi was to affirm this when she affably asided to Der Ling, "We will handle her pretty easily, I think."[3]

Cixi ordered eunuchs to fetch Kate's painting materials into the hall, including the six-by-four-foot canvas she had brought from Beijing. Der Ling had advised Kate that Cixi would not sit for anything smaller, and noted with exasperation that when Cixi saw the canvas she was "very much disappointed, as in her opinion even that was not large enough."[4]

Officials from the Zongli Yamen had told Kate also that Cixi would not be able to pose more than twice for her, a schedule that would have given her hardly enough time for a preliminary sketch. She would stretch this restriction a bit, but that was the least of her worries this first day in the unprepossessing darkness of the audience hall, which she studied frantically for a properly lit vantage point in which to begin her work.

Cixi, who had left the room, now re-emerged wearing a yellow silk gauze embroidered with fat purple wisteria, to be immortalized in one of the two official portraits Kate painted (the one that Cixi kept at the Summer Palace). Kate's eye for detail, trained in the richly observant school of fin de siècle French painting and now feasting on the visual smorgasbord before her, gives some idea of her plans for the portrait: "At the top button, from the right shoulder, hung a string of eighteen enormous pearls separated by flat pieces of brilliant, transparent green jade. From the same button was suspended a large, carved pale ruby, which had yellow silk tassels terminating in two immense pear-shaped pearls of great beauty!" It was a good thing she rejoiced in this splendid minutiae; she would need to fill up the huge canvas with it.[5]

After the eunuchs had placed the dragon-carved throne in the one place that gave Kate some light to work in, Cixi took her seat, and promptly at eleven o'clock, as announced by the chimes and tunes of eighty-five different clocks distributed about the room, the project began. "Beginning anything is momentous," Kate recalled. But aside from having a wall of blank canvas before her on one side and the empress dowager of China on the other, Kate was herself the object of attention of several rows of princesses, ladies-in-waiting, eunuchs, and servant girls, all standing "in breathless silence around, intently watching every movement, for everything touching Her Majesty is a solemnity."[6]

Sarah, standing in the crowd, was watching, too, but it was Cixi whom she studied. "While Her Majesty was posing for her portrait," she recalled, "two eunuchs knelt before her with communications. Her Majesty took one and perused it, then took the other . . . the intensity of her expression while reading spoke volumes," though it also said much about her inability to hold a pose while Kate sketched rapidly in charcoal across the towering canvas. Before Kate had done much more than block in the figure and the head, Cixi turned abruptly to her interpreter and said, "enough work had been done for that day."[7]

As the clocks ticked, Cixi came down from her throne in a rustle of silk gauze to inspect Kate's work. Politely, since Cixi had given her no more than about fifteen minutes of her time, Kate recalled that the dowager's personality was so strong she had "been able to get enough of her character into this rough whole to make it a sort of likeness," but it had not been long enough to accomplish anything satisfactory to the artist. However Cixi studied the sketch with the appraising eye of the talented amateur painter, then beckoned to Sarah and the others to come see. "The likeness pleased all," Sarah affirmed.[8]

After luncheon, an opera performance which Cixi narrated to her guests through Der Ling, and the giving of gifts, Sarah departed the palace wearing scented sandalwood bracelets Cixi had placed on her wrists. Even as Kate, delighted beyond measure by the success of the venture and the unexpected charm of Cixi, "had a curious feeling of having been transported into a strange world," Sarah went home with a similar sense of wonder but also a gratitude that at last the portrait project was begun. "The magnitude of this portrait painting is beginning to grow on me," Sarah told Laura. "What will the end be?" Kate might have asked the same. Over the next several months, there would be many starts and stops as Kate tried to keep up a regular schedule of sittings in a variety of settings, from the Summer Palace to the Forbidden City, none of them perfect for lighting or convenience; she would have to resign herself to having Der Ling and her sister stand in for the dowager when Cixi decided she could not pose any longer. And living with Lady Yu and daughters, Kate would have to resign herself to being watched at all times, though whether she knew this was by order of the empress dowager is unclear.[9]

What happened to Kate Carl, however, was much the same process as that which was transforming Sarah into an admirer and defender of China and the Chinese. As Kate was trying on the court gowns Cixi had had made for her, learning to use chopsticks and the Chinese language, exposing herself to the music, theatre, and ceremonials of Cixi's court, and studying the elderly woman whom she had come to paint and ended up adoring, Sarah was moving forward with her own larger project. It was an adjunct to the portrait: of building as many bridges between her world and that of Chinese women as she could and as they would allow. As she told an American friend:

> At first, as we look [at Chinese culture] we see nothing but confusion; we see no method, and everything seems to be done backwards; we see customs without meaning, education without value, religion without a redeeming feature; we are amused at

the people, at their style of clothes, of wearing their hair; at their modes of locomotion; their process of tilling the soil; their ancestor worship; their attitude toward women. We ridicule their amusements, and doubt their sincerity in all things. In fact, we deride, belittle, and woefully underrate everything Chinese . . . [But] if we can detect their line of thought, we can better comprehend their actions. Let us be unbiased, charitable, and watch to see if we cannot find that which we would assign to the good . . . It may be that we shall learn lessons of value to our own living.[10]

※ ※ ※ ※ ※

"I must tell you about my birthday," Sarah wrote to Laura on July 25, 1903. She had naturally been asked her age by her Chinese friends, there being no taboo about how old a lady was in a society where age brought respect from the young. Much had been made of Edwin's sixtieth birthday that spring: Cixi and the Guangxu emperor had gifted him with a fine sword with lacquer scabbard and the imperial monogram engraved on the blade. As Sarah's sixtieth birthday approached, these friends, who included the "beautiful, accomplished, young" wife of elderly Grand Secretary Wang Wen Chao, and her married daughter Mrs. Kao, began to ask her about her social schedule, finally requesting permission to visit her on the day of her birthday (July 24).[11]

"They said the sixtieth birthday is one of great note for the Chinese," Sarah noted. The sixtieth was special, because it was believed to be the start of a new cycle after a life of many children and much accomplishment. Wang brought out both the Chinese lunar calendar and the Western one, the better to synchronize them for Sarah's Chinese friends. Sarah wondered what they were up to, and asked one of the interpreters whether she should take her friends' interest seriously. "They surely are in earnest now," she was told. To be ready for them, Sarah and her American friend Maurine Campbell planned a birthday party.[12]

On July 23, gifts began to arrive at the temple-home. "Four most elegant, large embroidered birthday hangings in glass cases," Sarah enumerated for Laura, "lovely fans, beautiful ornaments, fragrant flowers, boxes of choice tea, boxes of delicious fruits, lotus seeds . . ." Her list went on and on, and did not include the gifts Cixi had sent to her a few days before. "How she learned about this day," Sarah wondered, "I never knew," but it was probably again the work of kind Lady Yu.[13]

The day of the birthday visit, Wang helped Sarah hang scrolls and display the gifts "in the most approved Chinese style." At noon the ladies arrived, and while they were having their tea Wang came in carrying a yellow card and two large boxes covered in yellow silk. "We all knew that Her Majesty had sent them," Sarah recalled. Inside, under the protective covering of lotus leaves, Sarah found flowers and ripe peaches. She gave each lady a flower; noting that they put them in their hair, she did likewise. The ladies explained to her what the gift meant. Peaches, for example, were considered the fruit of the immortals—the god of longevity, Shouxing, was usually depicted carrying one, and they were a traditional gift on the sixtieth birthday. The flowers were a rich lexicon: peach and oleander blossom meant "long life" and "rich in sustenance and beauty." Asters expressed "superior to circumstances." Perhaps the sweetest flower code of all belonged to the marigold, which spoke "words" that any sixty-year-old woman would love to hear: "beautiful in age." "Her Majesty has given you the best wishes that she could give anyone," the ladies told Sarah.[14]

Sarah was finding evidence that where East and West could clash, they could also embrace. "When the Chinese ladies visit me," Sarah told Laura, "I strive to make the visit interesting to them." She and Wang brought out her best Chinese and American possessions and Sarah and the guests talked about them, not to make comparisons so much as to find where there were common threads between the two cultures. This delighted Sarah's friend the Dowager Princess K'e, who told Sarah how, prior to the Boxer disaster, she had collected many foreign things, and studied photographs of foreign buildings and gardens, never imagining that she would one day be among them, in the home of Americans. "I am now permitted to look upon a living panorama," she enthused, much as Sarah herself did after visiting Chinese private homes.[15]

"I never expected to meet Prince Su again," Sarah told Laura, "or to meet his family"—indeed, it was surprising he had returned at all. The prince, whose palace had been destroyed in the Boxer siege, had fled Beijing with the empress dowager. When he returned to Beijing he had no home to come back to, nor his confiscated estates in Manchuria to rely on. Sarah was especially fond of Prince Su's sister, wife of the Mongolian Prince Gungsang Norbu, chief commissioner for Mongolian and Tibetan Affairs. Her "strong character and intelligence" attracted Sarah just as Cixi's did.[16] When the elderly mother of the Su siblings died, Sarah had Marian Headland send her sympathies to the family. With the family's thanks was included an unheard-of invitation "to go to their home of sorrow if we would thus honor them." Sarah recognized the uniqueness of the offer. "This was a very great departure," she wrote, "from the almost iron-clad customs of past centuries."[17]

Sarah and Marian Headland were received at the door of the Su home by the former Princess Su. White cotton served as mourning in old China, and all the servants, and the princess, were clad in it. The foreign women were guided to a south-facing building containing an altar room, with chambers opening to left and right for descendants of the deceased, separated by sex. Joining the women on the left, who knelt on white cushions facing the shrine, Sarah studied the faces around her. "Through their rough white cotton clothing, unpainted faces, unadorned persons, and wrapped heads," she observed, "their characteristic features and expressions shone forth in strength and beauty." None of the women turned to stare at the foreign lady in black who had joined them, as almost certainly would have occurred had a Chinese lady suddenly appeared at the cerements of a foreigner—it was simply accepted that she, like themselves, was there to honor the deceased princess.[18]

"Bells rang, cymbals tinkled, and uniformed musicians played their wailing music," remembered Sarah. "Friends of rank came and paid their respects, and brought their 'feasts' which were then placed upon the table back of the shrine." Sarah bowed to Prince Su before being taken into another courtyard. "Dowager Princess Su's long life of rank and honors, adorned with goodness, had reaped at her death a bountiful harvest in the outpourings of loving hearts," Sarah recorded. The courtyard was crowded with proofs of this: rows of flowering trees in painted porcelain pots, furniture and trunks filled with silks and satins; jewelry, fans, toilet articles, clothing—even her favorite dice and "ebony" chair; and servants to bring any of these things to her whenever should she desire. All, down to the dice, were made of papier-maché, "to be burned at their proper time and place" as offerings to the old princess beyond the Yellow Springs.[19]

When Marian Headland asked the daughter of Prince Su whether she really believed that her grandmother would require these things in the spirit world, the woman said, "Perhaps not, but she enjoyed her cards and dice, and the chair was such a necessity, that, whether she needs them or not, it is a comfort to us to get and send her everything she liked while she lived, and it helps us bear our sorrows."[20]

Later, Marian watched the burning of these spirit goods, which rose up "in a flame that could be seen for miles around. But in less time than it takes to tell it the whole was a heap of glowing ashes" in the empty street, urchins poking the embers with sticks. The mourners stayed for the brilliant flames, but nobody wanted to see the cold ashes.[21]

✳　✳　✳　✳　✳

Sarah found herself occupying an even more intimate place in the family of Grand Secretary Wang Wen Chao. On first hearing that Mrs. Wang was ill, Sarah had sent her a basket of flowers. The following day, the Wangs' nine-year-old daughter came to the legation door, her amah with her, bearing four boxes of tea in thanks for Sarah's floral gift. The girl was brought into the drawing room and seated, but each time a member of the Congers' extended family or other guests entered the room she rose respectfully in that display of flawless manners that Sarah loved. When Edwin came in, he was greeted with a graceful curtsy. Sarah adored the child and in any American household would have been forgiven for wanting to "take the little one in my arms and caress her." But Sarah knew that this was not the Chinese way. Soon after this, when Mrs. Wang was better, she called on Sarah herself. Her son had come with her, and he told Sarah he wished to thank Edwin personally for taking an interest in his mother's health. Wang introduced the elderly American man and the young Chinese boy, Sarah recalled, "and with all the grace and ease of an adult the little fellow acted his part." As she explained to Laura, "I assure you that these gracious manners are not confined to the higher classes . . . I have detected charming characteristics in the Chinese of which the foreigner dare not boast."[22]

Mrs. Wang had noticed how much Sarah loved children. On finding out about young Sarah Buchan in far-off America, she and her daughter

Mrs. Kao planned to make a set of clothing for the child. Then everything went silent. Sarah normally saw much of the two women, and though Mrs. Wang had been so ill, she had recovered. So when Sarah did not see her for a few weeks she wondered but did not pry. The news of Mrs. Wang's death came to her when Marian Headland brought Mrs. Kao with her on a visit to the legation. Mrs. Kao had waited, wanting to be the one to tell Sarah. "We talked of the good qualities of their dear one," Sarah recalled, "and of the happy hours that we had passed together." Sarah and her tiffins had meant so much to Mrs. Wang that, as Mrs. Kao told her, the dying woman's last request had been to see the group photograph Sarah had had made of her guests in the courtyard of the legation after one of their gatherings.[23]

Sarah ordered eight papier-maché pots, painted to look like the finest porcelain, filled with paper trees blooming with paper flowers in all colors, to be sent to the Wang mansion for the funeral. Then the next day, she and her sister Lavinia, who was staying with the Congers for the season, took sedan chairs to pay their respects. The grandeur of the elderly Princess Su's obsequies was absent, but she had been old and not far from death, while Mrs. Wang had died young, with children to leave to some other woman's care. The tragedy of this blanketed the Wang compound, where even the bright paper offerings of flowers, fruit, and money were dimmed. "Above an altar upon which incense was burning," recalled Sarah, describing the events later, "there was an excellent portrait of Mrs. Wang Wen Chao; before this portrait we bowed."[24]

Behind the shrine was the coffin, surrounded by mourning family members. It is a measure of the closeness Sarah had to this family that she was asked if she would like to join them at the coffin. At a Chinese funeral, the deceased commanded even more deference and honor than the still-living elderly; no one was permitted to approach the coffin who was not considered auspicious. That an outsider of both race and faith like Sarah would be invited to mourn with Mrs. Wang's immediate family was certainly unusual, possibly unprecedented. Suspecting this, Sarah first asked if other Chinese besides the family were allowed this privilege. When told that they were not, she thanked them and said "that as the rite was for her nearest and dearest, we would not enter." Influencing Sarah's decision may have been the endearing presence of Mrs. Wang's daughter. The girl curtsied to each lady, then came back to Sarah who, unable to resist, put her arms around the child but dared not kiss her. "My sympathy and love were shown in other ways," Sarah told Laura. When the guests were seated to a meal afterward, the girl, sitting between Sarah and Marian Headland, was seen to not touch her food. Sarah asked her why. "I cannot eat," she told her, looking up "with her big eyes and sweet expression." Sarah replied, "You are right, and neither do I care to eat," and the two, the sixty-year-old foreign lady and the nine-year-old Chinese girl, sat in solidarity, honoring the memory of the woman who would eat no more.[25]

Some time later, Wang Wen Chao arrived at the legation for a reception Edwin was giving for high Chinese officials. With him he brought a yellow silk box. Wang carried it to Sarah and read the note that was attached: "My wife had planned to make a suit of clothes for your granddaughter, and had begun the garments before her sickness, but left them unfinished. I have had them completed, and I bring them myself as a humble gift in her memory." Sarah opened the box and handled each garment with reverence before sending them on to Laura and Fred. "People may tell me," she wrote Laura, "that the Chinese lack feelings and ways of expressing them. My intercourse with these Chinese people teaches me quite to the contrary."[26]

"Dear Laura," Sarah asked her daughter, "teach [Sarah] the value of each of these many gifts so kindly sent to her from far-away China. Do not let the great number of them lessen their value. Each is as rich in its meaning as though it were the only one."[27]

✳ ✳ ✳ ✳ ✳

From contemplating the dead and their shrines, Sarah also experienced the happiest occasion of Chinese life (aside from the birth of a son), that of marriage. And she did so, as with funerals, in contravention of received Chinese custom.

The opportunity came through the vivacious Dowager Princess K'e, she who had dreamed of being in a real American household. A formidable aristocrat with the cynical mouth and laughing eyes of a woman who has seen more than her fair share of life's vagaries, the dowager princess was to Sarah a sort of accessible empress dowager. "She is a bright, educated, intelligent lady of high rank," Sarah observed admiringly, "and is queen of her home." Yet for all the stories Sarah had heard about the draconian habits of Chinese mothers-in-law, she never saw the dowager princess treat her daughters-in-law or indeed anybody with disrespect. She always appeared "gentle and tender," even to her servants.[28]

The dowager princess had already given Sarah a verbal invitation to the pre-wedding festivities for her youngest son and his bride. This was followed up by the arrival of large, red invitation cards. Sarah believed that this was the first time such an honor had ever been extended to foreign ladies by a Manchu family of high rank. At the dowager princess's mansion, Sarah was stunned by the beauty of the nuptial decorations. "The ladies of the household in beautiful embroidered gowns, exquisite in colorings, delicately painted faces, and elaborate festive head ornaments, came out from the large open door [of the house] to meet us near the centre of a paved court, which was beautifully decorated in red, the wedding color. What a picture!" Sarah enthused to Laura.[29]

Sarah was escorted to a reception room and introduced to the other guests, all Chinese, who, as at the Su and Wang funerals, welcomed her as one who belonged. She then was seated with them for a kind of performance she had never seen: a parade of rich and colorful wedding gifts, to the accompaniment of a Chinese orchestra. A Chinese lady guest explained to Sarah what each of the gifts meant as she looked on at the "extravagant dream-picture." The gifts were followed by servants carrying elegant pieces of furniture for the new bride's household. Sarah went to look at the bridal house with Dowager Princess K'e. "The entire front [of the house] was bedecked with wedding symbols," Sarah recalled. "Great papier-maché dragons were twined about the large teak columns on either side of the centre doorway [the heads and claws of which] reached out as if to protect the entrance." In contrast to the dragons, the Dowager Princess K'e threw open the doors, jubilantly showing Sarah all the pretty new things, including her future daughter-in-law's cache of jewelry, as they moved from room to room.[30]

Riding home in her sedan chair, Sarah thought over the events of the preceding few years. "I have accomplished much of my heart's great desire," she wrote, "to know the Chinese ladies in their homes; to get nearer to them and learn of them and perhaps to let them learn a little of the heart and ways of a foreign lady." One of the greatest lessons she had learned was that "human nature is about the same everywhere," that people were people, equal in all the basic traits of humanity. It was in recognizing this—in seeing herself reflected back from her Chinese friends, and them from her—that she had gained that "fuller view of life" she had missed when leaving Brazil several years before.[31]

✳ ✳ ✳ ✳ ✳

The portrait project continued, albeit at a pace dictated by Cixi's whims.

There were problems that Kate had not foreseen. For a painter trained in the avant-garde Académie Julian, any restriction was intolerable, but they rose afresh each day. "As the portrait progressed," she recalled, "I found myself constantly running up against Chinese conventionalities as to the way it was done." Cixi's courtiers (and Cixi herself) wanted details but no shadows. Kate persisted in her belief that if Cixi had had her way, being "artistic and progressive enough," she would have allowed Kate the leeway to add the perspective and shading that the artist believed was necessary to make the portrait live. Cixi, however, was of no such opinion, as Der Ling reports in her memoirs, and if her officials were telling Kate to limit the shadows, they were not doing so without her orders. "When I saw I must represent Her Majesty in such a conventional way"—in effect producing the one-dimensional, static and stylized composition style traditional for ancestor portraits—"I was no longer filled with the ardent enthusiasm for my work with which I had begun it." She was constrained, in effect, to paint with half her trained technique, a blow to education, pride, and artistry few painters could have endured.[32]

Cixi did not make the situation easier by summarily inviting Sarah out to the Summer Palace to see the work in progress. "I fully expected the portrait would be exhibited in the Throne-room," Kate wrote, "the only place where it had a proper light," but she again was disappointed (though never blaming the dowager). "After Her Majesty had greeted us," Sarah recalled, "and spoken many cordial words to each lady, we were invited to see the portrait." Sarah was taken in a palace chair "to a large building properly lighted for painting," she wrote, though again Kate was not at all of the same opinion. "Mrs. Conger was asked to look at it in the small room where it was kept when I was not working on it," she complained, which placed it at a disadvantage.[33]

With great ceremony, Chief Eunuch Li Lianying "removed the yellow covering over the 'Sacred Picture,' which hung flat against the wall in a very bad light, with annoying reflections." The small room was so crowded with spectators that "it was impossible to see the whole canvas at once." But Sarah loved it. "Surely, Her Imperial Majesty was there upon her throne," she recalled, "in all her Oriental splendor!"

> True to the Chinese idea there were characters, symbols, seals, and decorations. All spoke a silent, but positive language, and so did each of the thousands of pearls, large and small, and each of the other precious stones, which stood out beautifully before me in their richness. But that which was far more to me was the Imperial woman sitting there in her strength of character. As I gazed at the portrait I could recall a sweet tone of voice, a gentle clasp of hand, a cordial smile that bespoke a welcome not easy for any nationality to surpass. There is a chord in human nature when played upon by woman, that woman can hear and appreciate.[34]

Sarah felt that when the portrait was finally revealed in America, it would open the eyes of that nation to all that was "true to China."[35]

This the Americans would indeed do, Sarah was told by Cixi. "Her Majesty . . . said that she intended to send [the portrait] to the St. Louis Exposition in America," Sarah wrote to her sister, "and later she was going to present it to the United States Government. I expressed my great delight and said that from time to time I would visit the honored place and with renewed delight look upon a picture of Her Majesty's face, form and surroundings, the original of which I had so many times been permitted to look upon with true joy."[36]

Around this same time, Sarah met Prince Pulun, a descendant of the Qianlong emperor and an on-again-off-again heir to the dragon throne, who was part of the Chinese commission accompanying the portrait to St. Louis. He arrived at the legation apart from his wife, whose first visit to a foreign household this was, and Sarah wanted the princess to feel as comfortable and at home as possible. "Princess Pu Lun is beautiful in voice, conversation, manner, face, apparel and ornaments," Sarah remembered. When a return call was made to the princess's home, Sarah saw that some modern ideas had evidently penetrated the household, as both the prince and princess received her and Edwin, instead of Sarah having to go to the women's quarters at the back of the compound. "Their attitude toward each other as husband and wife and toward their guests was beautiful," she recorded. The highlight of the visit, however, came when Sarah told them how fond she was of children—she had still not met her own granddaughter in America. In came "two bright little boys," Sarah wrote, their manners "polite and full of grace" for children so young. Sarah knew that Princess Pulun had a baby son, and asked to see him. The boy was brought out by an amah and handed to her. "I really held in my arms that dear baby prince," Sarah told Laura. "He looked straight at me with a quiet, searching look. What did the little fellow think?"[37]

Having become this close to the couple, Sarah ventured one more request: that the gracious Princess Pulun be allowed to accompany her husband to the St. Louis Exposition. "I said that I should be delighted to have my people receive and know a representative Chinese Princess." There is no evidence that Princess Pulun went to America with her husband, but there are hints that Pulun was influenced in some degree by Sarah's push for the equality of women everywhere. Shortly after the exposition, the prince told a reporter for the *New York Times* that he saw the strength and confidence of educated American women as a model for the new woman of China. "That, I believe, is the secret of your great advancement," he said, "in all that pertains to the higher civilization. Your women are the companions of your men." That this was no mere lip service is proved by a letter written by Pulun's fellow commissioner, Huang Kaijia, to feminist educator May Wright Sewall, who had invited the prince to hand out diplomas at the Girls' Classical School, which she had founded in Indianapolis. The prince, wrote Wang, would be delighted to comply with Sewall's request, since he "has a very high opinion of American women."[38]

✳   ✳   ✳   ✳   ✳

Cixi had decreed, per her court astrologers, that the portrait for the exposition had to be completed by April 19, 1904. Though she had avoided the portrait up to now, as the deadline drew near she could not keep away from it. "She spent a great deal of time in my pavilion watching its progress," Kate recalled, "and expressed herself much delighted with it." There was much indeed to admire in the work despite the many restraints placed on its creator.[39]

Unlike the portrait Kate had started with, showing Cixi more than life-sized in her yellow gauze gown on a throne that exceeded the width of the canvas, the St. Louis image demonstrated what Kate had learned not just about Chinese art but about the dowager herself. If Cixi's figure dominated the first portrait, the second one placed her as the central feature in a grand mosaic, the sum total of which was the Qing throne. Gowned in yellow silk patterned with narcissus and "double long life" characters, Cixi wears her cape of three thousand pearls, each the size of a small bird's egg, a nacreous webwork draped across her shoulders like the "net of Indra" (a Buddhist concept of the interconnectedness of the universe). Unlike the first portrait, where Cixi is shown slightly turned from the viewer, the St. Louis portrait displays her face on and shadowless, a screen behind her alive with a flock of phoenix birds in flight—the phoenix being the symbol of the Chinese empress. Cixi herself designed the camphorwood frames for both portraits.[40]

Cixi invited the ladies of the foreign legations out to the Summer Palace to view the finished portrait on April 19. "As I was still working until the 'fateful hour,'" Kate wrote, "I did not go up to the Throne-room but awaited the ladies in my own place." The reaction was positive, especially from the dowager's ladies. The admiration received "from the Young Empress and the Ladies of the Court was almost embarrassing"—indeed, eunuchs always bowed whenever they saw the portrait through the windows of Kate's studio. When the imperial princes and officials came to see the portrait, it had to be moved out of the area reserved for women to the courtyard in front of Kate's pavilion; yet even Kate could not be present, having to content herself with listening to what comments she could understand from behind curtains. Even so, there would not have been much to hear from these inscrutable officials. "I must confess they revealed very little," Kate recalled. Probably afraid to say the wrong thing, they opted to say nothing. Perhaps Sarah was right: it took women to recognize the chord of sisterhood Kate had struck with this work of art.[41]

The portrait was now packed up in camphorwood box lined and covered with imperial yellow satin, and sent on its long voyage to the United States, kept upright the entire way to avoid placing it in the recumbent position of the dead. The train left Beijing bearing the "Sacred Picture" in a crate wrapped in silk covered in huge five-clawed dragons, seen off by a large delegation. On reaching San Francisco, where Prince Pulun had himself disembarked from the *Gaelic* a few weeks earlier, the portrait was placed on another train for St. Louis, where on June 19 it was opened in the presence of the prince and several American officials connected with the St. Louis Art Gallery and the Board of Fine Arts. "The Prince proposed the health of Her Majesty and the Prosperity of China," Kate was told, "which the assistants drank in sparkling champagne." Then the "Sacred Picture" was put on public display, "open to the gaze of the vulgar and the comment of the scoffer," Kate observed with unwonted asperity. The portrait was actually a hit at the exposition, if only for its exotic camphorwood frame, and the fact that it was exhibited alongside the pedantic portraiture of Julius Garibaldi Melchers and other turn of the century American artists. The *New York Times,* buying into the prevailing attitude that everything in China was out of proportion to reality, published a wry editorial about the portrait, which claimed it was, with frame, fourteen feet tall, but that this ungainly gift horse must not be looked in the mouth, comparing Cixi to a "choice palfrey . . . stiff with jeweled and embroidered housings and radiant in all devices of ornament." A year later, a reviewer of Kate's memoir of her several months at the imperial court would opine in the pages of the *New York Times* that she did not know how to paint at all, though this was more about her over-enthusiastic literary portrait of Cixi than the one she created on canvas. Yet truth be told, Kate had been forced by Cixi's demands into producing something far closer to propaganda art than portraiture.[42]

With its collection of international "villages" depicting Egypt, France, Morocco, Japan, Russia, and simulacra of a dozen other nations, the St. Louis Exposition offered a Chinese pavilion built to resemble Prince Pulun's palace in Beijing. While it was at first not thought worth as much potential concession revenue as the Japanese venue (all things Japanese having been the rage since the Meiji "revolution") it, too, was a hit, despite negative press that roused old stereotypes. Critics claimed that China had sent over for innocent American eyes to behold everything from opium pipes to mannikins of Shanghai prostitutes, women with bound feet, instruments of torture, and the other Eastern paraphernalia the Western world carried around in its imagination. For twenty-five cents (kids got in for a dime less), fair goers could watch demonstrations of Chinese theater, have their fortunes told, purchase silken items at a bazaar, have tea in a "Shanghai tea house" as dragon dancers wriggled through make believe streets, and even watch "religious rites" in a temple for an additional ten cents. These elements, while reflecting only a narrow slice of the real China, did help open people's minds to a China of culture, color, and exuberance, as did Kate's vivid image of the empress dowager, upstaging forgettable examples of fin de siècle Western portraiture.[43]

Following the exposition, Sir Chentung Liangcheng presented the portrait on Cixi's behalf to President Theodore Roosevelt in the White House Blue Room. It was only fitting, said the ambassador, "that the portrait of her Majesty should become the property of the United States Government, as a memorial of her abiding interest in the welfare and prosperity of the American people." President Roosevelt accepted graciously, asking Sir Chentung Liangcheng to convey to Cixi his government's "reciprocal regard and esteem for this country and its people."[44]

❋　❋　❋　❋　❋

Before Cixi's portrait had been packed for shipping, it was photographed by Xunling, the elder brother of Der Ling. A courtier who looked after the electrical plant at the Summer Palace, Xunling was trained in European photographic techniques. It was he who took the first photographs of the empress dowager and her court from 1903 to 1905. With its quicker turnaround time and its negligible demands on its subject's time, photography appealed more to Cixi than having her portrait painted. Before long she was being photographed around the Summer Palace grounds in a variety of poses, settings, and costumes (notably as Guanyin, goddess of mercy), often handling the cameras herself and watching with interest how Xunling developed the prints.

Sometime later that summer, after the "fateful" revealing of the St. Louis portrait to the ladies of the foreign legations, Der Ling's brother set up his bulky camera in a courtyard at the Summer Palace, and directed the servants to stretch between the pillars a painted canvas backdrop of bamboo and birds. A throne chair for Cixi was placed on a rich carpet laid over the paving stones. In this setting, Xunling photographed Cixi with Sarah, three other foreign women, and his own young daughter, Lili. A few commentators who have seen this picture, not familiar with prints of the original negative and having only small or poorly reproduced examples to judge by, have read into Cixi's expression impatience or arrogance, annoyance or boredom, as she sits on her throne, her left hand clasped in Sarah's right. Though the most striking feature of the photograph is certainly the fact that Cixi is touching a foreigner at all—the only time she was ever thus depicted—her expression does not support a negative interpretation. While age and a mild stroke made her face sag slightly, Cixi sits with easy poise, looking straight into the camera. The expressiveness of her eyes, often commented on by those who met her, shines with a striking immediacy, bright with incipient good humor yet sad as if contemplating some irreversible tragedy (as she had often had to do, and would have to do again before she died). Her lips are firm but not pressed—it is more as if she had just said or heard something funny and knows she has to remain still for the slow process of capturing her image; one had to retain the dignity of one's office even in a Kodak world. Cixi's hand lies gracefully in Sarah's gloved palm, which supports it with strength and determination. Sarah gazes into the lens with a boldly direct stare, her lips set in a smile both wise and challenging, as if to say to those who believed her a fool to love the Chinese and their empress dowager: "They are my friends, and could be yours, too, if you would only stop to look at them."[45]

17
Forbidden cities

Perhaps it was in the great Lama Temple in Beijing where Sarah had her most significant epiphany regarding the lot of Chinese women. While attending a Buddhist service there, she had looked around and been surprised to find herself the only female in the temple. Her reaction was not just that of a woman used to seeing women and men sitting side by side in churches in America. It was the feminism that moved such women as Margaret Sanger, Elizabeth Cady Stanton, and Mary Baker Eddy to look at the inequalities of the sexes and wonder what gave men the right to impose them. For Sarah, who often wrote of the "Father and Mother God," men had even less right to decide whether a woman should show herself in a house of worship. "Why should the worship of the Supreme Creator, Protector, and Sustainer of all good," Sarah asked, "be so hedged in by forms, ceremonies, laws and rituals, as to bar out woman?"[1]

"When I came to China," Sarah confided to a friend, "it was my unyielding effort, from the first, to learn all that I could of her people and from her people." Yet, as she found, "high walls, locked gates, curtained chairs and carts, and long-established customs" kept her from knowing the female half of China's population. "The streets of Peking were thronged with men," she recorded, "but women were seldom seen." She had patiently "listened for answers," doing what she could to penetrate these many "forbidden cities." From a desire to see and know these hidden women, Sarah settled down to work the system, and little by little, the locked doors opened. By this last year of her Chinese sojourn, and for all her reservations about some of their practices, Sarah believed that missionaries in China could be commended for one very important act: opening, and holding open, the door not just between China and the West, but between China's women and the world.[2]

Female missionaries in particular had been extremely helpful to Sarah in her own Chinese self-education. They had given her the key, through their services as interpreters and sources of insider knowledge, to unlock the doors she needed to get behind so that she could meet the real women of China. Had these missionary women not bridged the gap between her and Cixi, all the opportunities of standing together with the dowager, holding hands as they gazed at beautiful vistas, would not have helped her, or Cixi, know who the other woman really was.[3]

There were other foreign women in China who, in deploring the way foreign males abused China's sovereign rights, defended what one historian calls "a female kind of authority when they defended China." Unlike Sarah, who supported a woman's right to vote and thought a world without gender equality ("a grand brotherhood") a place not just off-kilter but an obstacle to a divine plan, many foreign women in China stood up for the Chinese but would not have dreamed of defending their own rights. Yet they often saw the two as intertwined. "According to the tenets of domestic ideology, authority was best applied indirectly," notes one historian, and at the very least, authority should be conducted at all times "according to the rules of decorum." American women had emerged from the Civil War in both the north and south embodying the woman's role as imparted by the Victorian age: to be the bearers of succor to their men, whether wounded in battle or weary after a hard day at work; to be the civilizing influence, teaching the children manners, and softening, if only by example, a husband's rougher edges. The women who came to China had, by and large, lived through the Civil War or were the daughters of women who had. They came to China emboldened by the Gospel or the spirit of adventure (evangelism demanding both) to bring that sense of decorum with which Victorian Christendom was imbued and offer it to people assumed to be living godless lives of error. These women literally believed themselves sent "to bear witness of that Light . . . which lighteth every man that cometh into the world." When some of them reached China, however, like Sarah their sympathy for the Chinese superseded the orthodoxy of Christian belief. Their missionary purpose was in many cases replaced by a crusade not just for light, but for the rights of the Chinese people. After all, as Pearl Buck, daughter of Chinese missionaries, wrote: "None who have always been free can understand the terrible fascinating power of the hope of freedom to those who are not free."[4]

Sarah wanted to "go to the self-sacrificing workers in the fields and see and study their work." To find them, in early November 1904, Sarah and Maurine Campbell started a three-month tour of southern China, covering several hundred miles in two months' time, up and down the Grand Canal and the Yangzi River.[5]

On November 13, Sarah and Maurine visited one of Shanghai's finest institutions for boys, the Nanyang College (a high school). Founded in 1896, Nanyang offered a course of seven years of English instruction to 250 boys and young men, including other foreign languages and a curriculum based on that found in foreign colleges. What most appealed to Sarah about Nanyang was that among the buildings on the luxuriantly landscaped campus was a temple to Confucius "where the college boys pay homage twice each month," Sarah wrote to Laura. "There is a gallery in the rear of this temple opposite the tablet where a choir of the boys sing while the others enter and *kotow* in front of the tablet."[6]

"Respect shown the great Confucius quite appealed to me," Sarah added, "as he is China's redeemer and saviour." In this opinion Sarah was in good company. Her friend Dr. W. A. P. Martin wrote that "among the sages of the pagan world he comes nearest to Christ in virtue and influence," a giver of laws and a respecter of what Confucius called "Heaven." "So consonant is his system with Christianity," Martin wrote in his book *A Cycle of Cathay,* "that the golden rule, in a negative form, is its first law, and charity and humility among its leading virtues."[7]

In Hangzhou several days later, one school stood out in particular. It was, of course, another institution for boys only, and Christian. "The service was conducted in both Chinese and English," Sarah reported to Laura. "They sang in English, 'No, Not One,'" the American hymn by Johnson Oatman and George Crawford Hugg that adjured "There's not a friend like the lowly Jesus"—a decidedly different attitude from the hierarchy of respect required by Confucian teaching. However, as with the Russian orthodox choir during the Boxer Uprising, Sarah heard in the massed voices a message of the potential for universal amity. "China has long sung alone," she wrote, "but little by little her people are joining the great sisterhood of nations." The only thing that gave her pause was that in teaching the Chinese another faith, missionaries were making it easy for them to forget their own culture. "Why should [the Chinese] be in haste to adopt ideas which they deem inferior?" she wrote. How would Americans like it, she pursued, if other nations came to the United States and set up schools "to educate our youth out of the customs and principles of our Government?"[8]

✳ ✳ ✳ ✳ ✳

During her journey, Sarah met three extraordinary women who embodied her ideals for East–West co-operation: Methodist missionary Gertrude Howe and her Chinese "daughters," Dr. Mary Stone and Dr. Ida Kahn.

The same age as Sarah, Howe had been in Jiujiang since 1872, where she taught at a Chinese girls' school with fellow American Dr. Lucy Hoag. The charismatic and self-willed Howe had put missionary noses out of joint by insisting that English be taught to students. Received wisdom at the mission was that Chinese, especially females, were not apt students of foreign languages. Yet they proved to be so under Howe's teaching, and achieved honors in all their other courses as well. Howe had also raised suspicions when, in the heat of summer, she declined to follow the other missionaries to the cool mountaintop resort of Kulin, preferring to remain in the foothills with the "flock of her [Chinese] grandchildren" in her "little hut-like house."[9]

In 1892, Howe showed she was willing to go even further for her students—she returned to the United States with two Chinese girls and three young men, setting up house in Ann Arbor. For the next two years, Howe took care of her two female charges not just financing their educations but cooking and cleaning for them. The girls studied medicine at the University of Michigan and "shocked" everyone by scoring highest in their class. But Howe was not surprised. When the father of Shi Meiyu, the girl who came to be known as Dr. Mary Stone, first brought his daughter to Howe and announced that she wanted to become a doctor of Western medicine, Howe had no doubt he meant it, though she told the girl's father—a progressive member of the local gentry—that first his daughter would have to learn English. This Mary did, at Howe's school, and with her partner Kang Aide, better known as Dr. Ida Kahn, she pioneered the cause of Chinese women doctors at a time when few women were even seen in public, let alone as professionals in the suspicious role of foreign-trained physicians. Dr. Kahn's route to becoming a doctor was more circuitous. A star pupil of Howe's, she had not revealed her interest in medicine until Howe happened to mention that a Shanghainese gentleman wanted her to marry his American-educated son—a pairing Howe would not have objected to. Just twelve years old, Ida did object. "I don't want to be betrothed. I want to study medicine," she told Howe. So she had joined Mary Stone in Michigan and graduated with her in 1896.[10]

Far from encountering immediate opposition on their return to China as certified physicians, Dr. Stone and Dr. Kahn were popular and in demand, and even played a role in the reforms of 1898. Kang Youwei's colleague and fellow survivor of the Hundred Days of Reform, Liang Qichao, wrote an article demanding that China make use of and encourage the talents of its female population. Howe heartily approved, believing that Mary Stone and Ida Kahn, who in addition to their foreign educations had never had their feet bound, were Liang's inspiration for the abolition of the ancient practice, a cause also upheld by missionaries throughout China.[11]

Sarah and Maurine met with Gertrude Howe and her two doctor foster-daughters in early December. Sarah knew that Dr. Stone and Dr. Kahn were "highly respected and beloved by their own people," having devoted their lives "in maidenhood to their country." She certainly approved of their method of reaching out to their people from across the gap of ignorance not only of female doctors but of Western medicine itself. "They work in harmony with these people," she wrote, "and thus gain access to their homes and their hearts"—something which she and the two female physicians had in common. "On this trip I am learning many things," she told Laura; "new ideas assert themselves, and old ideas are yielding." She found this to be even more the case when, later that month, Sarah and Maurine were guests of Mary C. Robinson, principal of the Girls' Boarding School in Zhenjiang. Opened on July 2, 1884, Miss Robinson's school had celebrated its first graduating class the year before Sarah and Edwin arrived in China—a class with all of two graduates. The second class, just three years later, grew to seven graduates, and at the time Sarah visited the school it had enrolled sixty girls, some paying and others scholarship students, divided into kindergarten, primary, and academic levels. "Natural feet and manual labor are among the requirements of the school," stated the author of the *Educational Directory for China*. If the curriculum for all three levels leaned heavily on all aspects of Christian instruction, as one would expect in a mission school, the girls were also well-grounded in music, geography, arithmetic, history, art, and, of course, the English language, as much their key to the world of the West as Chinese had been Sarah's key to the world of the East.[12]

As Sarah entered the school chapel, all the girls stood and sang for her and Maurine a song of welcome. "They had draped the American flag above our chairs in honor of our coming," she wrote, noting with approval that "above it [was] their own Dragon flag," the yellow pennant emblazoned with blue dragon that was to fly over China for only eight more years.[13] The day was filled with music, with students confidently singing part harmony and playing instruments. One little girl in the kindergarten was already an impressive musician, taught by a Chinese instructress who had got her start in life, like many unwanted daughters of the poor, abandoned on a doorstep (happily that of Miss Robinson). "With devoted care," Sarah observed, "she has grown into a trustworthy and competent co-worker for her people." Sarah was impressed by how absorbed the girls were in everything they did. Their lives at the school were not coerced but natural to them. They were, she felt, learning to be themselves even as they learned to become whatever they had it in them to be.[14]

While in Zhenjiang, Sarah also met Dr. Lucy Hoag, who had taught at the Jiujiang school with Gertrude Howe. Dr. Hoag had adopted a

Chinese girl, Sarah heard, and educated her. When it came time for the girl to marry, she chose a Chinese husband educated in America, who was now a professor at a school for boys located on an island in the Yangzi and subsidized by a wealthy Chinese patron. Sarah went to see the school and was shown through its classroom, library, gymnasium, and even the museum on campus. "What will be the future of China," she asked herself, "when these hundreds and hundreds of educated young people go out from these schools as a leaven into its vast population?" Especially when the females entered into Chinese society and began to make their mark, what changes might that bring?[15]

Dr. Hoag had arranged for her girls to surprise Sarah with a chorus of "God Be with You Till We Meet Again"; they then gave her an album of photographs of themselves at work at the school, images originally displayed at the St. Louis Exposition. She took this as a sign that what she had done for Cixi with the portrait project had been the right and useful thing. "The Chinese are reaching out for foreign ideas as never before," Sarah told Laura. "While in this attitude of thought, these ideas should be given to them abundantly."[16]

Sarah, too, on this last leg of her Chinese odyssey, was reaching out for Chinese ideas. "All along this wonderful trip," she wrote, "I am gratefully happy in my schooling. It almost seems as though I were taking a course in Heart and Mind University, and it has been my earnest prayer that I may learn lessons of value."[17]

✳ ✳ ✳ ✳ ✳

By the time Edwin met Sarah in Hong Kong in January, his decision to resign his post had been made. During the siege, many in the British legation contracted intestinal diseases from the water or food. Almost as many of those in the siege hospital were there not because of wounds, but due to dysentery or typhoid, and a majority of them had died. Edwin had managed to avoid that worst fate, but he could not avoid dysentery which he was never able to shake off. He was said to have lost thirty-five pounds during the siege. As Sarah wrote to Laura, after Edwin sent in his resignation to President Roosevelt he felt a great sense of relief. "He feels that he has spent enough time in China," she explained, "and in public service. We are going home to make for ourselves a fireside all our own, gather together our belongings, and enjoy them." It is possible also, as will be seen, that on top of all his other losses, Edwin had used up too many of his own resources, as diplomats of the day often had to do, to carry on any further in diplomatic work. Yet even then, duty called, as Sarah told Laura. During their vacation "your father received a cablegram from President Roosevelt transferring him from the Legation in China to the Embassy in Mexico." The appointment was a promotion "in recognition of work well done in China under most trying circumstances," and Edwin accepted. Though Mexico was, Sarah noted, "a crown to [Edwin's] political life," and as fascinating as it is to ponder what letters Sarah might have penned from Mexico City, it was not an honor Edwin was to wear for long.[18]

The Congers returned to Beijing on March 17. In their absence and that of Wang, who was with the Congers, the legation's second boy and staff had been preparing for two and a half weeks of nonstop farewell receptions. With packing and organizing for the voyage home, "we cannot go to all our friends," Sarah wrote, "therefore we ask them to come to us, as we must see them again."[19] Until the end of the month, Sarah and Edwin hosted suppers and tiffins for officials of the court and customs office, ladies of the court and missionaries, diplomats and princes. "All that I had to say to Wang," Sarah wrote, "was to tell him the color of flowers that I wished—red, yellow, white or pink—for the various tiffins and dinners, and this color it would be without another suggestion, and all beautifully arranged." That Sarah's Chinese lady friends were sorry to see her go is clear from their request of Marian Headland: What would Sarah most like for a farewell present? Knowing Sarah, Dr. Headland suggested photographs, and each woman presently sent her picture, often with her children, to the legation. "I shall many times through the years to come look at these pictures," Sarah wrote, "recall and hear again the words of these ladies, and feel the gentle hand touch, and read their thoughts through their lighted faces."[20]

Amid the dinners and packing, Sarah made time to see Dowager Princess K'e, who was ill. Sarah knew that, given their respective ages, they would most likely never see each other again. The visit "was a sad one," but was "precious to both of us." In an echo of the empress dowager, with whom Sarah had also arranged a final meeting on April 1, the dowager princess took rings off her fingers and placed them on Sarah's own.[21]

Perhaps the most meaningful of Sarah's farewell suppers was the one to which she and Edwin were invited by the British legation. "The French, British and German Ministers spoke in commendatory terms of my social efforts with the Chinese ladies," Sarah recorded, "including Her Majesty, the Princesses, and the families of Chinese officials. This I regard as a significant recognition, expressed as it was before their colleagues and to them." It was also proof to her many critics in China and abroad that she had not been a rogue operator, throwing a spanner into the gears of delicate Western diplomacy, but was working along with them (and in a more successful way) to bring East and West, China and America, closer together.[22]

Edwin's audience with the emperor and empress dowager took place before Sarah's, and had about it some of the same formality that colored all his diplomatic efforts. Though he had been minister, not full ambassador, the emperor awarded Edwin a special Order of the Double Dragon in recognition of his service to the Qing court as well as in honor of his nomination to the Mexican ambassadorship. Cixi gave him one of her scroll paintings, a study of amber and yellow chrysanthemums on a rich silk mounting. Edwin rather officiously declared he would place the painting in the care of the American State Department, still unwilling to trespass on the rule barring gifts from the throne of several years earlier.[23]

Forcing Cixi to obey foreign laws had never been Sarah's style, as she was to demonstrate again at their final meeting. When she arrived for her audience, Sarah and Cixi briefly observed the rules, then sat down together for a private talk, "as one woman to another." Sarah told the dowager about her trip to southern China, especially about the mission schools and what they were doing for young women and men. "She seemed deeply interested in hearing of her China as I really saw it," Sarah wrote, a point also made by Wu Yung four years earlier. They also talked about Katherine Carl's portrait. Kate was then already working on her memoir of her ten months at court, *With the Empress Dowager of China*, which she wrote for the same reasons Sarah had engaged her to paint Cixi's portrait, to counteract exaggerated and erroneous accounts in the press of the dowager and Kate's relationship with her. As much as she had chafed at the discipline of sitting for Kate's portrait, Cixi knew the importance of showing the West how she really was, for she would sit for another portrait later that year by Dutch painter Hubert Vos. In between these topics, the dowager also spoke of "our many interviews and visits together," and, Sarah added, "and of our understanding and friendship growing out of them." To commemorate this friendship, besides all the gifts she had given Sarah in her final weeks in China, Cixi had had a decoration made for Sarah, "the first of this high rank ever bestowed by China upon a foreign lady": a variation on the Order of the Double Dragon given to Edwin.[24]

Sarah's account of her final meeting with Cixi is unusually dry and matter of fact. We do not know what Sarah felt as she walked away from Cixi's palace, a wonderland she could not have imagined would ever be as familiar to her as it had become, or that the revered and reviled woman who made it her refuge would grow so close to her heart, knowing she would never see either again. Passing through courtyards, past bronze dragons and budding magnolias and clutches of cringing eunuchs for the last time, what she felt is closed to us. There is probably a reason behind that. There would be no more yellow journalism about the dowager weeping on her neck. Whatever occurred or was expressed between these two friends remains hidden behind the scrim of Sarah's straightforward account, which was further edited for publication several years later. Yet we have a hint that Cixi, watching "Kang taitai" disappearing back to her foreign world, was moved. Before Sarah could reach the palace gates, a woman she describes as an interpreter (possibly Der Ling) ran out to catch up with her. She explained to Sarah that Cixi had wanted her to have a special amulet, a "good-luck stone." In all the emotion, she had forgotten to present it before Sarah left the audience hall. The amulet was made out of a piece of blood-jade, a pale pink stone veined with darker red and carved in the shape of a hand. "Her Majesty had taken this good-luck stone from her person," Sarah was told, "and wishes to give it to you to wear during your long journey across the great waters, that you may safely arrive in your honorable country." According to Sarah's source at the imperial court, the amulet seems to have been ancient, having been in the imperial treasury since the early Tang. This was enough reason to revere it, but the jade hand had another history: it had been worn by

Cixi when she fled Beijing on August 14, 1900, a protective talisman on her journey.[25]

When Sarah reached the legation, she showed it to Wang. Greatly impressed, he said, "That Blood Stone grand thing. No Chinaman, much money, can't get like that." Sarah wore the jade hand for her journey home, and prized it for the rest of her life.[26]

✳ ✳ ✳ ✳ ✳

On April 4, Sarah and Edwin were at the Majiapu station, to board the train for Shanghai and their ship, the SS *Siberia*. Not just the current legation servants saw them off, but joining them to smile and wave through the smoke of firecrackers were all those who had worked for the Congers over the past seven years. "No honors could have been dearer to us," Sarah wrote, "than their presence on this parting occasion." Members of the Chinese Foreign Office were there as well, "and almost all the [foreign] diplomats," Sarah recalled, with Sir Robert Hart and many of the customs staff. (The Chinese band Sarah says was playing as the train pulled out was probably Sir Robert's.) With Sarah and Edwin as the train slid south were First Cook, that brave and ingenious master of the legation kitchen, and Wang, the two who had done so much for the Congers and Laura from the beginning, through the Boxer siege, and beyond. These two would stay with them until they boarded their ship for America. Two other passengers, the palace dogs given to Sarah by Cixi, were Lao Hu and Mo Yu ("Black Jade"), who had to find a place to sit amid the "beautiful flowers . . . piled high in our car."[27]

Sarah's first journey to Beijing from Tianjin had been punctuated by the acres of graves corrugating the flat Plain of Zhili, as if all of northern China were an enormous cemetery. China's walled and gated world had then been one of complete bafflement to her. Now, as she left a China she had come to love, from the train windows she saw these same graves. The Congers' departure date was ironically that of Qingming, the Clear and Bright Festival, when the spirits of the dead are honored. Families streamed from all points of the compass to honor their dead, carrying flowers, lighting incense, and bowing to the spirits of their ancestors. Seeing this ritual for the last time, Sarah now understood and appreciated it. "As I looked upon these decorated graves and reflected," she wrote, "I could detect kindred thoughts held by these Chinese people and by our own people at home."[28]

On reaching Hankou (now part of Wuhan), Edwin asked the viceroy of Hubei to grant Wang and First Cook hat buttons and *buzi* ("badges") of civil rank—they were given the ninth, with gold hat buttons and paradise flycatcher emblems. It was probably at this point that Sarah said farewell to Wang. Her letters from China are filled with examples of how important he was to the legation household. His ability to not only manage the compound but to make it comfortable and inviting for both Chinese and foreign guests was just one of his talents. To Sarah, Wang mattered in ways far above the management of her domestic sphere. Her reliance on and gratitude for his judgment for her dress and deportment in her visits to Chinese friends, and for his instruction in the mysteries of Chinese life, is evident on every page of her letters. She also prized his tender heart. Sarah tells how one day Wang came into the legation drawing room to find her crying. Sherza, the first dog given to her by Cixi, had had a fit and died in her arms. Though not a sentimental person, Wang lined a box with blue silk and helped Sarah place the body in it. Sarah chose a spot in the garden, and there he buried her. When the Congers moved to the Sanguanmiao, without being asked Wang disinterred Sherza's coffin and placed it in the grounds of the temple. Sarah later found flowers growing on the grave, and asked Wang who had planted them. "I did, Madam," he told her. "I thought Madam would like them there." Wang's was a tenderness that extended to her family, especially to Laura in the dark days of the Boxer Uprising. And he continued to care for her long after she had left China. When Wang observed that Sarah and Edwin were in tears on their first Christmas morning in China without Laura, he arranged on a table in the drawing room a gift and card with Laura's name on it, and set up her photograph nearby. It was as if, like an ancestor portrait, the photograph stood for the real person, and the table served as an altar. But this was no funerary altar mourning the dead, it was a veneration of life, allowing Laura to partake in her parents' Christmas from afar, and her parents to send their love on to her—a perfect example of what Sarah called the "wireless telegraphy" of the heart.[29]

After the *Siberia* began its journey across the Pacific, Sarah and Edwin sat together in their stateroom, talking of their Chinese experiences, in which both of them "detected many colorings in the brush-strokes of this life picture, seven years in the painting." In those seven years, which were utterly unlike anything they had expected, the Congers had been given "a broadness of thought that reaches high, far, and deep."[30]

"This thought," Sarah wrote, "is freighted with gratitude."[31]

18
Letters to China

Through 1905 and into 1906, Edwin had still planned to fulfill his ambassadorial obligations to Mexico—there was even talk of his running for governor of Iowa. Edwin's brother, Universalist minister Dr. E. L. Conger, lived in Pasadena, California, which is where the Congers themselves moved shortly after returning from China. It was there their new troubles began, starting with a rug.

In 1906, Sarah sold to a private Chicago dealer a Chinese carpet she had bought in Beijing for $90. For this silk carpet, purchased after the Boxer Uprising (and apparently not at one of the military auctions), she received the considerable sum of $6,910. This was a windfall large enough to purchase a lot on El Molino Avenue in Pasadena and have built on it the shingled Craftsman-style house later described as "a beautiful vine-covered bungalow," and "a veritable treasure-house of Chinese wonders." Sarah's sale could be seen as simply collector's luck, but with it came Sarah's first taste of the scandal that was to surround her entire Chinese collection.[1]

"Mrs. Conger bought the rug against the protest of her husband," ran a *New York Times* piece published on June 13, 1906, with tongue in cheek.

"Mr. Conger declared his wife would get cheated, but Mrs. Conger had her way." Sarah's judgment had been on the mark, though this discerning taste was to be held against her as proof of her sophistication and of her complicity in some sort of "racket"—readers were invited to ponder how could she *not* have known the carpet's value. The sale was pungent enough to attract the press. Later that month, the *New York Times'* catty "Topic of the Times" editor questioned Sarah's "Big Profit on a Fine Rug": "We are a little disquieted, or alarmed, or something, by the news—which may be only a report—that while in China Mrs. Conger bought for $90 a rug which has just been sold for $7,000. The bargain was good, as bargains go, but it was not exactly such a bargain as we would all like to have made too often by the wives of too many American Ministers." Given the sharpness of most Chinese antiques dealers, the writer speculates, surely Mrs. Conger must have wondered why she was getting such a good deal. Of course, perhaps she did not care, for it was "a morbidly tender conscience that recoils from palace loot after it has passed through several hands, or even one."

An anonymous letter writer from Brooklyn raised an issue that would haunt Sarah more seriously later on, that of import duty. "Was the rug appraised at $90 or at $7,000, or is the duty as yet to be levied?" asked "One Who Is Curious." The editor of "Topics of the Times" could not help following up with this same question, one "that could hardly be more trying and painful than that asked by one of our correspondents yesterday in regard to Mrs. Conger's now famous rug . . . Our own interest still centers in the disproportion between cost and price, but the tariff feature does have certain merits as a topic for purely academic debate"—making it clear that only an official investigation could clear up the controversy.[2]

While this scandal swirled, Edwin's health began to fail rapidly. As he continued to deteriorate, he was confined to his bed, where Sarah and Laura kept a vigil. On May 18, 1907, at the age of sixty-four, Edwin died in the house he and Sarah had just completed.[3] Though during the Boxer siege there had been criticism of Edwin's decisions and of his diplomatic abilities in general, the eulogies now poured in from papers as diverse as the *New York Times* and the *Oakland Tribune*, while the *San Francisco Call* dubbed him "the bulwark of the doomed foreigners in the Chinese capital." General Adna R. Chaffee lauded Edwin's effort to sort out the jumble of the post-Boxer Chinese landscape as "one of the largest and best of his works . . . In government and diplomatic circles," Chaffee added, "Minister Conger was very highly thought of. Government officials in China and Japan had the highest regard for his worth."[4]

In his will, which appointed no administrator (Sarah was named thus by a judge), Edwin left her an estate of no more than $1,100—and all she had in hand was $100, the rest consisting of a claim "against the state department for services rendered in the diplomatic corps" and the house she lived in—a particularly ironic situation considering Edwin had been a banker before he was a politician and diplomat. But then on accepting diplomatic office Edwin had entered a very expensive line of endeavor. In Edwin's day, there was usually a shortfall between what a diplomat had to spend and what he was able to cover with funds made available to him, which often included his own salary. Diplomats in the service of the United States were among the most poorly paid in the world, so that no man without a large private fortune could hope to sustain the expenses the job entailed. Mark Twain lambasted the American government for not seeing the folly of its practice or the benefit of ending it. The United States, he wrote, was like the little girl suddenly grown into the fashionable young lady who needed to be brought out in society and was becoming in this and all other ways "a thundering expense"; it was time to allocate proper funds and pay diplomats accordingly. "Think of a Seventeen-thousand-five-hundred-dollar ambassador!" Twain sneered at the prevailing pay rate. "Particularly for America . . . It is a billionaire in a paper collar, a king in a breech clout, an archangel in a tin halo."[5]

Former American minister to Germany, Charlemagne Tower, thought the salary issue a crucial matter of international dignity. "The national pride of every American demands that he shall represent his country properly," said Tower, "and live up to his station." Not only had Edwin been paid just a little over $13,000 per annum. In contrast to the practice of Britain, which owned its legations and also paid its diplomats handsomely, American diplomats had to rent their residences. Edwin would have had to fall back on his private fortune to bridge any deficits. How much of his money may have not only gone toward the reconstruction of the American legation but also as gifts to the Americans who had been ruined in the Boxer siege, not to mention the Chinese Christians of Beijing, we do not know. The Congers' many entertainments of Chinese officials and ladies would also have been expensive, involving not just the dinner but gifts; in a letter written to Laura about his and Sarah's first Christmas dinner for Chinese officials in 1901, Edwin groans over expenses that ran far beyond what had been budgeted for.[6]

Even as Sarah had been robbed of the years of happy retirement she had hoped to spend with Edwin, she was now forced to put the majority of her Chinese art collection, which she had hoped to also enjoy for years more, to auction. From February 19 to 22, 1908, through the American Art Galleries in New York City, 987 pieces from Sarah's collection were auctioned off at the Galleries' Madison Square South showrooms. Among the pieces offered were embroidered banners and hangings described in the catalogue as having their provenance in the imperial palaces and/or temples; another, a "Valuable Chinese Imperial Bell," was said to have been taken from the Temple of Agriculture during the Boxer Uprising. Another lot was a set of "Buddhist Temple Service Books," texts on Hua Yen Buddhism; these sixty volumes were said to have come from the Hanlin Library. There was also an "engraved tablet" from the Hanlin Library—one of the printing blocks that littered the site after the library's destruction. On the first day, sales totaled $7,893, as totted up by Sarah in red ink at the bottom of the page of her catalogue. Days two and three brought in $9,160 and $8,848.50 respectively. Day four was the most successful, bringing in $10,356, for a total of $36,207.50. However straitened her circumstances, and even deducting the auctioneers' fees, Sarah should have had enough to see her through the rest of her life. That debts may have had to be paid off first, and large ones, is suggested by the financial hardship that compelled her to move in with her daughter and son-in-law after 1920.[7]

This sale raised a storm that made the scandal of the Chinese carpet appear a mere comedy. A few days after the auction's end, the *Evening World* published what it hoped would be taken as an exposé. "United States Branded as 'Fence' for Permitting Sale of Goods Stolen from Peking by the Allies and Brought Here by an American Minister" blared the headline on a piece that used multiple correspondents as well as images of Sarah, Edwin, unnamed foreign ministers in Beijing, and foreign army officers grouped outside a gate of the Imperial City. Depicted as "gratified" to hear that her "loot" had sold for an enormous sum, Sarah was not blamed directly—that would be left for incendiary letter-writers and a United States congressman. But she was certainly implicated in the receipt of stolen goods, as was Fred Buchan, who was described as having arranged for the sale the previous summer, in his capacity of judge advocate of the Military Department of Missouri.[8]

"True, the American envoy [Edwin] and his young army aide, who afterward became his son-in-law, did not steal the imperial jade, ivory and bronze pieces, or the silks and embroideries," opined the *Evening World's* reporter, "but the thieves who did steal them found a market for them under the flag of the United States." Another column claimed that the Congers were somehow in cahoots with US Customs to bring in their "Chinese loot" duty-free. An official was interviewed in such a way as to make his every statement appear either naïve or blasé. "Asked if they came in free, he said, 'Why, of course. We admit free of charge all the goods that our own or foreign ministers or ambassadors wish to bring,'" and cited a section of the law code permitting this. The reporter then pounced with the information that Section 204 permitted such goods to be brought in free of duty only if they were not intended for sale. The official responded that the Conger objects had been imported several years earlier. As they had been judged to be the Congers' personal property, not future auction items, they were passed free. "We do not expect this privilege to be abused," the official was quoted as saying at the interview's end.[9]

Almost every newspaper report about the auction characterized Sarah's collection as "loot," and reporters gleefully named the society figures who flocked to possess a bedspread from the Forbidden City or a sacred bell from an imperial temple. They were even happier to identify organizations that came buying, like the Metropolitan Museum of Art and other American museums. On April 12, the *New York Daily Tribune* ran a piece on deliberations in the House of Representatives regarding diplomatic expenses. Texas Democratic representative James Luther Slayden rose to denounce "the recent sale in New York by Mrs. Conger, widow of the former Minister to China, of a valuable collection of 'loot' taken, he said, from the imperial palace of Peking, following the siege of that capital. He charged that the goods were all stolen, in the first place, but that that fact had not deterred Mrs. Conger from gathering the collection. It was, he said, sufficient to shock the morals of any civilized country."[10]

In the House, Slayden had asked that an article be read which outlined his outrage, the first sentence of which ran:

> 'How,' said a prominent foreigner in a New York Club on Saturday, 'would you Americans feel if, ten years after a Chinese raid on Washington, you heard of a Peking auction sale at which were offered many of the treasures of the White House and the finest residences of your capital?'
>
> Let us at once disclaim the slightest intention of insinuating that the present owner, or her personal representatives or relatives, had any hand in the looting of the imperial palaces which went on in Peking in the name of humanity and Christianity and civilization. We have every reason to believe the statement in yesterday's *Sun* that this collection is not the slow aggregation of years of indulgence in the collector's hobby, but represents the timely purchases of a practical woman with a taste for the beautiful, who found herself at an unlooked-for emergency in an exceptionally favorable position to obtain objects in which the whole world is interested.[11]

It was not that others had not indulged in the very same thing, the article continued. It was that the wife "of the American minister had . . . one great advantage over all others. She was able to bring her carefully selected loot into this country free of duty." The writer finished by stating that "we can think of no finer opportunity to demonstrate the innate courtliness and honesty of the American people . . . than for him to acquire the stolen property of the imperial family of China, and ship it back with the compliments of the whole people." Slayden's call for an investigation was ultimately retracted. But the damage was done.[12]

The fact that several objects *were* specially described in the auction catalogue as being of imperial provenance helped strengthen the story that Sarah had bought—or taken—known looted goods, even as they helped raise the bids on said objects. When we hear that Wang brought Sarah a pearl ring he had "found" in the street, should we question by what unorthodox processes Sarah obtained the rest of her collection? How did she come to have a cup from the Tongzhi emperor's wedding service, not something likely to have made its way out of the Forbidden City via normal means, or bells from the plough used by the Guangxu emperor at the Temple of Agriculture, or hangings from the imperial palace? Was there a connection between her visit to the looted imperial elephant stables, noted in her published letters on September 23, 1900, and the imperial silk elephant caparisons appearing for sale? Perhaps more to the point, how did she justify selling imperial things while Cixi was still living? Given Edwin's finances, surely Sarah knew that at his death there would be little money left. Had she in fact purchased art objects at a discount with a view to selling them later to compensate Edwin and herself for the expense of maintaining the legation and their policy of socializing with the Chinese?[13]

As with the carpet scandal, we do not know Sarah's reaction to this new criticism. For Laura's part, when interviewed by the *New York Daily Tribune* she insisted that the press coverage was "a tissue of falsehoods," without specifying why. "Any one with common sense" should be able to see that there was no truth in any of the stories being circulated about her mother's collection, Laura remarked. But her lack of details—or the paper's strategic editing—made it appear she was as blinkered toward her mother's "looting" as Sarah was blinkered toward her "loot." Fred does not seem to have entered the fray, at least not publicly.[14]

In Sarah's defense, we know that she had been collecting Chinese art and artifacts almost from her first day in China, and was given numerous presents by her Chinese friends, including the empress dowager. Because many of the objects in the catalog resemble those Sarah describes as being given to her over the years, the collection must represent in some part gifts as well as her own purchases. She owned thousands of objects. While hundreds were sold at the 1908 auction, she retained many more; her granddaughter still had several hundred pieces to bequeath to the Museum of Fine Arts, Boston, the Peabody Museum at Harvard, and the Peabody Essex Museum in Salem, Massachusetts in 1991. Though Sarah clearly suffered losses to her collection during and after the Boxer Uprising, it is not impossible that many objects escaped and were brought to America. What does not make sense is that she would spend the three months between the lifting of the siege and the crackdown on loot in Beijing haunting every sale, legitimate or not, in order to have accumulated such a huge collection. She and Edwin, having moved back to the ruined legation, were distracted by the effort of cleaning up the compound to make it livable again. That among the objects offered for auction were swords and other weaponry alleged to have come from Boxers could mean nothing more than that Edwin was presented with them after the uprising, or collected them from the grounds of the shattered American legation. That Sarah began to collect again after the dust settled in 1901 and 1902 is known, and we also know she was purchasing things on her trip through southern China with Maurine Campbell in 1904–05. If well after the end of the Boxer period she bought looted antiques in Beijing that were of imperial provenance, she was not alone. Those of us who have anything obtained through the Chinese antiques market after 1900 probably possess a few pieces of "loot" ourselves.

By the standards of the *United Nations Convention on the Means of Prohibiting and Preventing the Illicit Import, Export and Transfer of Ownership of Cultural Property,* adopted in November 1970, everyone who bought anything at the military auctions in Beijing in late 1900 and early 1901 would have been contravening Article 11, which categorically declares illicit the exporting of "cultural property under compulsion arising directly or indirectly from the occupation of a country by a foreign power." But the current concept of "national treasure"—the product of a culture defined on one hand as art and on the other as a sacred expression of the civilization which created it and that is inseparable from it—was not known. "Lots of Americans and Europeans in China thought that the Chinese culture they admired was in the past," writes Pamela Kyle Crossley. "There was a lot of attitude about saving the Chinese from themselves, and so on. They did not consider that there was such a thing as national ownership of national treasures." In other words, what critics of the post-Boxer redistribution of property were alleging was pure theft for profit, not the unlawful separation of artifacts from their culture of origin. Outright claims that objects offered were obtained under lurid circumstances, as part of the sales pitch, were a staple of business operating at the highest caliber of quality. In 1896, the New York firm of Vantine, specialists in Asian antiques, described a group of oriental carpets as "spoils from the temples, mosques and palaces of those mysterious and wonderful countries." But for the exciting circumstances of their looting and the "secret negotiations" involved in getting them out of their countries of origin to Vantine's New York showroom, discerning American collectors might never have laid eyes on them at all. In her critics' eyes Sarah's "theft" was compounded by the trick of using her diplomatic status to slip said loot under the duty radar—something too dishonorable to be American, though an act committed by plenty of Americans. The purchase of looted goods would also have sat ill with Americans who took pride in the official account of their nation's troops having been forbidden to loot in Beijing, and having allegedly stopped the imperial treasures from ending up on an auction table. The difficulty is that it is so difficult to tell loot from valid purchases. And more loot from 1860 can be traced than from 1900. In 1860, writes James Hevia, looting was "safely contained as an attribute of the lower ranks of soldiers." Most of what was taken came from a circumscribed area, Yuangmingyuan, and much of what made its way to foreign parts was labeled as coming from "the Summer Palace of the Emperor of China" or otherwise boldly proclaimed as having imperial provenance. In 1900, everyone was in on the looting, not least the Chinese themselves, who passed the property on to foreign purchasers, witting or un-, no questions asked.[15]

There is no simple answer to the question of origin of the objects Sarah sold, but she gives every indication of knowing they had originated in the palaces and temples of Beijing. But had the imperial court regarded these objects as the sacred treasures Sarah's critics did, surely they would have taken their complaints to the world press, if not to Sarah herself. Why does it appear no one did so? If the Chinese had a better sense of what a national treasure was than foreign pilferers, it was not demonstrated. Perhaps Cixi, nothing if not a realist, considered the objects lost to be so much water under the bridge—the cost of doing business with foreigners. After all, where the imperial Chinese throne was concerned, there was always more treasure stored away in warehouses all over China. In the scattered treasures and trinkets littering Beijing after August 14, 1900, who really knew what belonged to whom? But maybe the throne kept silent for a more important reason. The foreigners' boat had just recently settled itself into calmer waters. Cixi, wiser this time, may not have wanted to rock it again so soon.

✳ ✳ ✳ ✳ ✳

As if to make sure the world would still have what Sarah believed was an accurate image of the dowager, even if no-one ever saw Kate Carl's portrait of Cixi , Sarah prepared for publication her letters and diaries, written from 1898 till after her return from China in 1905.

Collected and published in 1909 as *Letters from China: With Particular Reference to the Empress Dowager and the Women of China,* the book was only a moderate success, going through a single edition. Sarah's second book, *Old China and Young America,* published in 1913, made even less of an impression on the reading public, despite its timely appearance the year after the Qing dynasty's fall and the rise of the Chinese republic. A small volume filled with many new photographs from the Congers' years in Beijing, as well as pictures of herself and her family serving as illustrations to some of the stories, *Old China and Young America* aimed to instruct children in comparing and contrasting the cultures of China and America through Sarah's experiences of both nations, including a chapter extolling the virtues of the empress dowager. It reinforced Sarah's primary themes: that as an old culture, China had much that young America could benefit and learn from, and that there were fewer differences between East and West than most people assumed.

Old China and Young America was easy for critics to ignore, as it came so many years after the Boxer Uprising and Cixi's death, and was aimed at young readers. What *Letters from China* had against it was Sarah's unapologetic friendship with the dowager, the dragon lady everyone now loved to hate, and her sympathies for the Chinese even after the Boxer siege. The *New York Times,* reviewing the book in May 1909, commended it for containing "some highly important letters," but the author was criticized for not providing more detail about day-to-day events during the Boxer Uprising, and for giving too much trust to the empress dowager. In fact in everything she wrote, it would be Sarah's friendship with Cixi which left her most open to attack. According to the *New York Times* reviewer, Sarah "said a good many nice things which are at variance with the world's estimate of the woman," and that it was likely "the Empress Dowager was on her good behavior while she was with Mrs. Conger and took pains that she should see her better side only." Again, first-hand experience did not matter; what the world thought, based on what the world digested from the sensationalist press, was what one should believe. (Not much has changed in that regard.)[16]

Coming as it did between Kate Carl's *With the Empress Dowager of China* in 1905 and Princess Der Ling's tell-all account of her service at court, *Two Years in the Forbidden City* in 1911, *Letters from China* has tended to be sidelined by these more vivid memoirs even today. In addition, others' records of Sarah—everyone from George E. Morrison to Lady Susan Townley, and even Der Ling—cast her in the role of Christian evangelist or stuffy elderly aunt, a sort of Hepzibah Pyncheon come to life. They, and those who might have been her readers, missed her authentic warmth and humanity. That Sarah was able "to see more in China than a potential market for western products and investments" and that "her sentiments [anticipated] by several decades many of the goals of contemporary feminist enthographers" was for a future era to recognize. Yet some of her contemporaries, including the American architect Sid Nealy, builder of the American legation, saw her contributions very clearly. "It is doubtful," Nealy wrote, "if the combined influence of the entire array of Ministers and Ambassadors representing Western civilization in Pekin, had half the effect of bringing the great Empress to a realizing sense of the needs of progress among her people, as did the modest little woman whose heart and soul was in this work." As Sarah stated, "I considered their customs and our customs to detect, if possible, some thought in common. I always succeeded in finding such a thought . . . Our friendships grew stronger; we trusted one another, and I have every reason to believe that our respect and affections were mutual."[17]

What no one seems to have appreciated were Sarah's more prescient comments toward the end of *Letters from China*—missed, perhaps, because they were so much more relevant to the future than the present:

> The time is coming—is now come—for a great work to be done in China. There is a wonderful awakening among these people, and a reaching for something outside of their great nation and their long-time customs and ideas. The Chinese had a claim of birthright and adhered to it; I too, had a claim of birthright and adhered to it. Between these two conceptions there was a great distance, but this distance was annihilated by the wireless telegraphy of the heart's sympathy.[18]

"There is a patriotic awakening in China," Sarah declared, "that seems to come from the depths of mind and heart." It was the awakening of China's women. She knew of what she spoke because she was kept abreast of the latest reforms by her female friends in Beijing. Writing to a niece in the fall of 1907, Sarah told her that "there are now seventeen Chinese girls' schools conducted and supported by Chinese ladies, some of them Princesses." In 1903, Cixi had complained to Princess Der Ling about being asked by one of Sarah's missionary friends if she would start up a school herself. Pleading she had no time, she shifted the project to the next highest lady at court, the imperial princess, who duly opened a school for girls in her palace. Sarah was delighted with this news, as with the information that Prince Su had started a private school in his house for the education of his many daughters and nieces. His sister, Princess Gungsang Norbu, founded a school that had already enrolled some one hundred and fifty Chinese women and girls, assisted by a Mrs. Chang, a Han lady friend of Sarah's who had unbound and regained the use of her feet. Princess K'e, too, had opened a school for the young women of her household. That these schools were mainly for the founders' own private circle was not significant—what mattered was that the old Chinese custom of not educating daughters was being turned around, woman by woman, girl by girl.[19]

Sarah had heard that some of her women friends had even started their own newspaper, solely for women. The paper was edited by Mrs. Chang, and was the first such women's daily to be published anywhere in the world. "Their woman's daily paper has a large circulation," Sarah noted with pride, "and is thoroughly read," a testament to the advancement of female literacy and part of the process of educating women, providing as it did summaries of world events, and instruction in arithmetic, physics, hygiene, and politics, interspersed with short stories. The paper even impressed the devout and cultivated ladies of the Women's Board of Missions in Portland, Maine. "One of the marvels of the age," wrote the board's Foreign Secretary Kate G. Lamson of Boston, "is the appearance of a daily paper for women in Peking, edited by a woman," which, though not produced by a Christian or espousing Christian beliefs, was providing for missionaries in China "a sphere for their own efforts."[20]

Sarah's goodbye to Cixi at the Summer Palace did not mean they had lost touch. Sarah refers to letters (no longer extant) sent to her from the palace. And after hearing of the disastrous San Francisco earthquake of April 18, 1906, Cixi sent the city $70,000 from her privy purse, perhaps as much because Sarah lived in California as because of the Chinese community; indeed, part of the donation was delivered directly to the American legation in Beijing. Cixi was said to have sent Sarah another dog from the imperial kennels, "a rare variety of canine, worth a great sum [which] has been one of the curiosities of Pasadena since its arrival in the Crown City."[21] And according to Sarah, Cixi also mailed her American friend what the latter calls "beautiful palace pictures," possibly exterior photographs of the Summer Palace taken by Der Ling's brother Xunling. One of his landscape efforts, a panoramic photograph of the entire palace complex, was such a favorite of Cixi's she liked to give it framed as a gift. If this was among the "palace pictures," it did not survive among Sarah's effects.[22]

Cixi died on November 15, 1908 of what is thought to be a case of the flu. Her death came a few hours after that of the Guangxu emperor and her nomination of the infant Puyi as his successor. A cottage industry of speculation arose almost immediately about the various ways in which the emperor might have met his end; Cixi was squarely blamed for all of them. She is still under scrutiny today after tests on the emperor's remains in 2008 detected suspiciously large amounts of arsenic in his hair and bones. That the Guangxu emperor had been sickly for years and made constant use of medicines in which arsenic was an ingredient— it was used, in the form of arsenic trioxide, for a variety of ailments— would certainly explain its presence. That no other toxins were detected would tend to rule out Cixi's having had him dosed with the quick-acting poison that would have led to him dying before she did. Fatal arsenic poisoning takes time and does not cause the sudden death needed in palace coups, though it could have masked an assassination by making his death appear to be from normal causes. There are theories that the Guangxu emperor's death was planned and executed by eunuchs. Or perhaps he had also contracted the flu. Regardless, for many in China and abroad Cixi's guilt is as much a given today as it was a century ago.[23]

In contrast to the many equivocal eulogies that appeared in newspapers across the globe, Sarah's was forthright. "The world's sympathy goes out to China on this day," Sarah wrote the day after Cixi's demise. "She lived a long life of usefulness, and with a strong hand, clear mind and loyal heart, guided the affairs of her country . . . Throughout this woman's life the world catches a glimpse of the hidden quality of China's womanhood. It savors of a quality that might benefit that of the Western World."[24]

✳   ✳   ✳   ✳   ✳

After 1920 Sarah, who had been living in the Pasadena house with her maid, chauffeur, and two boarders, sold the property and went to live with Laura and Fred. "She seems to have been short on cash," remembered her granddaughter. Sarah was the sort of grandmother that every child dreams of—she invited young Sarah to join her in her world, and readily joined Sarah in hers. "She had a desk set up in her room, so she could work," remembered Sarah Buchan Jewell. "She had a miniature desk made for me, and set up beside hers. It was so we could work together, she said." Sarah first lived with the Buchans in Washington, D.C., where in 1919 she tried to interest collector Charles Lang Freer in objects from her collection which she had kept back from the 1908 sale. One of these was the treasured brick she and her *mafu* had carried down from the Great Wall in May 1900, which had survived storage in San Francisco during the 1906 earthquake. Other objects had been gifts from the dowager or friends in China. That she offered them for sale rather than as gifts to the Smithsonian shows that she did not know Freer very well. Freer had built a gallery to house "one of the greatest art collections ever gathered by a single individual," which he sold to the Smithsonian Institution for $1 in 1915. He would not have been interested in dickering over Sarah's Chinese antiques. Thus the objects Sarah offered him were kept in the family, including the Great Wall brick; many were ultimately given to museums by Sarah's granddaughter in the early 1990s.[25]

Some time after 1929 (she does not appear in the 1930 Census), Sarah entered a Christian Science retirement home in Boston. She was almost 90. "She had become rather infirm," her granddaughter recalled, and could not live on her own. According to her granddaughter, she was then moved to the Christian Science Pleasant View Home in Concord, New Hampshire. When Sarah died in February 1932 there was no newspaper report and no obituary. Her body was quietly taken to California and buried beside Edwin's, both graves marked by simple granite plaques set into the ground. The remains of their son Lorentus were exhumed from the family plot in Iowa to be buried with his parents.[26]

In an age in which many of the reforms she worked for have been realized, Sarah Conger's controversial efforts to bring East and West into closer understanding have almost been forgotten. But her paramount belief that progress could benefit China's women as well as men is still redefining and broadening the role of Chinese women. It is unlikely that Sarah would have cheered on Mao's communists; the Cultural Revolution, with its destruction of art, literature, architecture, and people "tainted" by an imperial past, would have horrified her. But she surely would have approved of the improvement in women's status communism brought about. As American Jack Belden commented, "In the women of China, the Communists possessed, almost ready made, one of the greatest masses of disinherited beings the world has ever seen. And because they found the keys to the heart of these women, they also found one of the keys to victory over Chiang Kai-shek." From the day she had stood in the Lama Temple, wondering why women were not allowed, in Mao's future words, to hold up "their half of heaven," Sarah had rightly sensed that for China to function, its women had to be as much a part of life as its men.[27]

Sarah was convinced almost from the start, as were Kate Carl, Marian Headland, Princess Der Ling, and others who knew the dowager personally, that had Cixi been free to do so, innovations for the benefit of women would have been introduced more rapidly in China—not cars, planes, or trains, but the crucial innovation of women's education. When Sarah saw its first bloom in China she rejoiced in the woman she believed was responsible for it. "Private schools for girls of both the higher and lower classes are being started throughout China," Sarah wrote in 1907. "I am persuaded without doubt that this uniform action was quietly planned and sanctioned by the Throne, before this departure with its great responsibilities was taken." The world still disagrees with her where Cixi is concerned, but it is clear Sarah was part of the process that is still bringing freedom to the women of China.[28] "China belongs to her people," Sarah stated. Once the Chinese realized this, their activity would "awaken a slumbering strength which is all their own." That this strength was immense is clear in her characterization of an "Oriental 'dawn' and the Occidental 'twilight.'"[29]

All this had come to her, she insisted, through the "tender touch of a woman's heart": through her Chinese women friends, and especially through knowing and loving the Empress Dowager Cixi. "True friendship is sunshine to the day," Sarah wrote, "and a lamp to the darkness of night."[30]

Notes

Introduction

1. Buck, *Imperial Woman*, 352.
2. Na Genzheng, in discussion with the author, April 6, 2008; Martin, *The Siege in Peking*, 48.
3. Sarah Buchan Jewell, interviewed by the author, October 25, 2008.
4. Croll, *Feminism and Socialism in China*, 12–13.
5. Conger, *Letters from China*, 221.

Chapter 1   Farmer's daughter

1. Cherrington, "Universalism: A Kind and Gentle Religious Tradition was Once Dynamic in Galesburg," *Zephyr* (Galesburg, Illinois), January 18, 1996. According to the 1850 census for Elkhart, Indiana, the Pike family included an Augusta Pike, apparently Edward's 25-year-old sister, described by the census taker as an "idiot" (i.e., living with what we would now term mental retardation or an intellectual disability). So Sarah, nine at the time, grew up in an atmosphere of tolerance and understanding of yet another kind of marginalized person that Universalists believed should be treated with more respect, the mentally challenged.

2. The Pike daughters were: Mary, Sarah, Lavinia, and Fanny (US Census, City of Galesburg, Illinois, July 19, 1860). Being a farmer's daughter in the American Midwest certainly had its advantages: over a quarter of the women who went to Chinese missions were daughters of farmers, attributing their "missionary motivation" to the liberty of body and spirit they had known as girls growing up on farms. See Hunter, *The Gospel of Gentility*, 29.

3. Conger, *Old China and Young America*, 88–89, 95–96; Sarah Conger letter to Laura Conger Buchan, June 20, 1903. Sarah Pike Conger Papers, #991-12, Peabody Museum of Archaeology and Ethnology, Harvard University.

4. Conger, *Letters from China*, 296.

5. Seeley, *Manual of College Literary Societies*, 30–31; *Ladies' Repository* 38, p. 278; Conger, *Old China and Young America*, 119; Leonard, *Woman's Who's Who of America*, 199; Confucius, *The Four Books*, "Analects," 2(4): 135–136.

6. The Congers were also on the earliest complete list of abolitionists in Illinois, dated September 27, 1837. See *Illinois State Genealogical Society Quarterly*, XII, no. 3 (1980). For White Mayflower ancestry, see entries for F. Eaton/ S. Fuller/White, in van Antwerp et al., *Mayflower Families Through Five Generations*, vol. 1, 139.

7. US Census, City of Galesburg, Illinois, July 26, 1860; Webster, *Annals of Knox County, Annals of Galesburg*, available at http://www.usgennet.org/usa/ il/county/knox/annuals_knox_5.htm (accessed October 7, 2010).

8. Cherrington, *Zephyr*; Lombard College Yearbook, class of 1890, Knox College; Edwin Conger letter to Laura Conger Buchan, September 20, 1901, Sarah Pike Conger Papers, #991-12.

9. "Memory of E. H. Conger," *Republican Register*; "Conger, Edwin Hurd," entry in *Biographical Directory of the United States Congress*, available at http://bioguide.congress.gov/scripts/biodisplay.pl?index=C000675; Rex Cherrington, email correspondence with the author, August 25, 2008. First raised by Paul Raymond Kendall, president of Lombard College, Edwin's regiment was mustered in Knoxville, Illinois on September 1, 1862.

10. Entry for Edwin Hurd Conger in *Biographical Directory of the United States Congress* online. See "Memory of E. H. Conger," *Republican Register*.

11. Conger, *Old China and Young America*, 141–142.

12. Diary of Sarah Pike Conger, Vol. 1, Muscum of Fine Arts, Boston, 1991–217; Conger, *Old China and Young America*, 156–160; Doris Kearns Goodwin, *Team of Rivals: The Political Genius of Abraham Lincoln*, 486.

13. Obituary for Edwin H, Conger, *Daily Mail*, May 18, 1907; Lombard yearbook, class of 1890, Knox College; entry for Edwin Hurd Conger, *Biographical Directory of the United State Congress* online.

14. *The History of Dallas County*, p. 546; the Winterset, *Madisonian*, May 22, 1873.

15. Sarah Buchan Jewell, interviewed by the author, October 25, 2008.

16. "The Conger Family of Illinois," *Political Graveyard*, available at http://politicalgraveyard.com/families/15583.html.

17. Clipping from 1901 shared with the author by Rex Cherrington; Lombard yearbook, class of 1890, Knox College.

18. "Conger is Not a Candidate, But He Will Run If Urged," *Anaconda Standard*, April 26, 1901; Conger, *Old China and Young America*, 143–144.

19. Conger, *Letters from China*, 3.

20. Carpenter, *South America, Carpenter's Geographical Reader*, 523–524.

21. Ibid., 524–528.

22. Joseph, LeGrand, and Salvatore (eds.), *Close Encounters of Empire*, 173–196.

23. Conger, *Old China and Young America*, 119–120; Sarah Buchan Jewell, interviewed by the author, October 25, 2008.

24. Sarah Conger to Mary Baker Eddy, January 7, 1898. The Mary Baker Eddy Library for the Betterment of Humanity; Eddy, *Science and Health with Key to the Scriptures*, 468; Sarah Buchan Jewell, interviewed by the author, October 25, 2008; *Puritan* I, no. 9 (September 1897): 278.

25. *Puritan* I, no. 9 (September 1897): 278.

26. Sarah Conger to Mary Baker Eddy, January 7, 1898. The Mary Baker Eddy Library for the Betterment of Humanity.

27. Ibid.

28. Ibid.

Chapter 2   Mother of China

1. Hunt, *The Making of a Special Relationship*, 2–3.

2. Hamilton, *President McKinley, War and Empire*, vol. 1: 92; Mathisen, *Critical Issues in American Religious History: A Reader*, 406; Twain, "To The Person Sitting In Darkness," *North American Review*. If his personal library, part of which is now at the Yenching Library at Harvard, is anything to go by, Edwin Conger did a great deal of reading not just about China's past history but about its problems contemporary to his appointment as minister. He read everyone from British author Alexis Krausse, an expert on Asia who believed China was doomed to implode, to James Harrison Wilson, the former Civil War officer who brought to China and the Chinese of the 1880s his hopes and sympathies, and owned many of the major published Boxer siege accounts.

3. "China's Empress Dowager," *New York Times*, June 24, 1900. Unlike Denby, who merely "toyed" with participating in the partitioning of China, in his first year Edwin would urge Washington "to at least keep Manila and its hinterland as a step toward 'securing and holding our share of influence' in East Asia," helping to facilitate what Edwin termed a "commercial conquest." He little knew at the time, in choosing volatile Zhili province as the prime American field of operations, with what potent dynamite he was playing— that would come in late 1899 and especially in 1900. See Hunt, *The Making of a Special Relationship*, 176–177.

4. Der Ling, *Old Buddha*, 1–11.

5. Varé, *The Last Empress*, 5; Bland and Backhouse, *China under the Empress Dowager*, 1–7; Aldrich, *The Search for a Vanishing Beijing*, 115; Cixi's great-nephew, Na Genzheng, writes that Cixi was indeed born in Beijing, in a house on *Bidai* Lane. He provides a photograph of the house's gate in his 2005 book, *Cixi As I Knew Her* (*Wo suo zhidao de Cixi taihou*), p. 8. Another account of her origins was offered in 1991 in a Chinese study, *Cracking the Mystery of Cixi's Youth* (*Jie kai Cixi tong nian zhi mi*). See online version at http://www.tydao.com/suwu/lishi/cxss.htm.

6. Headland, *Court Life in China*, 9–11; Conger, *Old China and Young America*, 64–72.

7. Seagrave, *Dragon Lady*, 33.

8. Ibid. 32.

9. Ibid., 43. Also see Der Ling, *Old Buddha*, 1.

10. Seagrave, *Dragon Lady*, 43.

11. Sergeant, *The Great Empress Dowager of China*, 33–35; Hevia, *English Lessons*, 33.

12. Sergeant, *The Great Empress Dowager of China*, 45–46.

13. Hevia, *English Lessons*, 100.

14. Seagrave, *Dragon Lady*, 50–58; Sergeant, *The Great Empress Dowager of China*, 33–35; Headland, *Court Life in China*, 31. As late as 2009, pieces of Yuanmingyuan were still coming on the auction market and reopening old wounds. See "Twist in Sale of Relics Has China Winking," *New York Times*, March 3, 2009.

15. Der Ling, *Two Years in the Forbidden City*, 250–253.

16. Seagrave, *Dragon Lady*, 68.

17. Sergeant, *The Great Empress Dowager of China*, 41; Warner, *The Dragon Empress*, 85; Seagrave, *Dragon Lady*, 73–78.

18. Sergeant, *The Great Empress Dowager of China*, 42; Seagrave, *Dragon Lady*, 78–81; Rawski, *The Last Emperors*, 300.

19. Denby as quoted in Headland, *Court Life in China*, 36.

Chapter 3 High walls

1. Dong, *Shanghai 1842–1949*, 3–13.
2. Conger, *Letters from China*, 4 and 7–8.
3. Ibid.
4. Sarah Buchan Jewell, interviewed by the author, October 25, 2008.
5. Conger, *Letters from China*, 5.
6. Ibid.; Little, *Intimate China*, 321–325 and 336.
7. Scidamore, *China the Long-lived Empire*, 61–65.
8. Fei Shi, *Guide to Peking and its Environs Near and Far*, 7–8.
9. Conger, *Letters from China*, 5; Hunter, *Gospel of Gentility*, 1.
10. Zhang, *A Translation of the Ancient Book of Burial (Zan Shu) by Guo Pu (276–324)*, 41–46.
11. Hay, *Boundaries in China*, 15; Conger, *Letters from China*, 1–2 and 5. See also Hunter, *Gospel of Gentility*, 182.
12. Moser and Moser, *Foreigners Within the Gate*, 29–33; Scidmore, *China the Long-lived Empire*, 146.
13. Payen, "Besieged in Peking," *Century Magazine*, 453–454.
14. Coltman, *Beleaguered in Peking*, 177–178.
15. Payen, "Besieged in Peking," *Century Magazine*, 454.
16. Scidmore, *China the Long-lived Empire*, 145. Edwin received US$13,000 per year, see "Interesting Life History of Minister Conger," *San Francisco Call*, July 17, 1900.
17. Payen, "Besieged in Peking," *Century Magazine*, 454.
18. Hoe, *Women at the Siege*, 168–176.
19. Xiang, *The Origins of the Boxer War*, 134–137.
20. Conger, *Letters from China*, 5–7 and 19–21.
21. Ibid.
22. Ibid.
23. Ibid.
24. Ibid., 5–7, 19–21 and 33.

Chapter 4 Chinese Christians

1. Sergeant, *The Great Empress Dowager of China*, 163.
2. See Der Ling, *Two Years in the Forbidden City*, 175–179; Ching, *Chinese Religions*, 63.
3. Der Ling, *Two Years in the Forbidden City*, 175–179.
4. Sergeant, *The Great Empress Dowager of China*, 163–164.
5. Ibid., 166.

6.   See map in Little, *Intimate China*, 297.

7.   Two in Shandong, one in Manchuria, and another in Guangdong. See Sergeant, *The Great Empress Dowager of China*, 165–167.

8.   Kwong, *A Mosaic of the Hundred Days*, 58.

9.   Hunter, *Gospel of Gentility*, 24.

10.   Arlington and Lewisohn, *In Search of Old Peking*, 301–302.

11.   Hooker, *Behind the Scenes in Peking*, 2–4.

12.   Conger, *Letters from China*, 18; Arlington and Lewisohn, *In Search of Old Peking*, 302.

13.   Conger, *Letters from China*, 10.

14.   Ibid., 36. For another comparison of Asian men to women see Nealy, "Chinese Progress Due to an American Woman," *Boston Daily Globe*, November 26, 1911.

15.   Conger, *Letters from China*, 11–12.

16.   Ibid., 12.

17.   Ibid., 13.

18.   By the time they left China in 1905, Sarah and Edwin Conger had a number of significant books about China in their personal library, many gifts from their authors; they are now in the Harvard-Yenching Library.

19.   Conger, *Letters from China*, 14.

20.   Conger, *Old China and Young America*, 62–63; Conger, *Letters from China*, 200.

21.   Tsai, *Perpetual Happiness*, 211–212; Conger, *Letters from China*, 15.

22.   Conger, *Letters from China*, 14–16.

23.   Ibid.

Chapter 5   Daws in peacock's feathers

1.   Hart, *The I. G. in Peking*, vol. 2, Letter #1000, December 8, 1895.

2.   Hart, *The I. G. in Peking*, vol. 2, Letter #1116, September 25, 1898.

3.   Seagrave, *Dragon Lady*, 235.

4.   Conger, *Letters from China*, 23–24.

5.   Hart, *The I. G. in Peking*, vol. 2, Letter #1117, October 9, 1898.

6.   Conger, *Letters from China*, 25; Thompson and Macklin, *The Man Who Died Twice*, 189.

7.   Thompson and Macklin, *The Man Who Died Twice*, 190.

8.   Hart, *The I. G. in Peking*, vol. 2, Letter #1118, October 16, 1898.

9.   "Le Docteur Dethève et l'empereur Guangxu," Franzini in *Études chinoises* XIV, no. 1 (1995), quoted in *The Forbidden City: Center of Imperial China*, Gilles Béguin and Dominique Morel, Harry N. Abrams, Inc., 1997, 120–121.

10.   Conger, *Letters from China*, 26–27.

11. Ibid., 28–29.
12. Ibid.
13. Waley-Cohen, *The Sextants of Beijing*, 41.
14. Conger, *Letters from China*, 29.
15. Ibid.
16. Scidmore, *China the Long-lived Empire*, 150–151; Hart, *The I. G. in Peking*, Letter #1121 November 13, 1898.
17. Hart, *The I.G. in Peking*, Letter # 1121, November 13, 1898.

Chapter 6   Imperial audience

1. Scidmore, *China the Long-lived Empire*, 136.
2. Ibid.; Hart, *The I. G. in Peking*, Letter #1124, December 4, 1898.
3. For more on the train car, see Bredon, *Peking*, 140; Seagrave, *Dragon Lady*, 258.
4. Der Ling, *Two Years in the Forbidden City*, 134.
5. Hoe, *Women at the Siege*, 3; Conger, *Letters from China*, 40.
6. Little, *Round About My Peking Garden*, 50; Der Ling, *Two Years in the Forbidden City*, 113–115. On one occasion, Mrs. Archibald Little saw Guangxu leap happily from the imperial train carriage, very much like "many an English young man as he comes to his journey's end" (see Little, *Round About My Peking Garden*, 50).
7. Conger, *Letters from China*, 39; Seagrave, *Dragon Lady*, 260.
8. Conger, *Letters from China*, 39.
9. Der Ling, *Two Years in the Forbidden City*, 300–302.
10. Conger, *Letters from China*, 42.
11. Quoted in Seagrave, *Dragon Lady*, 261.
12. Hunter, *Gospel of Gentility*, 21.
13. Thompson and Macklin, *The Man Who Died Twice*, 189.
14. Quoted in Seagrave, *Dragon Lady*, 261; "Gossip in the Capital," *New York Daily Tribune*, June 23, 1900.
15. Conger, *Letters from China*, 43.
16. Conger, *Letters from China*, 43.

Chapter 7   Christmas in Beijing

1. Whyte, *Unfinished Encounter*, 71–77; Waley-Cohen, *The Sextants of Beijing*, 66–70.
2. Hunter, *Gospel of Gentility*, 25; Ching, *Chinese Religions*, 76; Conger, *Letters from China*, 45–46.

3.   Clark, *Our Journey Around the World*, 174; Diary of Sarah Pike Conger, Vol. 1, Museum of Fine Arts, Boston, 1991-217.

4.   Conger, *Letters from China*, 46 and 50; Hunter, *Gospel of Gentility*, 1; Ching, *Chinese Religions*, 69.

5.   Lao Tzu, *Tao Teh Ching*, 2 (translated by John C. H. Wu); Sarah Conger to Mary Baker Eddy, March 8, 1906, The Mary Baker Eddy Library for the Betterment of Humanity.

6.   Conger, *Letters from China*, 35.

7.   Ibid., 37–38.

8.   Ibid.

9.   Ibid.

10.   Darwin, *The Descent of Man and Selection in Relation to Sex*, 96.

11.   Conger, *Letters from China*, 33, 49 and 59–60; Whyte, *Unfinished Encounter*, 89; Edwin Conger letter of December 25, 1901, Sarah Pike Conger Papers, #991-12.

12.   Conger, *Letters from China*, 33, 49 and 59–60; *Tao Teh Ching*, 1.

13.   Conger, *Letters from China*, 43 and 50–51.

14.   For Fu Xuan quote, see Arthur Waley, *Chinese Poems*, 84–85; Conger, *Letters from China*, 50.

15.   Lang, *Chinese Family and Society*, 44.

16.   Pruitt, *A Daughter of Han*, 63–65; Croll, *Feminism and Socialism in China*, 20.

17.   Conger, *Letters from China*, 34–35.

18.   Ibid.

19.   Ibid.

20.   Ibid.

21.   Ibid.

22.   Ibid.

23.   Ibid., 47–48; Conger, *Old China and Young America*, 106.

Chapter 8   Unlocking the gates

1.   Arlington and Lewisohn, *In Search of Old Peking*, 153–155; Conger, *Letters from China*, 56–57. Sarah was also drawn to the Imperial Examination Halls, located not far from the observatory.

2.   Conger, *Letters from China*, 54–55.

3.   Arlington and Lewisohn, *In Search of Old Peking*, 157–158.

4.   Conger, *Letters from China*, 54.

5.   Ibid., 54–55.

6.   Ibid.

7.   Ibid., 45 and 59.

8.   Bredon, *Peking*, 251–252.

9.   See the photographs of Lancelot Giles in the Giles Pickford Collection, Australian National University, Canberra.

10. Bredon, *Peking*, 252 and 253–255.

11. Conger, *Letters from China*, 57.

12. Ibid.

13. Arlington and Lewisohn, *In Search of Old Peking*, 174–175.

14. Conger, *Letters from China*, 57.

15. Ibid., 57–58.

16. Ibid.

17. Ibid., 45 and 59.

18. Ibid., 49.

19. Ibid., 50.

20. Ibid.

21. Conger, *Letters from China*, 63–64 and 73.

22. Ibid., 73–74.

23. Ibid.

24. Ibid., 73; Scidmore, *China the Long-lived Empire*, 175–176.

25. Conger, *Letters from China*, 66 and 74.

26. Ibid.

Chapter 9   Gathering storm

1.   Crossley, *Orphan Warriors*, 190–191; Der Ling, *Two Years in the Forbidden City*, 216–222.

2.   "Tsi-An, Ruler of China, Dead," *New York Times*, November 16, 1908; David Hogge, in email correspondence with the author, May 15, 2009. One of the earliest positive Western accounts of Cixi was James Harrison Wilson's 1887 book, *China: Travels and Investigations in the Middle Kingdom*.

3.   Seagrave, *Dragon Lady*, 250–251.

4.   Thompson and Macklin, *The Man Who Died Twice*, 192–194.

5.   Kwong, *A Mosaic of the Hundred Days*, 207.

6.   Seagrave, *Dragon Lady*, 187.

7.   Ibid., 171–173.

8.   Hummel (ed.), *Eminent Chinese of the Ch'ing Period*, vol. 1, 405; Der Ling, *Kowtow*, 260–263.

9.   Quoted in Paul Clements, *The Boxer Rebellion*, 116.

10. Der Ling, *Old Buddha*, 239–242.

11. Ibid., 234–235; Headland, *Court Life in China*, 159; Wu, *The Flight of an Empress*, 203.

12. *New York Times,* July 6, 1900.

13. Little, *Round About My Peking Garden,* 51.

14. Conger, *Letters from China,* 75–76.

15. Ibid., 75–77. For the Declaration of Independence account see Preston, *The Boxer Rebellion,* 153; Payen, "Besieged in Peking," *Century Magazine,* 459.

16. Conger, *Letters from China,* 75–77.

17. Ibid.

Chapter 10   Shadow Boxers

1. Coltman, *Beleaguered in Peking,* 1 and 3–25.

2. Ibid.

3. Ibid.

4. Ibid.

5. Ibid.

6. Ibid.

7. Payen, "Besieged in Peking," *Century Magazine,* 453.

8. Conger, *Letters from China,* 87–88.

9. Ibid.

10. Ibid., 90.

11. Hoe, *Women at the Siege,* 30.

12. Cohen, *History in Three Keys,* 53–54 and 106–107.

13. Elliott, *Some Did It for Civilisation,* 305.

14. Sarah Conger to Charles Lang Freer, July 27, 1919. Charles Lang Freer Papers, Freer Gallery of Art and Arthur M. Sackler Gallery Archives, Smithsonian Institution.

15. Ibid.

16. Payen, "Besieged in Peking," *Century Magazine,* 454.

17. Quoted in Landor, *China and the Allies,* vol. I, 56–57; Payen, "Besieged in Peking," *Century Magazine,* 454.

18. Jessie Ransome, as quoted in Hoe, *Women at the Siege,* 23; Cohen, *History in Three Keys,* 83.

19. Conger, *Letters from China,* 90.

20. Hooker, *Behind the Scenes in Peking,* 6–11.

21. Ibid.

22. Ibid.

23. Myers' exploits during the Boxer siege inspired tales in the press of the day and, later, in Hollywood versions of himself, most notably in Nicholas Ray's 1963 film, *55 Days at Peking.*

24. "Foreigners in Peking," *New York Times,* July 16, 1900.

25. Conger, *Letters from China*, 93.

26. Kreiner, "American Missionaries and the Boxer Rebellion," *Sextant.*

27. Conger, *Letters from China*, 94.

28. Payen, "Besieged in Peking," *Century Magazine*, 454; Diary of Sarah Pike Conger, Vol. 1, Museum of Fine Arts, Boston, 1991-217; Hoe, *Women at the Siege*, 45–46; Martin, *The Siege in Peking*, 95.

29. Laura's ex-husband, George Landrum, had later enlisted in the 49th Iowa to fight in the Spanish–American War but died ten days after reaching his camp in Florida. See "Interesting Life History of Minister Conger," *San Francisco Call*, July 17, 1900.

30. Payen, "Besieged in Peking," *Century Magazine*, 455; "Interesting Life History of Minister Conger," *San Francisco Call*, July 17, 1900; *Puritan*, September 1897, vol. I (9): 278.

31. Conger, *Letters from China*, 95.

32. Ibid., 96.

33. Payen, "Besieged in Peking," *Century Magazine*, 455.

34. Coltman, *Beleaguered in Peking*, 58; Payen, "Besieged in Peking," *Century Magazine*, 455; Martin, *The Siege in Peking*, 104.

35. Payen, "Besieged in Peking," *Century Magazine*, 455.

36. Coltman, *Beleaguered in Peking*, 62–63.

37. Hooker, *Behind the Scenes in Peking*, 18–19.

38. Conger, *Letters from China*, 96; Payen, "Besieged in Peking," *Century Magazine*, 455.

39. Hoe, *Women at the Siege*, 64.

40. Ibid.; the print is featured opposite page 110 in Martin, *The Siege in Peking*.

41. Conger, *Letters from China*, 99; Payen, "Besieged in Peking," *Century Magazine*, 455.

42. "Besieged in Peking," *Century Magazine*, 455.

43. Payen, "Besieged in Peking," *Century Magazine*, 455; Hooker, *Behind the Scenes in Peking*, 25; Conger, *Letters from China*, 100.

44. Conger, *Letters from China*, 98 and 101–102; Hooker, *Behind the Scenes in Peking*, 20.

45. Hooker, *Behind the Scences in Peking*, 20.

46. Conger, *Letters from China*, 101.

47. Lynch, *The War of the Civilisations*, 106–110; Hooker, *Behind the Scenes in Peking*, 24.

48. Martin, *The Siege in Peking*, 75–76.

49. "The Last Letter of Bishop Favier," *Annals of the Propagation of the Faith*, LXVIII, vol. 460, 143, 144; Elleman, *Modern Chinese Warfare*, 126–128.

50. Diary of Sarah Pike Conger, Vol. 1, Museum of Fine Arts, Boston, 1991-217.

51. Diary of Sarah Pike Conger, Vol. 1, Museum of Fine Arts, Boston, 1991-217; Coltman, *Beleaguered in Peking,* 67.

52. Conger, *Letters from China,* 103.

53. Hooker, *Behind the Scenes in Peking,* 21 and 37–39; Coltman, *Beleaguered in Peking,* 68.

54. Hooker, *Behind the Scenes in Peking,* 21 and 37–39; Payen, "Besieged in Peking," *Century Magazine,* 455.

Chapter 11   Siege

1. Conger, *Letters from China,* 104–105.

2. Ibid., 106; Hunt, *The Making of a Special Relationship,* 161.

3. Der Ling, *Two Years in the Forbidden City,* 175–176.

4. "Chinese Officials' Reassuring Report," *New York Times,* July 2, 1900.

5. "Prominent Chinamen Quarrel," *New York Times,* July 30, 1900.

6. Conger, *Letters from China,* 106.

7. Ibid.

8. Hoe, *Women at the Siege,* 108–111.

9. Hooker, *Behind the Scenes in Peking,* 45–46.

10. Hoe, *Women at the Siege,* 107–108.

11. Diary of Sarah Pike Conger, Vol. 1, Museum of Fine Arts, Boston, 1991-217.

12. Moser and Moser, *Foreigners Within the Gate,* 35.

13. Payen, "Besieged in Peking," *Century Magazine,* 456.

14. Ibid., 460.

15. Diary of Sarah Pike Conger, Vol. 1, Museum of Fine Arts, Boston, 1991-217.

16. Conger, *Letters from China,* 109; Ruoff (ed.), *Death Throes of a Dynasty,* 83.

17. Hooker, *Behind the Scenes in Peking,* 41.

18. Martin, *The Siege in Peking,* 81–82.

19. Payen, "Besieged in Peking," *Century Magazine,* 457.

20. Conger, *Letters from China,* 110.

21. Captain Myers' report, September 26, 1900, available at http://www.history.navy.mil/index.html; Payen, "Besieged in Peking," *Century Magazine,* 457.

22. Payen, "Besieged in Peking," *Century Magazine,* 457.

23. Ibid., 461; Hoe, *Women at the Siege,* 149.

24. Diary of Sarah Pike Conger, Vol. 1, Museum of Fine Arts, Boston, 1991-217.

25. Hooker, *Behind the Scenes in Peking,* 55–56.

26. Ibid.

27. Ibid., 61–62.

28. Martin, *The Siege in Peking,* 87–88.

29. Diary of Sarah Pike Conger, Vol. 1, Museum of Fine Arts, Boston, 1991-217; Conger, *Letters from China*, 122; Coltman, *Beleaguered in Peking*, 206.

30. Diary of Sarah Pike Conger, Vol. 1, Museum of Fine Arts, Boston, 1991-217. In his book, *The Siege At Peking*, Peter Fleming claimed the Chinese set their rifle sights to maximum level, "for it was widely believed among the Chinese that the figures on the hind-sights governed the muzzle-velocity of the bullet." See page 76.

31. Ibid.

32. Weale, *Indiscreet Letters from Peking*, 137; Payen, "Besieged in Peking," *Century Magazine*, 457.

33. Martin, *The Siege in Peking*, 95; Payen, "Besieged in Peking," *Century Magazine*, 459.

34. Coltman, *Beleaguered in Peking*, 94–95.

35. Ransome, *The Story of the Siege Hospital in Peking*.

36. Conger, *Letters from China*, 110–111.

37. Ibid.

38. Coltman, *Beleaguered in Peking*, 96–97.

39. Payen, "Besieged in Peking," *Century Magazine*, 459.

40. Diary of Sarah Pike Conger, Vol. 1, Museum of Fine Arts, Boston, 1991-217; Guest Book from the American Legation, Museum of Fine Arts, Boston, 1991-220.

41. Conger, *Letters from China*, 115–116 and 143; Martin, *The Siege in Peking*, 118–119.

42. Payen, "Besieged in Peking," *Century Magazine*, 459.

43. Preston, *The Boxer Rebellion*, 154.

Chapter 12   Survival

1. Diary of Sarah Pike Conger, Vol. 1, Museum of Fine Arts, Boston, 1991-217.

2. Ibid.

3. Payen, "Besieged in Peking," *Century Magazine*, 459; Conger, *Letters from China*, 112–113; Sarah Conger letter to sister, December 16, 1901, Sarah Pike Conger Papers, #991-12.

4. Mary Pierce as quoted in "Anxiety in the Legations," *Nebraska State Journal*, October 28, 1900.

5. Lao Tzu, *Tao Teh Ching*, 9.

6. Conger, *Letters from China*, 113; Coltman, *Beleaguered in Peking*, 99–100.

7. Conger, *Letters from China*, 113.

8. Diary of Sarah Pike Conger, Vol. 1, Museum of Fine Arts, Boston, 1991-217.

9. Conger, *Letters from China,* 117–118.

10. Diary of Sarah Pike Conger, Vol. 1, Museum of Fine Arts, Boston, 1991-217; Conger, *Letters from China,* 119–120.

11. Conger, *Letters from China,* 159.

12. Ibid.

13. Ibid.

14. Eddy, *Science and Health,* 459.

15. Payen, "Besieged in Peking," *Century Magazine,* 462; Conger, *Letters from China,* 119–120 and 125; Martin, *The Siege in Peking,* 95.

16. Payen, "Besieged in Peking," *Century Magazine,* 461.

17. Conger, *Letters from China,* 130–132.

18. Ibid., 130–131.

19. Ibid.

20. Coltman, *Beleaguered in Peking,* 110.

21. Conger, *Letters from China,* 134; Hooker, *Behind the Scenes in Peking,* 124–125.

22. Coltman, 111–112; Conger, *Letters from China,* 135–136; *San Francisco Call,* July 23, 1900.

23. Conger, *Letters from China,* 135–136.

24. Ibid.

25. Ibid., 137.

26. *Davenport Republican*, July 22, 1900; "An Estimation of United States Minister Conger by an Old-time Friend," *Anaconda Standard,* July 29, 1900.

27. "Died at Peking," and "Lost Their Lives in the Massacre," *San Francisco Call,* July 17, 1900.

28. "New Hope for the Congers," *Post-Standard,* July 16, 1900.

29. Ibid.

30. Coltman, *Beleaguered in Peking,* 143.

31. Fredriksen, *American Military Leaders,* 192–193.

32. Captain Myers' report, September 26, 1900, available at http://www.history.navy.mil/index.html; "Mr. Conger Accuses Captain of Marine," *New York Times,* October 28, 1900.

33. "Mr. Conger Accuses Captain of Marine," *New York Times,* October 28, 1900; Sarah Conger letter of December 16, 1901, Sarah Pike Conger Papers, #991-12; Preston, *The Boxer Rebellion,* 168.

34. "Women Quarreled and a Man Suffered," *New York Times,* January 24, 1901.

35. Untitled articles in the *New York Times,* January 12, 1901 and May, 25, 1901; "Captain N. H. Hall Honored," *New York Times,* June 9, 1901; Hooker, *Behind the Scenes in Peking,* 80–82.

36. Untitled articles in the *New York Times,* January 12, 1901 and May, 25, 1901.

37. Hooker, *Behind the Scenes in Peking*, 80–81; Lynch, *The War of the Civilisations*, 19.
38. Lynch, *The War of the Civilisations*, 19 and 24–25.
39. Ibid.
40. Ibid., 24–25.
41. Lynch, *The War of the Civilisations*, 39–40.
42. Ibid., 60–61.
43. Ibid.
44. Ibid., 62.
45. Ibid.
46. Ibid., 63.
47. Ibid., 64–65.
48. Payen, "Besieged in Peking," *Century Magazine*, 466.
49. Ibid., 146.
50. Ibid., 144.
51. Giles, *The Siege of the Peking Legations*, 166 and plate 47. The fact that everyone at the time, including Sarah, seems to have understood Liu Wuyuan was male, leads me to assume that was indeed his sex, but that is not the final word on the subject. At least one writer believes Liu was female, based on the photograph by Lancelot Giles; certain features support this interpretation.
52. Conger, *Letters from China*, 145–146.
53. Ibid., 148–149.
54. Ibid., 148.
55. Hubbard, *Under Marching Orders*, 171; Mateer, *Siege Days*, 141.
56. Conger, *Letters from China*, 155.
57. Preston, *The Boxer Rebellion*, 206; Sarah Conger letter of October 16, 1901, Sarah Pike Conger Papers, #991-12.
58. Preston, *The Boxer Rebellion*, 234–244.
59. Ibid.
60. Hooker, *Behind the Scenes in Peking*, 174–175.
61. Ibid.; Preston, *The Boxer Rebellion*, 234–244; Coltman, *Beleaguered in Peking*, 141; Payen, "Besieged in Peking," *Century Magazine*, 467; Conger, *Letters from China*, 156–159.
62. Hooker, *Behind the Scenes in Peking*, 175.
63. Conger, *Letters from China*, 161.
64. Ibid., 161 and 183.
65. Ibid., 177.
66. Ibid., 161 and 183.
67. Ibid.

Chapter 13   Loot

1.   McNabb, *The Women of the Middle Kingdom,* 144–156.
2.   Sarah Conger to Fred Buchan and Laura Conger Buchan, January 16, 1902; Sarah Pike Conger Papers, #991-12;"The Court Back in Peking," *New York Times,* January 8, 1902;
3.   Diary of Sarah Pike Conger, Vol. 1, Museum of Fine Arts, Boston, 1991-217.
4.   Ibid.
5.   Hevia, *English Lessons,* 284; Boot, *The Savage Wars of Peace,* 96.
6.   Lynch, *The War of the Civilisations,* 146–148.
7.   Hevia, *English Lessons,* 235.
8.   Lynch, *The War of the Civilisations,* 177–179; Boot, *The Savage Wars of Peace,* 96. The pearl ring was later given by Sarah to her granddaughter Sarah Buchan Jewell. Sarah Buchan Jewell, interviewed by the author, October 25, 2008.
9.   Boot, *The Savage Wars of Peace,* 217 and 197–199; Hevia, *English Lessons,* 199 and Plate 30, 263.
10. Lynch, *The War of the Civilisations,* 156–160 and 177–181; Hevia, *English Lessons,* 217 and 219.
11. Conger, *Letters from China,* 163.
12. Ibid., 164 and 176.
13. Ibid., 165–166.
14. Ibid., 260–261.
15. Ibid.
16. Ibid.
17. Ibid.; Yoshihara, *Embracing the East,* 42; Hevia, *English Lessons,* 268.
18. Conger, *Letters from China,* 176.
19. "Empress Dowager's Many Perplexities," *New York Times,* December 16, 1900; Wu, *The Flight of an Empress,* 72–73 and 125. Luella Miner was told by a Chinese friend close to the court that Cixi had dressed in peasant style since her return to the Forbidden City on June 14, suggesting she was prepared to flee at any moment. See "The Flight of the Empress Dowager," *The Century Magazine,* March 1901, LXI(5): 777–780.
20. Der Ling, *Two Years in the Forbidden City,* 183.
21. Wu, *The Flight of an Empress,* 101–102 and 141.
22. Ibid., 72–74, 122–123 and 125.
23. Ibid., 104–106.
24. In support of this, Philip Sergeant wrote in 1910 that the Pearl killed herself out of fear that foreign soldiers would rape her, and Cixi did award

her posthumous honors for "protecting her virtue." See Wu, *The Flight of an Empress,* 148–154; Sergeant, *The Great Empress Dowager of China,* 247; Barmé, *The Forbidden City,* 101–102. For an account of Cixi's flight, see "Last Emperor's Cousin is Palace Clerk," *Telegraph,* August 4, 2004.

25. Wu, *The Flight of an Empress,* 152.

26. Ibid., 211.

27. Sergeant, *The Great Empress Dowager of China,* 256.

28. "The Court Back in Peking," *New York Times,* January 8, 1902. Sergeant, *The Great Empress Dowager of China,* 257–258.

29. "The Court Back in Peking," *New York Times,* January, 1902.

30. Hevia, *English Lessons,* 196; Sergeant, *The Great Empress Dowager of China,* 259.

31. For the photograph of Cixi see Moser and Moser, *Foreigners Within the Gates,* 121.

32. A native of Wyandotte, Kansas and graduate of the University of Kansas law school, Lieutenant Fred Erskine Buchan had served as a captain in the Spanish–American War. As leader of Operations and Training of the Second Army Corps in France during World War I, Buchan would be instrumental to breaking the Hindenburg line, and would be awarded the Distinguished Service Medal. Married to his college sweetheart, Lucinda K. Smith, in June 1898, he was widowed less than a year later. Fred met Laura when American troops entered the British legation on August 14, 1900. The marriage was described in the press as Laura's consolation for having made an unfortunate first marriage to George Landrum, though in fact it was also a consolation for the bereaved Fred (a fact never mentioned). Laura and Fred were married in Chicago at the home of Sarah's sister, Lavinia McConnell, with Mary Pierce as bridesmaid—she, too, had married an officer who entered Beijing with the American troops. Sarah was present at the ceremony. For further information, see "Miss Conger Married," *New York Times,* September 2, 1901; and "Fred Buchan Weds," *The Kansas City Journal,* June 5, 1898. For more information about Fred Buchan, see his obituary on the Arlington National Cemetery website at www.arlingtoncemetery.net/febuchan.htm; and "20th Kansas Infantry in the Spanish-American War," available at http://files.usgwarchives.net/ks/statewide/military/cob.txt.

33. Sarah Conger letter to Fred Buchan and Laura Conger Buchan, January 16, 1902, Sarah Pike Conger Papers, #991-12; Conger, *Letters from China,* 215.

34. Conger, *Letters from China,* 215.

35. Der Ling, *Old Buddha,* 291–292.

Chapter 14 Reconciliation

1. Conger, *Letters from China*, 216–217.
2. Ibid.; Sergeant, *The Great Empress Dowager of China*, 261–262.
3. Satow, *The Diaries of Sir Ernest Satow*, Vol. I: 1900–1903: 192–193, entry date January 28, 1902; Sergeant, *The Great Empress Dowager of China*, 260.
4. Conger, *Letters from China*, 294.
5. Townley, *The Indiscretions of Lady Susan*, 87. Lady Susan claimed later that at one meeting she climbed up on the dowager's bed and sat, as Cixi did, cross-legged beside her—an account to be taken with a large grain of salt.
6. Conger, *Letters from China*, 217–218.
7. Townley, *The Indiscretions of Lady Susan*, 87–89.
8. Conger, *Letters from China*, 218–219.
9. "Ladies Visit China's Ruler," *San Francisco Call*, February 2, 1902.
10. Sarah Conger letter to Fred Buchan and Laura Conger Buchan, January 16, 1902, Sarah Pike Conger Papers, #991-12; Headland, *Court Life in China*, 99–100.
11. Sarah Conger letter to Fred Buchan and Laura Conger Buchan, January 16, 1902, Sarah Pike Conger Papers, #991-12.
12. Lo, *The Correspondence of G. E. Morrison*, 178–179; Headland, *Court Life in China*, 101–102; Little, *Round About My Peking Garden*, 57; Sarah Conger letter of December 16, 1901, Sarah Pike Conger Papers, #991-12. Jane Hunter notes that there was in China a "wide-spread masculine fear" that the women's missionary movement was a front for the fight for women's suffrage and equal rights. See Hunter, *Gospel of Gentility*, 87.
13. Conger, *Letters from China*, 219–223; "Blames Diplomats in Peking," *New York Times*, February 4, 1902; Headland, *Court Life in China*, 101–102.
14. Conger, *Letters from China*, 234–237.
15. Ibid., 219–223 and 257; Willis, *Friendly China*, 114–115.
16. Nealy, "Chinese Progress Due to an American Woman," *Boston Daily Globe*, November 26, 1911; Conger, *Letters from China*, 252–253. Sarah was to be further credited in later years with influencing Cixi to modify or abolish "19 modes of barbarous punishment for offenses against the State." (See Nealy, "Chinese Progress Due to an American Woman," *Boston Daily Globe*, November 26, 1911.)
17. Conger, *Letters from China*, 223–224.
18. Sarah Conger to Mary Baker Eddy, March 8, 1906; Mary Baker Eddy to Sarah Conger, March 2, 1906 [Accession #L02621], © The Mary Baker Eddy Collection and used with permission; "Empress Defends Religion," *New York Times*, November 16, 1903; "Confucian Ethics," *New York Times*, November 17, 1903.

19. Conger, *Letters from China*, 254–255.

20. Ibid., 223–224.

21. Ibid., 225–226.

22. Ibid., 226–227.

23. Ibid.

24. Ibid., 227–228.

25. Sarah Conger to Laura Conger Buchan, October 27, 1902, Sarah Pike Conger Papers, #991-12.

26. Conger, *Letters from China*, 228–230.

27. Ibid., 286.

28. Ibid., 241.

29. Ibid., 274–275.

30. Ibid., 274–276.

31. *Chinese Creeds and Customs*, Vol. I, 45–54; Conger, *Letters from China*, 276.

32. Sarah Conger to Laura Conger Buchan, October 27, 1902, Sarah Pike Conger Papers, #991-12; *New York Times*, March 26, 1902.

33. Conger, *Letters from China*, 231–232; Conger, *Old China and Young America*, 50–52; Der Ling, *Two Years in the Forbidden City*, 176.

34. Sarah Conger to Laura Conger Buchan, October 16, 1901, Sarah Pike Conger Papers, #991-12; Carl, *With The Empress Dowager of China*, 52–56.

35. Conger, *Letters from China*, 232–233.

Chapter 15   Sisterhood

1. Sarah Conger letter of August 12, 1903, Sarah Pike Conger Papers, #991-12.

2. Little, *Round About My Peking Garden*, 25–26; Bredon, *Peking*, 297–208.

3. Holmes, *Burton Holmes's Travelogue*, 314–315; Na Genzheng, in discussion with the author, April 6, 2008.

4. Conger, *Letters from China*, 238.

5. Ibid.

6. Ibid., 239.

7. Ibid.

8. Ibid., 239–240; Sarah Conger to Fred Buchan and Laura Conger Buchan, August 12, 1903, Sarah Pike Conger Papers, #991-12.

9. Conger, *Letters from China*, 240.

10. Sarah Conger to Laura Conger Buchan, July 22, 1903, Sarah Pike Conger Papers, #991-12. Sarah Buchan was born on June 3, 1903 at Fort Assiniboine, Montana. She lived on several military bases throughout her childhood, from Kansas to the Philippines. She graduated from Wellesley College in 1925, and in 1926 married T. Edson Jewell, Jr., to whom she was

married for sixty-two years. She died in Needham, Massachusetts on August 2, 2009.

11. Conger, *Letters from China*, 247–248; Carl, *With the Empress Dowager of China*, xix.
12. Der Ling, *Two Years in the Forbidden City*, 184–185 and 195.
13. Ibid.
14. Ibid., 187–193.
15. Ibid., 184–185 and 195.
16. Carl, *With the Empress Dowager of China*, 221.
17. Headland, *Court Life in China*, 98–99; Der Ling, *Two Years in the Forbidden City*, 196–199.
18. Der Ling, *Two Years in the Forbidden City*, 196–199.
19. Conger, *Letters from China*, 248; Sarah Conger to Fred Buchan and Laura Conger Buchan, August 12, 1903, Sarah Pike Conger Papers, #991-12; Der Ling, *Two Years in the Forbidden City*, 203–204.
20. Der Ling, *Two Years in the Forbidden City*, 203–204.
21. Conger, *Letters from China*, 248; Der Ling, *Two Years in the Forbidden City*, 203–206.
22. Ibid.

Chapter 16   Portrait of a woman

1. Seagrave, *Dragon Lady*, 409–410; Edwards, "Imperial East Meets Democratic West: The St. Louis Press and the Fair's Chinese Delegation," *Gateway Heritage*, Fall 1996.
2. Conger, *Letters from China*, 271; Carl, *With the Empress Dowager of China*, 4–6.
3. Der Ling, *Two Years in the Forbidden City*, 229–240; Carl, *With the Empress Dowager of China*, 6–7.
4. Der Ling, *Two Years in the Forbidden City*, 229–240; Carl, *With the Empress Dowager of China*, 6–7.
5. Carl, *With the Empress Dowager of China*, 7–8; Der Ling, *Two Years in the Forbidden City*, 231.
6. Carl, *With the Empress Dowager of China*, 10–11.
7. Conger, *Letters from China*, 271; Carl, *With the Empress Dowager of China*, 11.
8. Carl, *With the Empress Dowager of China*, 11; Conger, *Letters from China*, 271.
9. Conger, *Letters from China*, 271.
10. Sarah Conger letter of January 15, 1904, Sarah Pike Conger Papers, #991-12.
11. Conger, *Letters from China*, 263–264.
12. Ibid.

13. Ibid., 264–266 and 269.

14. Ibid.

15. Ibid., 263–264.

16. Ibid., 264–265; Hummel, *Eminent Chinese of the Ch'ing Period*, 281; Crossley, *Orphan Warriors*, 272 note 65; Xu (ed.), *Regulations of the Republic of China Concerning Rule Over Tibet*, 11.

17. Conger, *Letters from China*, 284–285.

18. Ibid., 285–286.

19. Ibid., Lin, *My Country and My People*, 69.

20. Headland, *Court Life in China*, 301; Conger, *Letters from China*, 286–287.

21. Headland, *Court Life in China*, 301.

22. Conger, *Letters from China*, 288–289.

23. Ibid., 306–307.

24. Ibid.

25. Ibid.; Conger, *Letters from China*, 308. Julia Ching draws comparisons between the Confucian memorial dinner for the deceased and the Christian Eucharist "as a religious celebration of a common meal in which both living and dead take part." See Ching, *Chinese Religions*, 64.

26. Sarah Conger letter of January 15, 1904, Sarah Pike Conger Papers, #991-12.

27. Conger, *Old China and Young America*, 37–38, with photographs of Sarah Buchan and the young grand-niece of Duke Jung for comparison; Conger, *Letters from China*, 307–309.

28. Conger, *Letters from China*, 307–309.

29. Ibid., 279–280.

30. Ibid., 299–300.

31. Ibid., 300–305.

32. Carl, *With the Empress Dowager of China*, 161–163.

33. Ibid.; Conger, *Letters from China*, 291–293.

34. Conger, *Letters from China*, 291–293.

35. Ibid.

36. Ibid.

37. Ibid., 292.

38. Ibid., 312–314; "Prince Pu Lun Will Take Up The Cause of Woman in China," *New York Times*, July 3, 1904; Huang Kaijia to May Wright Sewall, May 7, 1904, May Wright Sewall Digital Collection.

39. Carl, *With the Empress Dowager of China*, 294.

40. Ibid.; Brook, *Vermeer's Hat*, 22.

41. Carl, *With the Empress Dowager of China*, 294–296.

42. Ibid.; for a photograph of the train, see Headland, *Court Life in China*, between 104–105.

43. "An Imperial Portrait," *New York Times,* June 27, 1904; "China's Dowager," *New York Times,* November 4, 1905; Ling, *Chinese St. Louis,* 51–52; Zheng, *The Social Life of Opium in China,* 184–185; Qiao, "China at the World Expo," *China Today,* 2009; Edwards, "Imperial East Meets Democratic West: The St. Louis Press and the Fair's Chinese Delegation," *Gateway Heritage,* Fall 1996; "China's Gift to America," *New York Times,* February 19, 1905.

44. For transcript of exposition program, see Truax, http://webpages.charter.net/mtruax/1904wf/home.htm; Carl, *With the Empress Dowager of China,* 297–300.

45. Dan, "The Unknown Photographer," unpublished article in the collection of the Freer Gallery of Art and the Arthur M. Sackler Gallery Archives, Smithsonian Institution; Diary of Sarah Pike Conger, Vol. 2, Museum of Fine Arts, Boston, 1991-218. Sarah's 1904 diary ends in early July. Nowhere before that does she mention posing for a photograph with the empress dowager.

Chapter 17   Forbidden cities

1.   Conger, *Letters from China,* 212.

2.   Ibid.

3.   Ibid.

4.   Ibid., 314 and 317; Hunter, *Gospel of Gentility,* 171–172; Mathisen, *Critical Issues in American Religious History,* 430; Gospel of John 1: 8–9 (King James); Buck, *What America Means to Me.*

5.   Conger, *Letters from China,* 317–318.

6.   Ibid.

7.   Ibid., 319–320; Martin, *Cycle of Cathay,* 287–288. Julia Ching mentions German philosopher Karl Jaspers' inclusion of Confucius in the ranks of Socrates, Jesus, and the Buddha: "In each case, we have a man who lived in a time of social crisis, and sought to respond to this through special teachings aimed at all people." See Ching, *Chinese Religions,* 52.

8.   Conger, *Letters from China,* 319–320.

9.   Ye, *Seeking Modernity in China's Name,* 120.

10. Ibid., 121.

11. Ibid., 122.

12. Conger, *Letters from China,* 330–331. Gee (ed.), *Educational Directory for China,* 105–106.

13. Ibid.

14. Conger, *Letters from China,* 335.

15. Ibid.

16. Ibid., 336–339.

17. Ibid.

18. Ibid., 341. Lombard College yearbook, Class of 1890, Knox College.

19. Ibid., 342.

20. Conger, *Letters from China*, 344.

21. Ibid., 347–348.

22. Ibid., 348–349 and 351.

23. Ibid., 349–350. Edwin kept the scroll, because it was given by his granddaughter to the Museum of Fine Arts, Boston, where the author examined it. The scroll bears an inscription by a court scholar named Lu Xiangzhun.

24. Ibid. Hubert Vos (1855–1935) painted two portraits of Cixi. One showed her as a young woman of thirty-five and obeyed her directive that there be no shadows. This portrait is still kept at the Summer Palace, where it was restored in 2008 by Anne van Grevenstein of the Stichting Restauratie Atelier Limburg. Vos painted a second portrait which he himself retained, showing how Cixi looked to him in 1905, an elderly but still vibrant woman of seventy. This portrait is in the collection of the Harvard Art Museum/ Fogg Museum.

25. Carl, *With the Empress Dowager of China,* xxi–xxii; Seagrave, *Dragon Lady,* 414–418; Conger, *Letters from China,* 352–354.

26. Conger, *Letters from China,* 352–354. The blood-jade amulet was later left to Sarah's granddaughter, Sarah Buchan Jewell. Sarah Buchan Jewell, interviewed by the author, October 25, 2008.

27. Ibid.

28. Ibid., 354–355.

29. Ibid., 356. Sarah Conger to Laura Conger Buchan, July 8, 1903, Sarah Pike Conger Papers, #991-12; Conger, *Letters from China,* 370. See Edwin Conger to Laura Conger Buchan, December 25, 1901, Sarah Pike Conger Papers, #991-12, in which Edwin tells Laura that her mother has taken Wang's cue and set up a blue and white vase filled with "magnificent white chrysanthemums," in front of which they had placed a Christmas card for Laura. This bouquet "shall be the altar where we shall worship today," Edwin told his daughter.

30. Conger, *Letters from China*, 358–359.

31. Ibid.

Chapter 18 Letters to China

1. "Upsets Plan for Conger," *New York Times,* April 7, 1905; "Noted Diplomat Near Death at Pasadena Home," *Los Angeles Herald,* May 16, 1907.

2. "Big Profit on a Fine Rug," *New York Times*, June 16, 1906; "Big Profit on a Fine Rug," *New York Times*, June 19, 1906; "Mrs. Conger's Rug Once More," *New York Times*, June 20, 1906.

3. "Ambassador Conger Quits," *New York Times*, August 23, 1905; "Edwin H. Conger Dies at Pasadena After Long Illness," *San Francisco Call* May 19, 1907; "Noted Diplomat Near Death at Pasadena Home," *Los Angeles Herald*, May 16, 1907.

4. "Ex-Minister Conger Dead," *New York Times*, May 19, 1907; "US Minister Conger Dies," *Oakland Tribune*, May 19, 1907; "Edwin H. Conger Dies at Pasadena After Long Illness," *San Francisco Call* May 19, 1907; "Edwin H. Conger Obituary," *Los Angeles Herald*, May 18, 1907.

5. "Edwin H. Conger Dies at Pasadena After Long Illness," *San Francisco Call*, May 19, 1907; "Statesman Left Small Estate," *Los Angeles Herald*, June 8, 1907; Twain, "Diplomatic Pay and Clothes," January, 1899, reprinted in *The Complete Essays of Mark Twain*, 251–259.

6. Sarah Conger letter postmarked September 3, 1903, Sarah Pike Conger Papers, #991-12; Sarah Conger letter of December 16, 1901, Sarah Pike Conger Papers, #991-12; Edwin Conger letter of September 8, 1901, Sarah Pike Conger Papers, #991-12. For diplomatic pay, see Markus Mösslang and Torsten Riotte (eds.), *The Diplomats' World: The Cultural History of Diplomacy, 1814–1914;* "Charlemagne Tower on the Ambassador's Handicaps," *New York Times*, November 1, 1908; Edwin Conger letter of December 25, 1901, Sarah Pike Conger Papers, #991-12.

7. *The Conger Collection* catalogue, February 19–22, 1908, Museum of Fine Arts, Boston, APP.1991.4 (Sarah Conger's own copy); Sarah Buchan Jewell, interviewed by the author, October 25, 2008.

8. "United States Branded as 'Fence,'" *Evening World*, February 25, 1908.

9. Ibid.; "Conger Sale Brings $9,044," *New York Times*, February 22, 1908.

10. *New York Daily Tribune*, April 12, 1908; Congressional Record, April 18, 1908, Vol. 42, Part 5, 60th Congress/1st Session, 4930–4931.

11. Congressional Record, April 18, 1908, Vol. 42, Part 5, 60th Congress/1st Session, 4930–4931.

12. Ibid.

13. Conger, *Letters from China*, 174; "Chinese Antiques Sold," *New York Times*, February 20, 1908. The Tongzhi wine cup, now at the Peabody Essex Museum in Salem, Massachusetts, was identified because it matches the service in the Palace Museum in Beijing. The elephant caparisons were purchased by the Metropolitan Museum of Art.

14. "Mrs. Conger's Sale of Relics," *New York Daily Tribune*, February 25, 1908.

15. Crossley, letter to the author, August 27, 2008; Hevia, *English Lessons*, 208–211; "Peking Relics in Washington," *New York Times*, June 7, 1901; Yoshihara, *Embracing the East*, 36; United Nations, *Convention on the Means of Prohibiting and Preventing the Illicit Import, Export and Transfer of Ownership of Cultural Property*, Article 11, 139, available at http://portal. unesco.org/en/ev.php-URL_ID=13039&URL_DO=DO_TOPIC&URL_ SECTION=201.html (accessed October 7, 2010).

16. *New York Times*, May 29, 1909.

17. Croll, *Wise Daughters From Foreign Lands*, 101; Borzo, "Our Lady In Peking," *Annals of Iowa* 39, no. 6 (1968): 413; Croll, *Feminism and Socialism in China*, 57–58; Conger, *Letters from China*, 370; Nealy, "Chinese Progress Due to an American Woman," *Boston Daily Globe*, November 26, 1911.

18. Conger, *Letters from China*, 370.

19. Ibid., 371–374.

20. Ibid.; *New York Times*, November 15, 1906.

21. *New York Times*, April 25, 1906.

22. "Last Emperor's Cousin is Palace Clerk," *Daily Telegraph*, August 4, 2004; "Sommerpalastseintritts-kartensammler Na Genzheng" ("Na Genzheng, Collector of Admission Tickets to the Summer Palace") CRI On-Line Deutsch, October 13, 2005, available at http://german.cri. cn/311/2005/10/13/1@37065.htm (accessed October 7, 2010).

23. McCartney, "Now the Chinese Know: The Guangxu Emperor was Poisoned. But by Whom?" *The Times*, November 4, 2008; Rust and Soignet, "Risk/ Benefit Profile of Arsenic Trioxide," *The Oncologist* 6, Suppl. 2 (April 2001): 29–32; Mino and Yamada, "Detection of High Levels of Arsenic and Mercury in Some Chinese Traditional Medicines Using X-Ray Fluorescence Spectrometry," *Journal of Health Science* 51 (2005): 607–613; Chiang, "Application of arsenic trioxide for the treatment of lupus nephritis," *Committee on Chinese Medicine and Pharmacy Yearbook 2006*, CCMP 95– RD–006. Available at http://www.ccmp.gov.tw/en/research/result_detail.asp ?relno=51&selno=0&no=95&detailno=1020. The latter article discusses the use of arsenic trioxide, long a traditional Chinese medicine for everything from gastrointestinal disorders (from which we know the Guangxu emperor suffered) to cancer.

24. Conger, *Letters from China*, 376–377.

25. Sarah Buchan Jewell, interviewed by the author, October 25, 2008; Sarah Conger to Charles Freer, July 17, 1919, Charles Lang Freer Papers, Freer Gallery of Art and Arthur M. Sackler Gallery Archives, Smithsonian Institution; 1920 US Census; 1930 US Census.

26. Sarah Buchan Jewell, interviewed by the author, October 25, 2008.

27. Croll, *Feminism and Socialism in China*, 1 (quoting Jack Belden, *China Shakes The World*).

28. Conger, *Letters from China*, 372.

29. Ibid., 374–375.

30. Ibid., 371.

Bibliography

Diaries and Correspondence

Bailey Willis Papers. Huntington Library, Pasadena, CA.

Charles Lang Freer Papers. Freer Gallery of Art and Arthur M. Sackler Gallery Archives, Smithsonian Institution, Washington, D.C.

Diary of Sarah Pike Conger. Vol. 1: 1898–1900. Accession number 1991-217. Museum of Fine Arts, Boston, MA.

Diary of Sarah Pike Conger. Vol. 2: 1900–1902. Accession number 1991-218. Museum of Fine Arts, Boston, MA.

Guest Book from the American Legation, Museum of Fine Arts, Boston, 1991-220.

The Mary Baker Eddy Library for the Betterment of Humanity, Boston, MA.

May Wright Sewall Digital Collection. Marion County Public Library, Indianapolis, IN.

Sarah Pike Conger Papers, #991-12. Peabody Museum of Archaeology and Ethnology, Harvard University, Cambridge, MA.

Secondary Sources

Aldrich, Michael. *The Search for a Vanishing Beijing: A Guide to China's Capital Through the Ages*. Hong Kong: Hong Kong University Press, 2006.

Almanach de Gotha. Gotha: Justus Perthes, 1899.

Almanach de Gotha. Gotha: Justus Perthes, 1900.

Anaconda Standard. Anaconda, MT. Daily. Articles used from 1900 to 1901.

Arlington, L. C. and W. Lewisohn. *In Search of Old Peking*. Peking: Henri Vetch, 1935.

Barmé, Géremie. *The Forbidden City*. Cambridge, MA: Harvard University Press, 2008.

Béguin, Gilles and Dominique Morel. *The Forbidden City: Center of Imperial China*. Translated by Ruth Taylor. New York: H. N. Abrams Publishers, 1997.

Belden, Jack. *China Shakes the World*. New York: Harper and Bros., 1949.

Bickers, Robert and R. G. Tiedemann (eds.). *The Boxers, China, and the World*. Lanham, MD: Rowman and Littlefield, 2007.

Biggs, Chester M., Jr., and Chester M. Biggs. *The United States Marines in North China, 1894–1942*. Jefferson, NC: McFarland and Company, 2003.

Bland, J. O. P. and Sir Edmund Backhouse. *China under the Empress Dowager, Being the History of the Life and Times of Tzu Hsi*. London: Heinemann, 1910.

Boot, Max. *The Savage Wars of Peace: Small Wars and the Rise of American Power*. New York: Basic Books, 2002.

Borzo, Henry. "Our Lady in Peking," *Annals of Iowa* 39, no. 6 (Fall, 1968): 413.

Boston Daily Globe. Boston, MA. Daily. Articles used from 1905 and 1911.

Bredon, Juliet. *Peking: A Historical and Intimate Description of its Chief Places of Interest*. Shanghai: Kelly and Walsh, Ltd., 1931.

Brook, Timothy. *Vermeer's Hat: The Seventeenth Century and the Dawn of the Global World*. Toronto: Viking Canada, 2008.

Buck, Pearl S. *Imperial Woman*. New York: John Day Company, 1956.

———. *What America Means to Me*. Manchester, NH: Ayer Company Publishers, 1973.

Cameron, Meribeth E. *The Reform Movement in China 1898–1912*. New York: Octagon Books, Inc., 1963.

Capt. Myers' report, September 26, 1900. Available at Naval History and Heritage online http://www.history.navy.mil/index.html (accessed October 7, 2010).

Carl, Katherine A. *With the Empress Dowager of China*. New York: The Century Co., 1907.

Carpenter, Frank George. *South America, Carpenter's Geographical Reader*. New York: American Book Company, 1899.

Chen Xiaomei. *Occidentalism: A Theory of Counter-Discourse in Post-Mao China*. Lanham, MD: Rowman and Littlefield, 2002.

Cherrington, Rex. "Universalism: A Kind and Gentle Religious Tradition was Once Dynamic in Galesburg," *Zephyr* (Galesburg, IL), January 18, 1996.

Chiang, Bor-Luen. "Application of arsenic trioxide for the treatment of lupus nephritis," *Committee on Chinese Medicine and Pharmacy Yearbook*. 2006. CCMP 95-RD-006. Available at http://www.ccmp.gov.tw/en/research/result_detail.asp?relno=51&selno=0&no=95&detailno=1020 (accessed October 7, 2010).

Chinese Creeds and Customs, Vol. I. Hong Kong: South China Morning Post, 1956.

Ching, Frank. *Ancestors: 900 Years in the Life of a Chinese Family*. London: Harrap, 1988.

Ching, Julia. *Chinese Religions*. New York: Orbis Books, 1993.

Christian Science Sentinel. Articles used from 1902.

Clark, Francis E. *Our Journey Around the World: An Illustrated Record of a Year's Travel of Forty Thousand Miles Through India, China, Japan, Australia, New Zealand, Palestine, Greece, Turkey, Italy, France, Spain, etc.* Hartford, CT: A.D. Worthington and Company, 1895.

Clark, George B. *Treading Softly: US Marines in China, 1819–1949*. Santa Barbara: Greenwood Publishing Group, 2001.

Clements, Paul. "The Boxer Rebellion: A Political and Diplomatic Review." Doctoral dissertation, Columbia University, 1915.

Cleveland, Harold Irwin. *China At War with the World: The Story of the Boxer Outrages and History of the Flowery Kingdom*. Philadelphia: American Book and Bible House, 1900.

Cohen, Paul A. *History in Three Keys: The Boxers as Event, Experience, and Myth*. New York: Columbia University Press, 1997.

Coltman, Dr. Robert. *Beleaguered in Peking: The Boxers' War Against the Foreigner*. Philadelphia: F. A. Davis Company, 1901.

Confucius. "Analects." In *The Four Books*, 123–428. Translated by James Legge. Taipei: Taiwan Culture Book Co., 1970.

The Conger Collection catalogue, February 19–22, 1908, New York. APP.1991.4 (Sarah's own copy). Museum of Fine Arts, Boston, MA.

"Conger, Edwin Hurd." Entry in *Biographical Directory of the United States Congress*. Available at http://bioguide.congress.gov/scripts/biodisplay.pl?index=C000675 (accessed October 7, 2010).

"The Conger Family of Illinois," *Political Graveyard*. Available at http://politicalgraveyard.com/families/15583.html (accessed October 7, 2010).

Conger, Sarah Pike. *Letters from China: With Particular Reference to the Empress Dowager and the Women of China*. Chicago: A. C. McClurg and Co., 1909.

———. *Old China and Young America*. Chicago: F.G. Browne and Co., 1913.

"Cracking the Mystery of Cixi's Youth" (Liu Qi). Available at www.tydoo.com/suwu/lishi/cxss.htm (accessed October 7, 2010).

Croll, Elisabeth. *Feminism and Socialism in China*. New York: Schocken Books, 1980.

———. *Wise Daughters from Foreign Lands: European Women Writers in China*. London: Pandora, 1989.

Crossley, Pamela Kyle. *Orphan Warriors: Three Manchu Generations and the End of the Qing World*. New Jersey: Princeton University Press, 1990.

Daily Mail. Galesburg, IL Daily. Articles used from 1907.

Daily Telegraph. London. Daily. August 4, 2004.

Dan, Lydia. "The Unknown Photographer." Unpublished article, written in 1982. Freer Gallery of Art and the Arthur M. Sackler Gallery Archives, Smithsonian Institution, Washington, D.C.

Danby, Hope. *The Garden of Perfect Brightness: The History of the Yüan Ming Yüan and of the Emperors who Lived There*. London: Williams and Norgate Ltd, 1950.

Darwin, Charles. *The Descent of Man and Selection in Relation to Sex*. London: John Murray, 1871.

Davenport Daily Leader. Davenport, IA. Daily. Articles used from 1900.

Davenport Republican. Davenport, IA. Daily. Articles used from 1900.

Der Ling. *Two Years in the Forbidden City*. New York: Moffat, Yard and Company, 1911.

———. *Kowtow*. New York: Dodd, Mead and Company, 1929.

———. *Old Buddha*. New York: Dodd Mead and Company, 1929.

"The Diplomats' World: The Cultural History of Diplomacy 1814–1914." *Studies of the German Historical Institute London Series*. Oxford: Oxford University Press, 2008.

Dong, Stella. *Shanghai 1842–1949: The Rise and Fall of a Decadent City*. New York: Harper Collins, 2000.

Eberhard, Wolfram. *A Dictionary of Chinese Symbols: Hidden Symbols in Chinese Life and Thought*. London: Routledge, 1986.

Eddy, Mary Baker. *Science and Health with Key to the Scriptures*. Boston, MA: The First Church of Christ, Scientist, 1971.

Edwards, Sue Bradford. "Imperial East Meets Democratic West: The St. Louis Press and the Fair's Chinese Delegation," *Gateway Heritage,* Fall 1996.

Elleman, Bruce. *Modern Chinese Warfare, 1795–1989.* London: Routledge, 2001.

Elliott, Jane E. *Some Did It for Civilisation, Some Did It for Their Country.* Hong Kong: Chinese University of Hong Kong, 2002.

Evening World. New York, NY. Daily. Articles used from 1908.

Favier, Pierre-Marie-Alphonse, "The Last Letter of Bishop Favier," *Annals of the Propagation of the Faith*, vol. LXVIII, no. 460. Supplement to the American Edition, Baltimore: Society for the Propagation of the Faith, June 1905.

Fei Shi. *Guide to Peking and its Environs Near and Far.* Tianjin: Tientsin Press, Ltd., 1924.

Flaherty, S. F. *Our Regiment: A History of the 102nd Illinois Infantry Volunteers.* Chicago: Brewster and Hanscom Printers, 1865.

Fleming, Peter. *The Siege at Peking.* London: Readers Union Rupert Hart-Davis, 1960.

Franzini, Serge. "Le docteur Dethève appelé en consultation par l'empereur Guangxu: documents rassemblés et commentés" (Doctor Dethève's appointment with the Guangxu emperor: Collected documentation with commentary), *Études chinoises* XIV, no. 1 (Spring 1995). Available at http://www.afec-en-ligne.org/IMG/pdf/14-1.Franzini.pdf (accessed October 7, 2010).

"Fred E. Buchan," Obituary. Arlington National Cemetery Website. Available at www.arlingtoncemetery.net/febuchan.htm (accessed October 7, 2010).

Fredriksen, John C. *American Military Leaders from Colonial Times to the Present.* Santa Barbara, CA: ABC-CLIO, 1999.

Galesburg Register Mail. Daily. Galesburg, IL. Articles used from 1963.

Gee, Nathaniel Gist (ed.). *Educational Directory for China.* Suzhou: Educational Association of China, 1905.

Giles, Lancelot. *The Siege of the Peking Legations.* Perth: University of Western Australia Press, 1970.

Gill, Gillian. *Mary Baker Eddy.* Cambridge, MA: Perseus Books, 1998.

Godden, Rumer. *The Butterfly Lions: The Pekingese in History, Legend and Art.* London: William Clowes and Sons Limited, 1977.

Goodwin, Doris Kearns. *Team of Rivals: The Political Genius of Abraham Lincoln.* New York: Simon and Schuster, 2005.

Hamilton, Richard F. *President McKinley, War and Empire: President McKinley and the Coming of War, 1898.* Piscataway, NJ: Transaction Publishers, 2006.

Hart, Sir Robert. *These from the Land of Sinim: Essays on the Chinese Question.* London: Chapman and Hall, 1901.

———. *The I. G. in Peking: Letters of Robert Hart, Chinese Maritime Customs, 1868–1907*. Cambridge, MA: The Belknap Press of Harvard University Press, 1975.

Hay, John (ed.). *Boundaries in China*. London: Reaktion Books, Ltd., 1994.

Headland, Isaac Taylor. *Court Life in China*. New York: Fleming H. Revell, 1909.

Heinrichs, Waldo H., Jr. *American Ambassador: Joseph C. Grew and the Development of the United States Diplomatic Tradition*. Oxford: Oxford University Press, 1986.

Hevia, James Louis. *English Lessons: The Pedagogy of Imperialism in Nineteenth Century China*. Durham, NC: Duke University Press, 2003.

The History of Dallas County. Des Moines, IA: Union Historical Company, 1879.

Hoe, Susanna. *Women at the Siege: Peking 1900*. Oxford: Holo Books, 2000.

Holmes, Burton. *Burton Holmes's Travelogue: Down the Amur; Peking; The Forbidden City*. New York: Travelogue Bureau, 1917.

Hooker, Mary [Polly Condit Smith]. *Behind the Scenes in Peking*. Oxford: Oxford University Press, 1987.

Hu Piyun (ed.). *Historical Photos of Old Beijing*. Beijing: Beijing Publishing House, 1995.

Hubbard, Ethel Daniels. *Under Marching Orders: A Story of Mary Porter Gamewell*. Washington, D.C.: Review and Herald Publishing Association, 1905.

Hummel, Arthur W. (ed.). *Eminent Chinese of the Ch'ing Period (1644–1912)*. Washington, D.C.: United States Government Printing Office, 1943.

Hunt, Michael H. *The Making of a Special Relationship: The United States and China to 1914*. New York: Columbia University Press, 1983.

Hunter, Jane. *The Gospel of Gentility: American Women Missionaries in Turn-of-the-Century China*. New Haven: Yale University Press, 1989.

Illinois State Genealogical Society Quarterly XII, no. 3 (Fall 1980).

"Interview With The Lukens: Eliza Jane Carr and George Lukens" Thomas Tredway Library, Augustana College. Available at www.augustana.edu/library/SpecialCollections/Biography/lukens.html (accessed October 7, 2010).

Joseph, Gilbert M., Catherine C. LeGrand, and Ricardo D. Salvatore (eds.). *Close Encounters of Empire: Writing the Cultural History of US–Latin American Relations*. Durham, NC: Duke University Press, 1998.

Kansas City Journal. Kansas City, MO. Daily. Articles used from 1898.

Kentuckian. Hopkinsville, Kentucky. Daily. Articles used from 1904.

Kreiner, Jared. "American Missionaries and the Boxer Rebellion," Christopher Newport University History Department, *The Sextant* No. 6/7 (Summer 2007), 1–16.

Kwong, Luke S. K. *A Mosaic of the Hundred Days: Personalities, Politics and Ideas of 1898*. Cambridge, MA: Harvard University Press, 1984.

———. "No Shadows," *History Today* 50, no. 9 (September 2000).

Ladies' Repository (A Universalist Monthly Magazine for the Home Circle) 38, ante-1876.

Landor, A. H. S. *China and the Allies*. Vol. I. New York: Scribner's, 1901.

Lang, Olga. *Chinese Family and Society*. Hamden, CT: Archon Books, 1968.

Lao Tzu. *Tao Teh Ching*. Translated by John C. H. Wu. Boston: Shambhala Library, 2003.

Leonard, John William (editor-in-chief). *Woman's Who's Who of America: A Biographical Dictionary of Contemporary Women of the United States and Canada, 1914–1915*. New York: American Commonwealth Company, 1914.

Lin Yutang. *My Country and My People*. New York: J. Day Co., 1935.

Ling Huping. *Chinese St. Louis*. Philadelphia: Temple University Press, 2004.

Little, Archibald. *Intimate China: The Chinese As I Have Seen Them*. Philadelphia: Hutchinson and Co., 1901.

———. *Round About My Peking Garden*. Philadelphia: T. Fisher Unwin, 1905.

Liu, Lydia H. *The Clash of Empires: The Invention of China in Modern World Making*. Cambridge, MA: Harvard University Press, 2006.

Lo Hui-min (ed.). *The Correspondence of G. E. Morrison*. Cambridge: Cambridge University Press, 1976.

Lombard College Yearbook, Class of 1890, Knox College.

Los Angeles Herald. Los Angeles, CA. Daily. Articles used from 1907.

Lynch, George. *The War of the Civilisations: Being a Record of a "Foreign Devil's" Experiences with the Allies in China*. London: Longmans, Green, and Co., 1901.

Mackerras, Colin. *Western Images of China*. Oxford: Oxford University Press, 1999.

Madisonian, Winterset, IA, May 22, 1873.

Martin, W. A. P. *A Cycle of Cathay, or China, South and North*. New York: Fleming H. Revell, 1897.

———. *The Siege in Peking: China against the World*. New York: Fleming H. Revell, 1900.

Mateer, Ada Haven. *Siege Days: Personal Experiences of American Women and Children during the Peking Siege*. New York: Revell, 1903.

Mathisen, Robert R. *Critical Issues in American Religious History: A Reader*. Waco, TX: Baylor University Press, 2001.

McCartney, Jane. "Now the Chinese Know: The Guangxu Emperor Was Poisoned. But by Whom?" *The Times*, November, 4, 2008.

McNabb, R. L. *The Women of the Middle Kingdom*. New York: Young People's Missionary Movement, 1907.

Miner, Luella, "The Flight of the Empress Dowager, from Information Derived from One of Her Suite," *The Century Magazine*, vol. LXI, no. 5, March 1901.

Mino, Yoshiki and Yasujiro Yamada. "Detection of High Levels of Arsenic and Mercury in Some Chinese Traditional Medicines Using X-Ray Fluorescence Spectrometry," Pharmaceutical Society of Japan, Tokyo. *Journal of Health Science* 51(5), 607–613.

Moser, Michael J. and Yeone Wei-Chih Moser. *Foreigners Within the Gate: The Legations at Peking*. Oxford: Oxford University Press, 1993.

Mösslang, Markus and Torsten Riotte (eds.), *The Diplomats' World: The Cultural History of Diplomacy, 1814–1941*. Oxford: Oxford University, 2008.

Na Genzheng. *Cixi as I Knew Her* (*Wo suo zhi dao de Cixi taihou*). Beijing: Gold Wall Press (Jincheng Chubanshe), 2004.

Nealy, Sid. "Chinese Progress Due to an American Woman," *Boston Daily Globe*, November 26, 1911.

Nebraska State Journal. Lincoln, NB. Semi-Weekly. Articles used from 1900.

New York Daily Tribune. New York, NY. Daily. Articles used from 1900 and 1908.

New York Times. New York, NY. Daily. Articles used from 1894 to 1909 and 2009.

Oakland Tribune. Oakland, CA. Daily. Articles used from 1905 and 1907.

Page, Brian. *Beijing: Then and Now*. San Diego: Thunder Bay Press, 2007.

Paludan, Ann. *Chronicle of the Chinese Emperors: The Reign-by-Reign Record of the Rulers of Imperial China*. London: Thames and Hudson, 1998.

Payen, Cecile. "Besieged in Peking," *Century Magazine* LXI, no. 3 (January 1901): 453–459.

Pensacola Journal. Pensacola, FL. Daily. Articles used from 1909.

Post Standard. Syracuse, NY. Daily. Articles used from 1900.

Preston, Diana. *The Boxer Rebellion: The Dramatic Story of China's War on Foreigners That Shook the World in the Summer of 1900*. New York: Walker and Company, 1999.

Pruitt, Ida. *A Daughter of Han: The Autobiography of a Chinese Working Woman*. Palo Alto: Stanford University Press, 1967.

Puritan I, no. 9. New York: Frank A. Munsey Co. (September 1897).

Qiao Tianbi. "China at the World Expo," *China Today*, 2009. Available at http://www.chinatoday.com.cn/ctenglish/se/txt/2009-05/15/content_195965.htm (accessed October 7, 2010).

Ransome, Jessie. *The Story of the Siege Hospital in Peking*. London: Society For Promoting Christian Knowledge and New York: E. and J. B. Young and Co., 1901.

Rawski, Evelyn S. *The Last Emperors: A Social History of Qing Imperial Institutions.* Berkeley: University of California Press, 1998.

Republican Register. Mt Carmel, IL. Daily. Articles used from 1907.

Robert, Dana L. *American Women in Mission: A Social History of Their Thought and Practice.* Macon, GA: Mercer University Press, 1998.

Roberts, George E. "The Opium Habit in Iowa." Third Biennial Report, Iowa State Board of Health. Des Moines, IA: Iowa State Board of Health, 1885.

Ruoff, E. G. (ed.). *Death Throes of a Dynasty.* Kent, OH: Kent State University Press, 1990.

Rust, Deborah M. and Steven L. Soignet. "Risk/Benefit Profile of Arsenic Trioxide," *The Oncologist* 6, Suppl. 2 (April 2001): 29–32.

San Francisco Call. San Francisco, CA. Daily. Articles used from 1900 to 1908.

Satow, Sir Ernest. *The Diaries of Sir Ernest Satow, British Envoy in Peking (1900–06).* Vol. I: 1900–1903. Edited and annotated by Ian C. Ruxton. Self-published. 2006. Available at http://www.lulu.com/content/249070 (accessed October 7, 2010).

Scidmore, Eliza Ruhama. *China the Long-lived Empire.* New York: The Century Co., 1900.

Seagrave, Sterling. *Dragon Lady: The Life and Legend of the Last Empress of China.* New York: Random House, 1993.

Seeley, I. C. *Manual of College Literary Societies.* Kalamazoo, MI: Chaplin and Ihling Bros., 1871.

Sergeant, Philip W. *The Great Empress Dowager of China.* London: Hutchinson, 1910.

"Sommerpalastseintritts-kartensammler Na Genzheng" ("Na Genzheng, Collector of Admission Tickets to the Summer Palace"), October 13, 2005, CRI Online Deutsch. Available at http://german.cri.cn/311/2005/10/13/1@37065.htm (accessed October 7, 2010).

Spence, Jonathan D. *The Gate of Heavenly Peace: The Chinese and Their Revolution, 1895–1980.* New York: Viking Press, 1981.

———. *God's Chinese Son: The Taiping Heavenly Kingdom of Hong Xiuquan.* New York: W. Norton and Company, 1996.

———. *The Chan's Great Continent: China in Western Minds.* New York: W. W. Norton and Company, 1998.

The Student. Knox College. Articles used from 1947.

Thompson, Peter and Robert Macklin. *The Man Who Died Twice: The Life and Adventures of Morrison of Peking.* Sydney: Allen and Unwin, 2004.

Townley, Lady Susan. *The Indiscretions of Lady Susan.* New York: D. Appleton and Company, 1922.

Truax, Mike. Transcript of St Louis Exposition Program. Available at Mike's 1904 St Louis World's Fair Web Pages http://webpages.charter.net/mtruax/1904wf/home.htm (accessed October 7, 2010).

Tsai, Henry Shih-shan. *Perpetual Happiness: The Ming Emperor Yongle*. Seattle: University of Washington Press, 2001.

Twain, Mark (Samuel Langhorne Clemens). "Diplomatic Pay and Clothes." January 1899. Reprinted in *The Complete Essays of Mark Twain*. Cambridge, MA: Da Capo Press, 2000.

———. "To The Person Sitting In Darkness," *North American Review* (February 1901).

"Two Pioneers in the Orient," *Quarterly News* 16, no. 4, 253–256 (Winter 1979–80). Held at the Mary Baker Eddy Museum and Historic Sites, Longyear Historical Society.

van Antwerp, Lee D., Arthur H. and Katherine W. Radasch, Robert M. and Ruth W. Sherman. *Mayflower Families Through Five Generations*. Vol. 1. Plymouth, MA: General Society of Mayflower Descendants, 1975.

Varé, Daniele. *The Last Empress*. New York: Doubleday, Durant and Co., 1936.

Waley, Arthur. *Chinese Poems*. London: George Allen and Unwin, 1946.

Waley-Cohen, Joanna. *The Sextants of Beijing: Global Currents in Chinese History*. New York: W. W. Norton and Company, 1999.

Warner, Marina. *The Dragon Empress: The Life and Times of Tz'u-Hsi Empress Dowager of China 1835–1908*. New York: MacMillan Company, 1972.

Washington Herald. Washington D.C. Daily. Articles used from 1909.

Washington Post. Washington D.C. Daily. Articles used from 1905.

Weale, B. L. Putnam (Bertram Lenox Simpson). *Indiscreet Letters from Peking*. New York: Dodd, Mead and Company, 1907.

Webster, Martha Farnham. *Annals of Knox County, Annals of Galesburg*. (Commemorating Centennial of Admission of Illinois as a State of the Union 1818) published in the *Republican Register*. Galesburg, IL, 1921.

Whyte, Bob. *Unfinished Encounter: China and Christianity*. Glasgow: William Collins Sons and Company, 1988.

Willis, Bailey. *Friendly China: Two Thousand Miles Afoot Among the Chinese*. Palo Alto: Stanford University Press, 1949.

Wilson, James Harrison. *Travels and Investigations in the Middle Kingdom*. New York: D. Appleton and Company, 1887.

Wu Yung (Yü-Ch'uan). *The Flight of an Empress*. Transcribed by Liu K'un. New Haven, CT: Yale University Press, 1936.

Xiang Lanxin. *The Origins of the Boxer War: A Multinational Study*. London: Routledge Curzon, 2002.

Xu Xingsheng (executive editor). *Regulations of the Republic of China Concerning Rule Over Tibet (1912–1949)*. China National Center for Tibetan Studies, China No. 2 History Archives. Beijing: China Intercontinental Press, 1999.

Ye Weili. *Seeking Modernity in China's Name*. Palo Alto: Stanford University Press, 2001.

Yoshihara, Mari. *Embracing the East: White Women and American Orientalism*. Oxford: Oxford University Press, 2003.

Zhang Juwen. *A Translation of the Ancient Book of Burial (Zan Shu) by Guo Pu (276–324)*. New York: Edwin Mellen Press, 2004.

Zheng Yangwen. *The Social Life of Opium in China*. Cambridge: Cambridge University Press, 2005.

Index